ECHOES OF SILENCE
Avadhut Gita Revisited

Karl Renz

ECHOES OF SILENCE
Avadhut Gita Revisited

Karl Renz

Concept by
Sanjay Inamdar

Compiled by
Manjit Achhra

Translated and Edited By
Sanjay Inamdar & Manjit Achhra

Once King Yadu (ancestor of Krishna) met Avadhut Dattatreya on the way. Impressed by his enigmatic carefreeness, the King was drawn towards him. He humbly prostrated before Dattatreya and asked, 'Sir, may I know how is it that you seem to be so happy? What is the source of your happiness, though you appear to be like a beggar? Who are you? May I know your whereabouts and a little of your history?'

Dattatreya did not say who he was. He merely said, 'I am happy because of what I am, not because of what I have'.

ECHOES OF SILENCE Avadhut Gita Revisited

Copyright © 2013 Karl Renz

First Edition: October 2013

PUBLISHED BY
ZEN PUBLICATIONS
A Division of Maoli Media Private Limited

60, Juhu Supreme Shopping Centre,
Gulmohar Cross Road No. 9, JVPD Scheme,
Juhu, Mumbai 400 049. India.
Tel: +91 9022208074
eMail: info@zenpublications.com
Website: www.zenpublications.com

COVER & BOOK DESIGN
Red Sky Designs, Mumbai

ISBN 978-93-82788-84-3

All rights reserved. No part of this book may be reproduced or transmitted in any form or by any means, electronic or mechanical, including photocopying, recording, or by any information storage and retrieval system without written permission from the author or his agents, except for the inclusion of brief quotations in a review.

Contents

Preface	10
Introduction	12
Chapter One	15
Chapter Two	121
Chapter Three	172
Chapter Four	232
Chapter Five	265
Chapter Six	307
Chapter Seven	341
References	359

Other Books by Karl Renz
- A Little Bit Of Nothingness
  81 Observations On The Unnamable
- Worry and be Happy
  The Audacity of Hopelessness
- The Song of Irrelevance
  Meditation of what you are
- Heaven and Hell
- Am I - I Am
- May It Be As It Is
  The Embrace of Helplessness
- If You Wake Up, Don't Take It Personally
  Dialogues in the Presence of Arunachala
- The Myth of Enlightenment
  Seeing Through the Illusion of Separation

Other Books by Zen Publications
- Redemption Stories: Unwasted Pain
- A Duet of One
- Pursue 'Happiness' And Get Enlightened
- Pointers From Ramana Maharshi
- Enlightened Living
- A Buddha's Babble
- A Personal Religion Of Your Own
- The Essence of The Ashtavakra Gita
- The Relationship Between 'I' And 'Me'
- Seeking Enlightenment – Why ?
- Nuggets of Wisdom
- Confusion No More
- Guru Pournima
- Advaita and the Buddha
- It So Happened That... The Unique Teaching of Ramesh S. Balsekar
- Sin and Guilt: Monstrosity of Mind
- The Infamous Ego
- Who Cares?!
- The Essence of the Bhagavad Gita
- Your Head in the Tiger's Mouth
- Consciousness Writes
- Consciousness Speaks
- The Bhagavad Gita – A Selection

Preface

The impossibility of satisfactorily introducing Karl Renz or whatever he says to readers was conveniently circumvented by us so far in our earlier compilations of his talks into books simply by using the facility of not doing so, leaving readers to get an unfiltered and unobjectivised taste of Karl directly.

We apologize this time, however, for the intervention as it was difficult to retain that facility in this compilation, where Karl, here, is in what he could term as 'good company' of Dattatreya which necessitated this deviation.

While editing Karl's book 'Song of Irrelevance', I happened to go through the 'Avadhut Gita (song of the free) of Dattatreya' (incidentally Ramesh Balsekar's copy which he had gifted me) and was pleasantly shocked to discover the complementary nature of the 'songs' sung by these two. Discovering someone whose words resonate so harmoniously with the motor-mouth prattle of Karl's empty words, (for me, a rarity matched recently only by Nisargadatta Maharaj, Ranjit Maharaj, Ramana Maharishi and UG) was like a cherry on the Karl cake. Excited, I experimented juxtaposing verses from the Avadhut Gita along with selective dialogues (or more appropriately, monologues) of Karl from the book's manuscript for fun. The concoction turned out to be a flamboyantly audacious and mind blowing jugalbandi (jamming session) of these two. The idea of this book took root then.

It may be noted that before discussing the idea of this book with him, Karl was unaware of Dattatreya or the Avadhut Gita. He did not concern himself in any way about the content, quality, production or post-production issues pertaining to this (or any earlier) book. About this book, Karl joked " He (Dattatreya) says the same things like me, but in much fewer words. It's going make me look stupid for using so many words"! Karl added, "He is far more polite, unlike me!"

Interestingly, 'Karl' (name given by his parents) in German means 'free man, strong' - not very different from the word 'Avadhut' which, in layman terms, may be roughly understood as 'the free one - of the highest possible order, who has transcended both bondage and freedom'.

The Sanskrit verses have been incorporated in this book to facilitate their independent interpretation, authentication and verification as a certain amount of divergence in interpretation has crept into the various available translations. For this book the translation of verses is done by myself and Manjit Achhra assisted by references to translations of Swami Ashokananda, Swami Abhayananda, Sri Jaya Chamarajendra Wadiyar, Banmali Chaturvedi and others.

Anyone familiar with the Avadhut Gita of Dattatreya would agree to the sheer audacity of this extreme Advaita text. The stunningly paradoxical proclamations found here leave little room, if any, for the reader to honestly arrive at any comprehensible imagination of Reality, striking at the root - imagination itself, which is found to be the impediment to Reality. It is perhaps this 'intellectually untouchable' nature of the Avadhut Gita that renders this ancient scripture unsusceptible to relative interpretation, thereby retaining its eternally enigmatic and uncatchable nature- remaining forever, a double arrowed pointer to ↔ Absoluteness Itself!

Sanjay Inamdar
September 2013

INTRODUCTION

*L*ao Tzu says – The Tao that can be spoken, is not the real Tao, The name that can be named is not the real name. In that sense, can we call silence as truth? No! Says Karl-Who needs to be quiet to be quiet? Silence is not sitting somewhere and not saying anything. That's still saying too much. That's talking too loud – someone who is not saying something.

This book presents unparalleled dialogues from Dattatreya's Avadhut Gita and talks with Karl Renz. Dattatreya is an ancient Indian Avadhut encompassing the trinity of Brahma, Vishnu and Shiva, collectively known as Trimurti. The name Dattatreya can be divided into two words - 'Datta' (meaning given) and 'Atreya' referring to the sage Atri, his physical father.

Dattatreya was born to sage Atri, who was promised by Shiva, that he himself would incarnate as his son. Since the Absolute subsumes all three aspects of the trimurti, Dattatreya is usually depicted with three heads, symbolising Brahma, Vishnu and Shiva; past, present and future; and the three states of consciousness: waking, dreaming and dreamless sleep. They also symbolize the three states of manifestation: creation, sustenance and destruction.

In the Nath tradition (to which Nisargadatta Maharaj and Ranjit Maharaj belonged), Dattatreya is recognized as an Avatar or an incarnation of Shiva and as the Adi-Guru (Primal Teacher) of the Adinath tradition. This further developed to the Navnath (Nine Lords) tradition.

An 'Avadhut' is someone who has cast away all attachments by virtue of the fact that he is 'liberated' from bondage, attachment and suffering. In fact, the 'Avadhut' Dattatreya is a rare sage who is 'liberated' from both 'bondage' and 'liberation'.

The Dattatreya Upanishad praises the Avadhut as the one who bestows the highest character of sentience and bliss, who is in the guise of a child, a mad-man, a devil. (baalonmatta-pishaaca-veshaaya)

Once Dattatreya dove into a lake and stayed there for many years to evade an entourage of sages pursuing him. The sages, however, remained on the banks of the lake awaiting his return. Dattatreya emerged from the water naked and in the company of a beautiful woman. The text further relates that he made love to her, drank liquor and enjoyed singing and music. In spite of this, the sages did not abandon him. Dattatraya, accompanied by his shakti, continued to engage in these practices and was meditated upon by those longing for moksha.

The Avadhut Gita (Song of the Free) is a wonderful compilation of the highest thought recorded in text by two of Dattatreya's disciples, Swami and Kartika in the 9th century. The true dating of this Gita, however, remains unknown. Originally a work of seven chapters, a spurious and misogynistic eighth chapter may be a later attempt to append sexual morality to the Nath tradition by some conservative ascetic(s). Some of the ideas in this Gita are however common to both Shaivite and Buddhist Tantras.

The wise man prattles about the truth says Dattatreya. Karl would say, for me it would be the same as the high, profound or brmm... brmm.... There's no difference. Makes no difference. All the day brmm... is no different than talking all the day about the substratum and the absolute and the highest of the highest. And all the levels of the underlying truth. Different resonance but that what is resonating to itself would not be different in nature.

In that sense, one may sit silent and still be really talking loud. On the other hand, you may say whatever and they are just empty words. Nothing gets spoken in that.

This book is organized in seven chapters as the original Avadhut Gita with each verse presented in Sanskrit along with the translation and corresponding 'match' from Karl's talks. What's truly remarkable is that two men, having no common background or influence speak in such a similar pattern that it's hard to imagine that they are not actual commentaries.

That is what makes it more alive, as there is no one trying to prove or justify any verse. It's just like a pattern in a kaleidoscope that has repeated itself amongst million other possibilities.

Today as the probabilistic view of the universe; the idea of universe itself gets challenged, more and more physicists talk like mystics. All that can happen has already happened. This would endlessly repeat itself like a solid block. In that sense, patterns repeat and in a rare possibility appear exactly the same.

Enjoy this rare blend of east and the west, traditional and contemporary, prattles of... whatever! And with all the words, all the highest of the highest, does anything really get said?

Manjit Achhra
September 2013

Chapter One

ईश्वरानुग्रहादेव पुंसामद्वैतवासना ।
महद्भयपरित्राणाद्द्विप्राणामुपजायते ॥ १॥

*By God's grace alone,
the desire for non-duality arises in inwardly stirred men;
To save them from great fear. [1:1]*

K: If grace is after you, if that depression happens, because there is a senselessness happening, the world makes no sense any more, marriage makes no sense, money makes no sense, nothing can satisfy you, you become depressed. But that deep rest is because grace is already after you. Because you coming closer to that what is peace, and that never needs any sense of life, there is no meaning in it. It never needs any meaning. And if the Self wants to be that again what is Self, not knowing anything and not needing anything, you will be depressed. The closer you come to that what is rest, you as a phantom will be depressed. I take it as a good sign.

– *May It Be As It Is* p82

येनेदं पूरितं सर्वमात्मनैवाअत्मनात्मनि ।
निराकारं कथं वन्दे ह्यभिन्नं शिवमव्ययम् ॥ २॥

How shall I pay my salutations to That
which is formless, non-dual, auspicious and inexhaustible;
Who fills all this with His Self
and also fills the self with His Self. [1:2]

K: This is all the vibration of the light you are. Imagine! The Indian mythology is very clear in it. The nature of the first penis is to penetrate whatever is there. So you always try to penetrate yourself by whatever means, by whatever possibility.

At first you penetrate the space, the yoni, the cosmic vagina you penetrate and try to find the end of light in that infinite space. And you cannot find the end of light but you vibrate in infinite ways to fill up that space. By that you fill up the whole universe, the whole milky ways, whatever is there, is you trying to penetrate yourself and you trying to find yourself in that infinite space.

All is absolute. The absolute light, the absolute space and the absolute possibilities of all possible vibrations of that light. All of that is what-you-are. So being what-you-cannot-not-be is being That and that is Nisargatta's 'I Am That'. And through That, there is no second. And you cannot not be what-you-are. That is the way you are living yourself.

You are light living in all possible ways of light vibrating in all ways. Vibrating and non-vibrating, knowing and not knowing, all whatever is! But by none of that you will know your nature. You cannot know your nature. In any relative whatever you do or not do, whatever knowing or not knowing, it is a realization of what-you-are but not that what-you-are. So what to do?

– Heaven And Hell p112

K: First there is awareness, the light of Shiva. And then comes space, and the lingam starts to vibrate, and then in that absolute vibration creates all that can be created as information of vibration. This is all vibration of energy. Even the scientists would say you can't find any matter. It's just vibration of light, that's the closest you can get. But that what is light you still don't know. And that is Para-Brahman. And knowing him as Brahma he knows himself as light, as creator, starting to know himself. And the love affair comes later. It's just innocent vibration, in an innocent space. And then out of that innocent penetration, comes all that – look at it! And then that what came out of it wants to know why. 'Why did this bloody vibrator start to vibrate?' 'If he wouldn't have started to vibrate I would not have this problem!' 'How can I stop this bloody vibrator?' 'So now I meditate and try to stop this bloody vibrator!' 'And I go deeper and deeper and if it doesn't stop I try everything'. That's called self-inquiry or meditation. You try to stop the vibration of light. Amazing!

– *May It Be As It Is* p202

पञ्चभूतात्मकं विश्वं मरीचिजलसन्निभम् ।
कस्याप्यहो नमस्कुर्यामहमेको निरञ्जनः ॥ ३॥

The whole universe composed of five elements
is like water in a mirage;
To whom shall I pay my salutations?
I am One and without imperfection. [1:3]

Q: For me, the most challenging thing with you is not that you contradict yourself, but behind that there is a solid block of concrete that you cannot do a fucking scratch. That's the real annoying thing for me...

K: Everyone wants to scratch that. I always point to that which can never be touched.

Q: But what is it?

K: I have no idea. I talk to you and I see the same. That what is what-you-are is as solid as it can be. For me it makes no difference, but you are in the impression that you can be touched or changed like a leaf in the wind and of course you feel controlled by something. But in what I Am there is no believer, no belief system that can be moved by something.

But if I look at you, I see the same – the unmovable. It's always there. There's always that and nothing else as the unmovable itself. So I cannot even take it as a compliment because for me there is only That, but why not? Give me compliments. You cannot help me with that either.

Q: [Another visitor]: That what you call unmovable, is what others would call God?

K: Call it underwear – forget it.

Q: But what is meant by That?

K: Call it That which has no second and the absence of the second which cannot be touched by anything. Not even by itself. So, call it whatever.

– The Song Of Irrelevance p23

आत्मैव केवलं सर्वं भेदाभेदो न विद्यते ।
अस्ति नास्ति कथं ब्रूयां विस्मयः प्रतिभाति मे ॥ ४॥

All this is nothing but Self;
There is neither difference or non-difference,
or the absence of difference or non-difference;
How, then, can I say that it is or is not?!
I am wonderstruck. [1:4]

K: You don't have to remember, you are That anyway. Don't try to remember, just be That. Don't make it a concept, I just point to something. When I say – you're the absence of the presence, I just point to the fact that you cannot be found in any presence. You cannot find what-you-are, because you are the absence of the presence. And in the absence, you have not lost yourself because your presence cannot be lost in the absence.

But now in the presence, you're the presence which cannot be found in the presence. By whatever present moment, you cannot find yourself. If you can find yourself, you could be something that could be found and that already is hell. Now you found yourself. You claim that you're a human, you know yourself and that already is hell.

So, you better be the absence of any idea of what-you-are. Because what you can find are ideas, concepts, sensational images and all kinds of experiences. But in all those experiences, you cannot be found. You cannot find yourself in the experiencer, experiencing, what can be experienced. If you really look for yourself, you cannot find yourself anywhere. No way to find yourself. You pretend that you're in the experiencer, but if you really look for it, you cannot find yourself.

That's actually Nisargadatta's Ultimate Medicine – look for the speaker and you cannot find that. By not having found who-you-are, you just remain in the absence of – what? You're not even a loser. Because if you would have been a loser, you could have found yourself. As you could not lose yourself, you're neither the loser or the finder. You're just – who knows? Who needs to know? But still you are! The laziest you can be, which has never done anything. Never active nor inactive, neither doing nor not doing – neither.

That's the famous neti-neti, you're neither that or That and That never needs to have any idea about acceptance or tolerance. Acceptance, tolerance only applies to the phantom concept world. Love, hate, all needs someone who calls something – something and has an idea about something. And that's the root thought 'I' – that always creates problems which would not be there without it. That's called mind.

— *Worry And Be Happy p75*

वेदान्तसारसर्वस्वं ज्ञानं विज्ञानमेव च ।
अहमात्मा निराकारः सर्वव्यापी स्वभावतः ॥ ५॥

*The essence and the basis of Vedanta
is this Knowledge – This Supreme Knowledge:
'I am Self, formless, all-pervasive by my very nature'. [1:5]*

Q: When Sri Ramana was asked, 'When will realization of the Self be gained?' he replied, 'When the world, which is what is seen, has been removed there will be realization of the Self, which is the Seer.' What is the true understanding of the world?

K: The world is there the moment the 'I' appears. Out of this 'I' the spider creates the world surrounded by creation, then the 'I am' as formless consciousness. Then the creative force of the 'I am' creates all this information, which we call world. So this information of universe or world is consciousness in form, coming out of the non-form of formless consciousness.

Consciousness creates by simply getting into form. That which is world is actually consciousness in action, like Shiva dancing with himself and creating this universe out of his dance. The essence of everything that is form and non-form is consciousness. All there is, is consciousness - as cosmic consciousness.

Q: And how to remove the world?

K: By being as you are. If there is Self and nothing but Self then there is no world anymore. That is the only way out: to see that there was never any such thing as world, that world in its essence is consciousness, and consciousness is all that there is. Consciousness is your absolute realization, but you are not your realization. You are that which is realizing itself through consciousness. So you are the very source of consciousness. It is not even consciousness, but consciousness is your infinite body, or your infinite realization. Then there was never any world, mind or obstacles at all because at this realization everything collapses. That is the only realization that I know: to see that the Self is ever realized. And for this there is nothing to do or not to do. Simply be That, which is Self.

– Interview

K: You are all this, in essence, as you are the I of the "I," the I am of the "I-am," and the I am so of the "I am so." You are always That which is existence itself, That what is Heart of whatever is and is not.

In this sense, you are That which is emptiness and you are That which is fullness. But you are not emptiness and you are not fullness. So be That, as you cannot not be it. By whatever you try, you cannot leave what you are. There is no advantage to be here, there, or there, and no disadvantage.

Whatever idea of advantage or whoever tells you this is like "awareness" or something special, whenever you make a landing place, you are separating yourself from something else, from That which is separation. Whenever you make a landing place, you separate from That. By making emptiness what you are, you separate yourself from fullness. Whatever you define, whatever "divine" idea you have, is separation. But you cannot separate yourself.

– Eight Days in Tiruvannamalai p47

यो वै सर्वात्मको देवो निष्कलो गगनोपमः ।
स्वभावनिर्मलः शुद्धः स एवायं न संशयः ॥ ६॥

There is no doubt that I am That God who is the Self in all;
Shining, space-like by nature, free of defects and pure. [1:6]

K: Abidance in the Self is like simply being That which is Heart, which is prior to that "I"-thought, and then staying prior to that "I"-thought. Being That from which the "I"-thought comes. Staying in that Source, as that Source you are, by seeing that "I"-thought comes in the morning into whatever form of "in-form-ation," but That which you are is prior to that.

Q: It's actually not possible.

K: Nothing else is possible. You cannot not abide, as you are That anyway. You are That which is the Source of that "I"-thought, what is Heart itself, and in that Heart, the "I"-thought as an "in-form-ation" flowers or blooms. But you are not what is coming as an "I"-thought, so stay in That which is permanent, absolutely permanent, as solid as it can be, that Heart itself, unmoved by that idea. That is abidance. Be that unmoved Heart itself—which was never touched or untouched, never shaken or changed in any sense—simply by seeing that "I"-thought already as a phantom thought and staying at That which is prior to that thought.

– *Eight Days in Tiruvannamalai* p132

अहमेवाव्ययोऽनन्तः शुद्धविज्ञानविग्रहः ।
सुखं दुःखं न जानामि कथं कस्यापि वर्तते ॥ ७॥

I alone am immutable, indestructible and infinite
– pure consciousness itself;
I know neither pleasure nor pain as occurring to anything. [1:7]

K: I'm singing the glory of forms. You can enjoy them because you're not part of it. You like everything because you don't need it. That is the singing of songs of glory of informations that give you pure joy, because you don't need it. Because they cannot bring you joy. That's the joy of emptiness of forms.

Your nature, which you can say is the joy that doesn't need joy, is enjoying all informations of... And no one needs them. It's a dance of information which is pure joy because there is no need for it. It's a pure entertainment of life, but it doesn't need to make sense or anything. You don't get more or less by any of this information. So, they're pure beauty.

– *Worry And Be Happy* p77

न मानसं कर्म शुभाशुभं मे
न कायिकं कर्म शुभाशुभं मे ।
न वाचिकं कर्म शुभाशुभं मे
ज्ञानामृतं शुद्धमतीन्द्रियोऽहम् ॥ ८॥

I have no mental activity, good or bad;
I have no bodily activity good or bad;
I have no verbal activity, good or bad.
I am the nectar of Jñana*, beyond senses, pure. [1:8]

---

* Jñana in the *Avadhut Gita* does not refer to objective knowledge/ knowingness, consciousness or awareness which are the terms generally used to depict Jñana. It is used as pointer to the Absolute itself.

Q: Do you believe in thoughts?

K: No. I don't believe in thoughts. For me all of that is a reaction of – you don't know what. And I don't have to know where it comes from because for me nothing ever comes and nothing ever happens.

Why should I know where it comes from? What would be the use of it? What would I gain if I know where it comes from? And who would be the gainer of knowing where it comes from? Who needs that advantage? Questions after questions...

The answer is always – 'me'. And that's already an idea!

Q: If you know where it comes from, we can be a bit more alert...

K: Where does the 'me' come from? And who wants to know where does the 'me' comes from? Only me!

Q: The Self...

K: The Self doesn't need to know anything, only the 'me' needs to know. So the 'me' creates the problems which would not be there without the 'me'. Now you create the problem because you would not exist without the problem.

An idea creates the idea that the idea needs to know the idea and where it comes from. But without the idea of 'me' there would not even be an idea. A concept needs to know where the concept comes from.

– *Heaven And Hell p17*

मनो वै गगनाकारं मनो वै सर्वतोमुखम् ।
मनोऽतीतं मनः सर्वं न मनः परमार्थतः ॥ ९ ॥

Mind is indeed like space, Mind is indeed in all directions;
The Mind is the past, Mind is all;
But in reality there is no mind. [1:9]

Q: Is there a difference between mind and consciousness?

K: No, they are the same in nature for sure – just different words for... so, never-mind. If you want to blame someone, you call it mind. If you want to pray to the same thing, you call it consciousness.

That's the way it is! If you want to find someone who is guilty, you call it mind and if you want to find someone who can help you, you call it consciousness. But it's not different.

So, if you want to blame it, you call it the devil and so if you want to have someone who can help you, you call it God.

– *Bombay 2013*

Q: So that means that the reporter will always be? I mean, I hear the mystics talking about the "no-mind" state–

K: Yeah, if you would recognize yourself in that "me," in the reporter, in whatever you experience, consider it as no different from what you are. You are That which is the experience, experiencing what is experienced, in essence, as you are That which is. In That, there was never any mind, there is no anything, there is nothing that can disturb you, as That which is freedom itself cannot be disturbed by freedom.

That freedom is the absence of a second. So whatever is there is an entertainment of talking, the Self is talking with the Self. So what? Self-entertainment. And who needs then the Self to shut up? What other Self?

So what is with this "no-mind"? The absolute no-mind is if you see that whatever is, is the Self and being it. By being absolutely what you are, you are That which is existence itself. So you are That. There never was, never will be, any mind. So what is then the no-mind? There's neither mind nor no-mind. Both are ideas.

And who needs a "no-mind"? The mind. Only the mind minds the mind. Never mind!

— *Eight Days in Tiruvannamalai*

अहमेकमिदं सर्वं व्योमातीतं निरन्तरम् ।
पश्यामि कथमात्मानं प्रत्यक्षं वा तिरोहितम् ॥ १०॥

I, the only one am (I am) all this, transcending space and
all-pervasive; I am devoid of distinction;
How, then, can I see the Self as perceived or beyond
perception?! [1:10]

Q: As I understand, it is the subject that perceives all the objects?

K: No. The subject is already experienced by That what is experiencing the object. There's no need for it. It's just the way it happens.

Q: So, there are two sides of the coin, subject and object?

K: No. Subject-object is just one side of the coin. The other side of the coin is the absence of the subject-object – presence-absence. In the presence there is a seer, seeing what can be seen. The other side is the absence of seer, seen, what can be seen. So, there are two sides of what-you-are. You are the Absolute Self – the coin, and one side of the coin is the presence of experience and the other side is the absence of experience. In the presence there is always a presence of the seer – 'me', experiencer, experiencing what can be experienced. That's the presence. It starts very subtle with the presence of awareness, but already there is an 'I'.

Q: The subject in this case is consciousness?

K: Consciousness is one side of you That plays the subject and the object. It plays all the roles. There's a conscious side and an unconscious side. On one side you are conscious in this dream of consciousness and the other side is the absence of the dream of consciousness. But you are in the presence and in the absence of the dream of consciousness. Both are your sides. So, you cannot get rid of the consciousness or the absence of consciousness. But in consciousness, this is all there is – whatever you can experience. Whatever can be, is in consciousness. But what-you-are is with and without it.

– Worry And Be Happy p16

K: There is only That which is existence itself, because when you are That which is seeing, then you are whatever is – there is no separation. When you are That which is the experiencer, you are That which is experiencing and what is experience, as you are that existence absolute.

So you are That which is the experiencer, but you are not the experiencer. You are That which is the person, but you are not the person. You are That which is the body, but you are not the body. So if you are That which is, then you are what is the experiencer, that experiencing, and what is experienced—in the presence of that and in the absence too. Then there is no difference. In the presence of what is world, or in the absence of the world, only That which is, is.

And That has no idea of being That or not. So even to say you are That which is seeing, you are not seeing, you are That which is seeing. And by being That which is seeing, you are what is seer and what is the whole world. Because then whatever is, is Heart. As you are That which is the world, you don't know the world anymore, because whatever is, is what you are. So in that moment, you are not the seer, not the seeing, nor the seen, as you are That which is. In the presence and in the absence. It makes no difference any more.

In order to exist, the experiencer needs the presence of experiencing and something to experience. But That which is the experiencer doesn't need the presence of an experiencer experiencing blah, blah, blah. This is absolutely independent of any circumstance. All the circumstances need circumstances, the experiencer needs a circumstance of experiencing, but That which is the experiencer doesn't need anything.

– Eight Days in Tiruvannamalai

त्वमेवमेकं हि कथं न बुध्यसे
समं हि सर्वेषु विमृष्टमव्ययम् ।
सदोदितोऽसि त्वमखण्डितः प्रभो
दिवा च नक्तं च कथं हि मन्यसे ॥ ११॥

Thus you are One; Why, then, do you not understand;
That you are the unchangeable One, equally perceived in all?
O mighty One, ever-shining, unrestricted; Where, for you, is
there any distinction of day and night ?! [1:11]

K: Parabrahman in its Absolute absence of any presence of any experience, is that what he is in its nature and is never losing its nature. Then it starts dreaming itself in a dream-like realization of seven possible ways. But in none of them it can get found or lost, that is all. But try to find yourself in one of the seven states, in the presence or absence or personal or impersonal makes you relative. Even the impersonal states are relative states. Natural state doesn't know any state. Your natural state is being what you are, neither knowing nor not knowing what you are. There is no Absolute knower or not knower present or absent. There is knowledge without even being aware of knowledge. That knowledge doesn't even need to be aware of knowledge or conscious of knowledge or anything. From there which is knowledge is realizing itself as a personal knower or an impersonal knower. Then there is a knower who knows or an impersonal knower in knowing what can be known in the oneness experience. Only separation experience, where the knower is different from what he knows or where the knower is one from what he knows.

But both are relative. Both are different. In the dream, you can say that impersonal is better than the personal but only in the dream. For what you are, it's neither. In what you are, there is no discriminator who discriminates between personal and impersonal.

And where there is discrimination between personal and impersonal, it's already too late. There starts the relative discriminating between better and not so good, advantage-disadvantage all of that. It comes as a pair. Even oneness and separation comes together.

Ramana is a rare one who said when there is oneness there is twoness, instantly. It comes together as day and night. Then you shift through all of them or so it seems like but what you are never shifts through anything and what shifts through something is a fisherman who wants to fish something. Always tries to catch a bigger fish, an impersonal fish because he thinks that the impersonal fish tastes better than the personal fish. Both stink. All the fishes stink after a while.

– Am I – I Am p65

आत्मानं सततं विद्धि सर्वत्रैकं निरन्तरम् ।
अहं ध्याता परं ध्येयमखण्डं खण्ड्यते कथम् ॥ १२॥

Know the Self always to be everywhere, one and uninterrupted;
I Am That which meditates and That which is meditated upon;
Why, then, do you divide the indivisible?! [1:12]

K: You meditate. Because your nature is meditation as consciousness, and that meditation means you have no expectation of a result. So you are as you are. You are that meditation, which is meditation in nature, action without intention.

Simply see, there is no result coming out of whatever is done or not done. By no understanding can you become what you are. In spite of knowing or not knowing, you are. So if you are totally in spite of whatever you can know or not know, then there is meditation because you cannot not realize yourself.

And realizing yourself is meditating about That which you are. Out of that meditation, the whole dream starts. This dream is meditating about what you are as consciousness. This is a manifestation of what you are. That is meditation without intention.

At the moment intention is part of the meditation; it becomes a personal "me," because there is an advantage idea. "By meditating, I can become what I am looking for, what I am longing for." You make yourself an object of desire, of a goal. Then you are in that control business. You become "the meditator." You are doing meditation.

But you have to be meditation. There is no doership in meditation. That is the "I am" meditating about That which is "I am." That's all.

– *Eight Days in Tiruvannamalai p172*

K: The nature of meditation is – there's action without intention. There's no cause in it, it's not be- cause. It's just – Pang!

– *Worry And Be Happy p50*

न जातो न मृतोऽसि त्वं न ते देहः कदाचन ।
सर्वं ब्रह्मेति विख्यातं ब्रवीति बहुधा श्रुतिः ॥ १३॥

You are never born nor do you die; You never have a body; 'All is Brahman'– the scriptures declare this truth in various ways. [1:13]

K: You always commit the murder. You committed the murder now by thinking there are persons. Even that you think you are born, you committed murder. You murdered yourself. You committed suicide by just believing you have a body is suicide. That you are born is suicide.

So you are a murderer already and you should be punished for that. Life time you got already and a death penalty on top of it, by believing that you are born. Happy Birthday!

Look! Instant punishment! The moment you are born, you got a lifetime on top of a death penalty. Then you fear that something may happen to you. Just by your committing suicide, by believing that you are born you are punished with a lifetime on this bloody earth.

– Heaven And Hell p59

स बाह्याभ्यन्तरोऽसि त्वं शिवः सर्वत्र सर्वदा ।
इतस्ततः कथं भ्रान्तः प्रधावसि पिशाचवत् ॥ १४॥

That which is outside and inside is yourself;
You are the auspicious One; ever existing in every circumstance,
under all conditions; Why, then, are you deluded and why do
you run around like a ghost?! [1:14]

K: That's maybe why I don't go back to Tiruvannamalai anymore, because there are too many disciples running around who claim to be a disciple of someone who never took any disciples. What a falsity, running around this mountain now. But the mountain doesn't care. Someone claiming to be - I could... But I am too lazy for that. I have no interest in cleaning up. Otherwise I would have to destroy the whole universe. But I did already. How can I destroy what is not there? Just by being what you are you destroy everything.

Whatever you can imagine is destroyed.

— May It Be As It Is p108

संयोगश्च वियोगश्च वर्तते न च ते न मे ।
न त्वं नाहं जगन्नेदं सर्वमात्मैव केवलम् ॥ १५॥

*Union and separation owe their existence neither
to you nor to me; There is no you, no me, nor is there any
universe; All is verily the Self alone. [1:15]*

K: I don't see anything.

Q: Why? Is it because everything is a lie?

K: No. Because What I Am is not a seer. How can I see something? What I Am never sees anything. The seer sees what can be seen. But all of that is part of the seer, the story of the seer but is not what 'I Am'. You cannot make That what I Am the story of a seer. Whatever you see is already past, you know that. You need to explain what you see. There needs to be an explainer for what you see, otherwise there is not even seeing.

You have to name a tree to see a tree. You have to name the universe, that there can be a universe. That there is a seeing and a seer, he has to name himself.

— Heaven And Hell p145

शब्दादिपञ्चकस्यास्य नैवासि त्वं न ते पुनः ।
त्वमेव परमं तत्त्वमतः किं परितप्यसे ॥ १६॥

An outcome of the five senses you are not,
nor do they belong to you; You are the supreme Reality.
Why, then, do you bother?! [1:16]

K: I tell you whatever you can experience is a lie. Anything, whatever, there is no exception.

Q: That is the nature of experience?

K: That is the nature of any sensational experience. Whatever you can experience is a lie and a lie always starts with an experiencer. So it starts with a lie and it continues with lies. And whatever you can know, is a lie. The lie starts with a knower. The knower, the knowing, what can be known – it's all ignorance. It's all false, from the beginning. Whatever comes from that field of knowledge and whatever can be known or not is all part of it. It's all part of it, there is no exception. Knowledge will never be found in one of that. Whatever you find is lower and higher lies, deeper lies and higher lies. Lie, lie, lie, lie. That is lila.

And thank God you cannot find the end of lies. No beginning of lies and no end of lies. So in the nature, even the lies are knowledge. As even they are absolute in their nature, they are real-lies. There is a reality of lies. But you cannot find reality in the lies. The nature of it is already real. But not one lie is better than the other. But if you make one lie more or less higher or lower, then you rely on – whatever.

So it's easier to see everything as a lie. That's the good company. Being the absolute liar talking to the absolute liar. That is the good company of the absolute liar talking to the absolute liar who is listening. Because even the Self cannot know the truth. Even the absolute cannot know itself. So whatever the absolute is saying to the absolute is a lie. Even the pointers are pointers of lying.

Q: When the absolute is saying that 'I'm saying lies', doesn't it become the truth?

K: No. No.

Q: When you say that the nature of everything is a lie, doesn't that become the truth?

K: No. You don't have to pronounce it. The moment you pronounce it, it becomes a lie again. That's why the Neti-neti is so profound. Neti-neti means lie, lie, lie, lie and not lie, lie, lie, truth.

– Heaven And Hell p140

जन्म मृत्युर्न ते चित्तं बन्धमोक्षौ शुभाशुभौ ।
कथं रोदिषि रे वत्स नामरूपं न ते न मे ॥ १७॥

For you there is neither birth nor death, nor is there a mind;
For you there is neither bondage nor liberation,
nor good nor evil; Why, then, do you shed tears, my child?!
Name and form apply neither to you nor to me. [1:17]

K: So the question is like, did something happen to you anyway? The pointer is always like since you were a baby, whatever you can remember is what you are and that never changed. Through all your so-called life, all your beginning and ends, all your changes, all your deep disasters, personal whatever, there is That what you are uninterrupted and unchanged. There was never any change in what you are.

But you cannot even know what it is. But it is That what you are, totally unchanged. Maybe there is a more or less memory functioning of cluster of events that are clustered around some imaginary 'I', but even that doesn't change you. You are still that what you were as a baby – unaffected, never had any effect. The whole story never had any effect to what you are.

So what you are was never affected by any of these immense tragedies of your personal events and being born is quite tragic. But you were already That before you were born and since you were born, nothing happened to what you are. There are so many happenings, you can count them, very intense and very touching but nothing happened.

So, if I point to that, it's That which you cannot not be which is already there. So it's not something new, it is most natural that you cannot not be. It's not a new discovery or something; it doesn't need a discovery channel or something. That's why they call it the open secret and not the closed underwear.

– *Am I – I Am p196*

अहो चित्त कथं भ्रान्तः प्रधावसि पिशाचवत् ।
अभिन्नं पश्य चात्मानं रागत्यागात्सुखी भव ॥ १८॥

O mind, why do you wander about deluded, like a ghost?
Behold That indivisible Self;
Renouncing passion – be happy. [1:18]

K: Everyone runs around an enlightened sausage in the Ramana Ashram and thinks he can gain something by that. A mummified body, radiation of light, and everyone is running around and falling down in front of a sausage, on top of a lingam. I like it! How stupid can it get? Look at it! Just look at the divine stupidity! Running around Kailash, prostrating. Yet all of that has to happen.

And all of that is unavoidable. In spite of no one needing it, it has to happen. In spite of the universe being as it is already and God being absolute, and all being complete, all little aspects of meditation, of whatever, have to be done, will be done, is already done. No way out! I still call it stupid. But you cannot avoid being dumb enough to believe in yourself. You will always again believe in what you are, and in believing what you are you left yourself. But by that believing in what you are, even in the experience of having left yourself, you haven't left yourself. It's an experience of the believer having left what is the believer.

But even by that you haven't left. And then you maybe remember your religion, you come back. But by going back and by remembering no one goes back. But still it happens. So you cannot avoid all these experiences. What to do?

I can only point out none of that can deliver what you are looking for. You rather be here now what you are and don't postpone that what never needs to look anyway. But even that is too much. Who needs that? But still I have to say it. This paradox you cannot break. In spite of everything you are, but still this happens. You have to realize yourself. You cannot not realize yourself.

– May It Be As It Is p161

त्वमेव तत्त्वं हि विकारवर्जितं
निष्कम्पमेकं हि विमोक्षविग्रहम् ।
न ते च रागो ह्यथवा विरागः
कथं हि सन्तप्यसि कामकामतः ॥ १९॥

You alone are indeed the Reality;
One, devoid of change, unaffected and the nature
of freedom itself; Neither attachment nor aversion apply to you;
Why, then, do you suffer, seeking the objects of desires?! [1:19]

K: The Gnostic's have this snake sign where the head is looking at its own tail. And the head thinks that the tail is a different snake. So it fears himself because the tail is moving and the head is not moving. And then the head fears the tail. So it becomes a fairy tale – the whole thing. [Laughter] Then he wants to control his own tail – the other snake. Then he asks, where does the movement come from? You are the movement and you are asking where does the movement come from? What an idea!

Your tail is moving and you ask why is the tail moving? And who is moving here? Can that be me? No! It's very instant fear. You cannot avoid it. There is a lover and the beloved in the best form because there is loving and caring. With love-caring, becomes love-hating. Both come together. Loving and hating comes together as one side of... care taking.

– Heaven And Hell p21

K: Out of an "okay" always comes a "not okay" again. You have to live with it. Even to call it "predestination" is trying to control it, because by understanding it as predestination, that freedom or that peace that comes by that is depending on that idea. So, whatever you do, you make yourself dependant on that understanding of predestination. You cannot step out of it. No way out.

That detachment is so totally attached to that detachment. When I am asked what you do, I say—Be totally attached to what you are, be that absolute being, as you cannot not be attached to what you are, being that attachment itself. You cannot leave what you are.

In absolute identification, there is no separate identification anymore, and the separate one is simply dropping—but that cannot be done. That absolute identification that you are That: cannot be done—you have to be It! But not by any understanding, not by choice, not by anything, as you are That anyway, as you cannot not be it, that's all! So be It!

– Eight Days in Tiruvannamalai

वदन्ति श्रुतयः सर्वाः निर्गुणं शुद्धमव्ययम् ।
अशरीरं समं तत्त्वं तन्मां विद्धि न संशयः ॥ २० ॥

*Scriptures declare the Self to be attributeless, pure,
inexhaustible, formless, existing equally everywhere;
Know me to be That without an iota of doubt. [1:20]*

Q: You said that in absolute nothing, there is Absolute...

K: I never said that. Nothing is not Absolute. The nature of nothing is Absolute and the nature of everything is Absolute, but 'nothing' is not Absolute. If 'nothing' would be Absolute, there would be no-everything. If 'nothing' would really be the nature of things, then this would be not what is. Then 'nothing' would be different to this.

How can anything that is different to this be the Absolute without a second? Only that. How can that be? How can nothing be the Absolute? How can emptiness be the Absolute?

Whatever you say or don't say – it is not. It has no attribute or no-attribute, neither it has nor it has not. Neither it is nor it is not, it neither exists nor doesn't exist. Whatever you say is false. Whatever you say, whatever you don't say, whatever you hear, think or not think is all false. False, false, false, false, false!

Because whatever you come up with or not come up with needs opposites, needs to exist. Even emptiness needs to exist to be emptiness.

– *Am I – I Am p147*

Q: When you say consciousness is looking for itself, it's all the time impersonal...

K: It is never impersonal. It doesn't even know impersonal and personal. Why should it be impersonal? You cannot give any attribute to That. By making it impersonal, you already create it as an opposite to personal.

Q: In the way you are experiencing yourself...

K: I don't experience myself – Thank God! I can never experience what I Am, so I can never experience myself. Hallelujah! That's all I can say.

– *The Song Of Irrelevance p22*

साकारमनृतं विद्धि निराकारं निरन्तरम् ।
एतत्तत्त्वोपदेशेन न पुनर्भवसम्भवः ॥ २१॥

Recognize that with form to be unreal and formlessness to be eternal; Receiving the teaching that expounds this truth, there is no possibility of rebirth. [1:21]

Q: The realization is that there is a lie, that everything is formless...

K: But even that goes away too. Everything is formless, is that a truth?

Q: That there is no form...

K: Is that truth? Whatever you can pronounce and find out, would be covered again. Whatever you say now is separation because the non-form is different from form and formlessness. Then you make another level – emptiness. Then you say I realized that emptiness can never get more or less. Sounds good! Then the opposite of emptiness would not be true.

Q: But that's the nature of language...

K: No. You cannot escape in language. Don't blame language, you can do better. Many people come to me and claim that they have realized something. That they went to a deep place where no one was, there was just emptiness and there was no one to find. They really found a place where there was no one. So, is this not truth and that was truth? Who makes a difference – When I was not it was true and now when I am, it's true. Who makes this difference?

– Worry And Be Happy p24

Q: Will you talk about the difference between the "I" and the "I am"? I'm confusing those two. You were saying the "I am" is formless and the "I am so-and-so" is form—

K: Yeah, and what is the pure "I" is formlessness. This is the Source of form and non-form, which is awareness. There is not even the idea of "non-form." There is no second in awareness. There is not even space. The "I am" is already space-like, formless consciousness. And out of that space, or emptiness, comes form. "In-form-ation." Both come together at once, as polarity, form and non-form, as one. Both come together out of what is awareness.

Q: So the "I am" is potential form?

K: No, even the "I am" already is form-like. Even the non-form is a kind of form. They both come together. There is no form without non-form. There is no-emptiness without fullness. Both come together at once out of what is the Father, the awareness.

– Eight Days in Tiruvannamalai p299

एकमेव समं तत्त्वं वदन्ति हि विपश्चितः ।
रागत्यागात्पुनश्चित्तमेकानेकं न विद्यते ॥ २२॥

The wise claim that Reality is One and homogeneous in nature;
Through renunciation of attachment, mind and its manifold
expressions cease to exist. [1:22]

K: UG Krishnamurti was once flying on a plane to America and an American was sitting next to him. Americans always ask – What are you doing? Where do you come from? How much money do you make? He asked UG – What is your profession? UG said – I am retired. From what? From retirement! [Laughter] Then the American was quiet for the rest of the flight.

That's like Vashistha pointing out – you retire from retirement because you cannot retire from yourself. You renounce renunciation – by being what-you-are. There will never be any possibility of renouncing anything because renouncing is ignorance. You cannot renounce what-you-are. You devote devotion. What is there that is not you? How can you devote something? Does anything belong to you at all? What can you devote? What can you give?

– *Worry And Be Happy p117*

अनात्मरूपं च कथं समाधि-
रात्मस्वरूपं च कथं समाधिः ।
अस्तीति नास्तीति कथं समाधि-
र्मोक्षस्वरूपं यदि सर्वमेकम् ॥ २३॥

How can that which is the nature of non-self be samadhi?*
How can that which is the nature of self be samadhi?
How can that which is the nature of presence or the absence be samadhi? If all is one and of the nature of freedom,
how can there be samadhi?! [1:23]

* Samadhi is usually described as a non-dual state of consciousness or mind in which the consciousness of the experiencing subject becomes one with the experienced object.

Q: What is the difference between the samadhi and the A-ha moment?

K: The samadhi of awareness is a personal samadhi. You still take it personally that you are the screen where nothing happens and the world is different from what-you-are. There are projects but you are established in awareness. But that's still a personal awareness. The thirst for yourself cannot be stopped by that personal awareness. You always come back and you are as thirsty as before.

Q: Can I know that it's only a samadhi?

K: Many masters talk about it. They know and they claim that they're established in That. Then they tell you, you will be better off, if you follow me. I can teach you to reach that place. So, they give you a reference point where they claim to be established in. They speak from there and I believe them. It's authentic. But it's a reference point and any reference point is a relative one. Then they tell you that it's an advantage. Yes, it is an advantage. I believe it but a relative advantage of a personal advantage. If you are looking for that, go for it.

But I sit here and tell you That the absolute advantage – not needing any advantage, is your nature. And just by being what-you-are, nothing has to be done. But if you are interested in a personal advantage, then you go to someone who can give you that. I have no interest in that.

My absolute interest is [small mischievous pause] – I have no idea!

– *Worry And Be Happy p213*

विशुद्धोऽसि समं तत्त्वं विदेहस्त्वमजोऽव्ययः ।
जानामीह न जानामीत्यात्मानं मन्यसे कथम् ॥ २४॥

You are the all pervading pure essence, disembodied, unborn and imperishable; How, then, can you think in terms of knowing or not-knowing your Self?! [1:24]

K: When God knows himself he is the most stupid guy on earth ever known. God not knowing himself he is Knowledge himself. But God knowing himself he is total ignorance, but still what he is. So he is absolute Ignorance as he is absolute Knowledge. So his absolute Nature is in absolute Knowledge no different than in absolute Ignorance. It never is changing his absolute Nature. But in the absence of knowing he is absolute Knowledge. In the presence of knowing, he is absolute Ignorance. You can even say the nature of ignorance is Knowledge. So what has there to happen? The only little suffering part is: you want to have it! You are greedy. And even people who do self-inquiry they want to earn it, they want to gain it. There is something personal on their agenda. They want to escape from something with it. But it is never meant like that. I am not here to end suffering. I have no interest in ending suffering.

— *May It Be As It Is p187*

K: Who cares about an enlightened phantom? Only the other phantoms. It always needs a community of ignorant ideas and one of them maybe is a master-ignorant. The master of ignorance! There are no masters of knowledge. How can there be a master of knowledge? How can there be a master of Heart? You can only be a master of shit. [Laughter]

And I call it shit, because it is shit — compared to what is your chit — the knowledge, whatever you realize, whatever you know, whatever has a knower or can know — is shit. Even knowing himself, is shit — shit knowing shit. Sat-shit-ananda. Sometimes it's unavoidable, the phantom will always carry a story and sometimes it's a story of 'no-story' — the story of being unborn. Even that is a story.

— *Worry And Be Happy p26*

तत्त्वमस्यादिवाक्येन स्वात्मा हि प्रतिपादितः ।
नेति नेति श्रुतिर्ब्रूयादनृतं पाञ्चभौतिकम् ॥ २५॥

Scriptural proclamations like 'That thou art'
expound the truth of Self;
For that which is unreal and composed of the five elements;
The Shruti proclaims as neither this nor that. [1:25]

Q: What is being said here is a lot of Neti-Neti, not this, not this...

K: It's all Neti-Neti. It's all negative-negative. It's leaving the unpronounced positive aside. The positive will never pronounce itself as whatever it is or not that what you can pronounce is already the negative of the positive. It's not different from the positive but whatever you can pronounce is the negative of that what is the positive.

It's like the realization of that what is Reality, but it's not different from it. But whatever you can experience cannot give you the experience of what you are, it's all negative. It's all Neti-Neti. Not this, not this, not this can ever give you the experience of what you are. It's all negative.

Q: Not this not this not this can never give you the experience of what you are?

K: Yes because the experience of what you are is always there and never needs to be given. You don't need the experience of existence because what you are already is That what is That.

Q: It's Neti-Neti, but Neti-Neti is not a path?

K: It's a permanent Neti-Neti. You just be that what you don't have to know to be.

Q: No reference points, no concepts...

K: There is an absolute reference point of being what you cannot not be which doesn't need any reference point. That what needs a reference point will always be a relative one and will always be a different one and will never be good enough.

Q: That what you cannot-not-be is a reference point but cannot be the reference point...

K: Absolutely. You cannot not be That what never needs a reference point. Be that what doesn't need a reference point, being that what is the absolute reference point of that what you cannot-not-be.

Q: No reference point to the concepts, they dissolve...

K: A concept, a ghost needs a reference point. The me always needs a reference point which is relative because when there would be no relative there would be no me anymore. The me survives in only relative experiences. It always needs a reference to something else. It always needs duality, it lives by duality. If there would be no duality it could not exist.

So what it is doing, even trying to get enlightened, he confirms that there is one who is unenlightened. He trying to wake up confirms the one who is unawake! He tries to realize himself and confirms the one who is unrealized. So whatever is coming from that doer or non-doer is trying to survive.

The ghost, the doubtful me always needs doubtful actions to survive as that what is a doubtful me. Even claiming, I am so sincere, I am honest, I only live for truth or whatever. Just doing it confirms the one who needs it. Fantastic! Even doing it you confirm the one who survives by that. That will never stop. That is the way you realize yourself.

Neti-Neti is the best, was always the best and always will be the best. The deep-deep sleep pointer is always good. The deep-deep sleep means in deep-deep sleep there is total absence of anyone who is or is not, and still what you are is what it is. From there comes the presence.

But to know yourself as presence as that what doesn't need the presence to be That what it is. That is what you are.

– Am I – I Am p95

आत्मन्येवात्मना सर्वं त्वया पूर्णं निरन्तरम् ।
ध्याता ध्यानं न ते चित्तं निर्लज्जं ध्यायते कथम् ॥ २६॥

The self is filled by the Self and is ever pervaded by it;
When there is no meditator or meditation;
Why, then, does your mind meditate shamelessly?! [1:26]

K: If the Self is really after the Self, it will kill the Self – just by being that. The idea of Self cannot remain. God totally and absolutely concentrates on himself, on That what is God. The idea of God would cease away, just by That. That's called the rising of the inner sun and by that inner sun, of absolute knowledge, all that what you can imagine ceases away like butter in the sun.

You cannot even avoid rising of the inner sun – the darkness, the mystery of what-you-are. It will even chase the relative light away. If Shiva wants to destroy the idea of Shiva, it will destroy it when it destroys it and not one second before. And whatever the shadow has done before – it was just a joke. And with That – what is the sun – all those vipasanna techniques and all the meditation and all what you have done, is just peeing in the wind.

– The Song Of Irrelevance p207

शिवं न जानामि कथं वदामि
शिवं न जानामि कथं भजामि ।
अहं शिवश्चेत्परमार्थतत्त्वं
समस्वरूपं गगनोपमं च ॥ २७॥

Not knowing Shiva (Absolute), how can I speak of Him?
Not knowing Shiva, how shall I worship Him?
If That what I am is itself that Absolute Reality;
The all pervading essence – boundless like space. [1:27]

Q: As I understand it, it doesn't have any criteria – neither internal nor external...

K: Yeah. Having absolutely no idea of what-you-are and what-you-are-not. Don't forget what-you-are-not. You neither know what-you-are and what-you-are-not. That's the absolute absence of any idea. If you know what-you-are-not, you still claim to know what-you-are. No. You neither know what-you-are or what-you-are-not.

Q: You can't even say you are not the phantom?

K: No. When there is the phantom, I am the phantom. When there is no-phantom, I am not the phantom. I can never be not That. This just-is, but I Am with and without. I Am with that experience of a phantom and I Am without that experience of a phantom – that's all. But I Am not the one experiencing the phantom and then being the Reality and saying that I Am the Reality and what I experience is not real. I cannot even say that.

I have absolutely no idea of what is real and is not real. I have absolutely no idea of any reality or realization. Because first you need to have an idea of reality and then realization and all of that. If you ask me, it's all fucking fiction.

– *Worry And Be Happy p110*

K: The Self is another false. Whatever you call Self is false. God, Self, whatever. False, false, false. Whatever can be reached even by Self is false reaching. Whatever you can come up with – is separation, it's two. What Self can reach what Self? And who is there to reach what? One false reaching another false. False, false, false.

Whatever you can say is a lie and see everything is a lie. Especially the one who tells you everything is a lie is a liar. So don't rely. What else can you do? The liar has to always rely and he is lying and lying and lying, just to stay in this life as a liar. You rely only on lies because only a liar needs to rely on lies. Then you become a real-lies-ator. Then real-lies your reality.

Then you lie and lie and lie. Then you think that by some lies, you can get out of the lie. Then you need masters who tell you lies, who claim that they found a way out. That they know their true nature. Oh my goodness! What kind of true nature would that be which could be known by someone? Especially by masters, all liars from the beginning to the end.

– Heaven And Hell p139

नाहं तत्त्वं समं तत्त्वं कल्पनाहेतुवर्जितम् ।
ग्राह्यग्राहकनिर्मुक्तं स्वसंवेद्यं कथं भवेत् ॥ २८॥

The 'I'-thought is devoid of reality;
Reality – the all pervading essence,
Is devoid of the need of imagining itself;
Is devoid of distinctions of perceived and perceiver;
How, then, can the 'I'-thought be that which is aware of Itself?!
[1:28]

Q: Ramesh Balsekar says that you are the ego. I am struggling with that. I feel that ego is totally different. If you have the sense of doership, that is the ego, if not, you are not the ego. But Ramesh always said 'You are the ego. You will die as an ego'. That concept is something which I am not able to accept. Could you enlighten me on that?

K: What is meant by it is you are That what is the ego, but that what is the ego doesn't have an ego.

Q: I didn't get you.

K: Yes, if you would get me, there would be no ego anymore. So the ego fights for his schizophrenic idea of me. There is an ego who has an ego. And that means duality. A me who has a me. There is a me-me. And then what Ramesh is pointing to, you are That what is the ego. And the ego came and will be gone as that what is what you call ego. But the ego doesn't know any ego. Only in ownership there are two egos. And then one ego wants to get rid of the other ego.

Q: I cannot understand, there are not two egos.

K: But it needs two egos to know an ego.

Q: Something I can't get into my head. Is it I and the ego? If I feel I am not the doer, somebody else is the doer, then they say the ego is not there. But as long as they feel 'I am the doer', that is the ego.

Ego is something which is different from you and it doesn't exist at all. You imagine it exists. But I was told by Ramesh 'you are the ego'. That is the way the contradiction is coming. Until then I have accepted that I am not the ego.

K: That was what I was talking about. That one who is not the ego is still the ego. That's why I said there are two egos. One who is not the ego and sees an ego. There is two. One who is different from the ego. Then there are two egos.

Q: This is my down-to-earth question, not an imaginary one. What I heard from so many people is 'you are different from the ego'. And if you are feeling that you are doing something that is the ego that gives you this feeling. But this is what I am trying to practice now: I am not the doer; somebody else is the doer, that is what I have been told. I am trying to accept that. If I am not the doer, but I am feeling I am the doer, that feeling is considered an ego. I want to know if that is correct thinking or not correct thinking. That's all I want to know.

K: Whatever you understand now is depending on one who needs to understand. That's called ego. There is a need, a needy I, which needs to understand. That's called ego. That's an experience. You experience one who needs some understanding to get rid of that ego, because there is dis-ease, a not-pleasurable experience. Because there is a me which is always longing for something. There is always something wrong with it. So that's called ego. And you are right: what you can experience you cannot be. But that experience you cannot get rid of. It will be there. That experience of a me which is misery, the me-sery of the me, which is the ego, will always be there. But the me, which is an experience of misery, which is an experience of one who is doing something, is sometimes there and sometimes not. So who is there without it?

— May It Be As It Is p69

अनन्तरूपं न हि वस्तु किंचि-
तत्त्वस्वरूपं न हि वस्तु किंचित् ।
आत्मैकरूपं परमार्थतत्त्वं
न हिंसको वापि न चाप्यहिंसा ॥ २९ ॥

Reality realizes itself in infinite forms, but is not an entity;
Realization is of the nature of Self, but is not an entity;
Devoid of injury or non-injury;
The Self is verily the supreme Truth. [1:29]

Q: It's too late, but still the time is there...

K: Where? No one could ever prove time. You repeat something what you heard about but no one could ever prove time. Time just means two – separation. But no one could ever prove it. The whole quantum physics, the whole scientists could not even find matter. It may not matter. Maybe there is not even two.

Where is the movement? They can only say sometimes it's a particle, sometimes it's a wave. But they cannot find the movement. Where is the movement? What is moving? And where? And who is observing it? And who is witnessing? If you really look for it, you cannot find anything.

Where is something? The moment you look for it, it's gone.

Only when you not look at it, it can be there. But when you look at it, it's gone. Crazy!

– *Heaven And Hell p21*

विशुद्धोऽसि समं तत्त्वं विदेहमजमव्ययम् ।
विभ्रमं कथमात्मार्थे विभ्रान्तोऽहं कथं पुनः ॥ ३० ॥

You are the all pervading essence
– pure, bodiless, unborn and imperishable;
Why, then, do you have any delusion about the Self?!
How, indeed, can I be deluded?! [1:30]

K: The ultimate medicine – Being That, what is in dying not dying and in birth, not born. You cannot avoid one experience. The experience of birth, you could not avoid. But you're not born in that experience, because prior to that experience you have to be, during and beyond.

So, nothing ever happened. It's just a pointer that shit happens, but in that shit happening – what to do?

I can only point to that helplessness. You cannot avoid as shit. You cannot avoid knowing yourself, but any moment you know yourself, it's an experience of unhappiness – you cannot avoid it. You cannot avoid the misery. You can only realize yourself in misery and you have to realize yourself. You're that what has to realize itself – if you like it or not.

– *The Song Of Irrelevance p91*

K: You cannot not fall in love with yourself. You simply wake up to imagining awareness as light, as you cannot not wake up to that awareness. And out of that awareness, you fall in love with "I am" and "I am so-and-so." This is the nature of it. You cannot not do it. You are the helplessness. You cannot avoid anything!

Your helplessness means you are That without a second. It means there is no control. There's absolute controllessness, because there is no second to control.

The beauty of "no second" is that there is no second who can control you. Whatever is there is an imagination of separation and oneness, and whatever ideas are there are because you imagine something. And all those imaginary sensations cannot touch what you are. That's all. They are simply dream-like imaginings. And you are That, but they will never change what you are, as they can never touch or move you one inch.

Q: So is the mistake we make to make a separate world in it?

K: No, you are not in it. You are it. The crazy idea that you take this [Karl slaps his own leg] as being born, as your limited existence, you cannot avoid. But now, you as the Self place yourself in front of That whatever that is sitting here, just to be reminded, "Hey, come on, this cannot be! You're joking! You must be joking to take that as real, as being born!" Ha, ha, ha.

— *Eight Days in Tiruvannamalai p75*

घटे भिन्ने घटाकाशं सुलीनं भेदवर्जितम् ।
शिवेन मनसा शुद्धो न भेदः प्रतिभाति मे ॥ ३१॥

When the pot is broken,
The space within it merges with the infinite space,
and becomes undifferentiated;
As pure Mind, no differences remain,
between the mind and Shiva. [1:31]

Q: The body is vibration of energy that has a given an information of form...

K: Yeah and when this vibration is not functioning anymore, the vibration collapses and naturally goes to the 'I Amness'. Energy cannot get lost.

Q [Another visitor]: So is there a vibration that gives life to a body?

K: It does not give life to anything. The energy in that vibration that you call life, it doesn't give any life. That what is energy – is life and it doesn't give any life to anything. It just shows itself as That, but it doesn't give any life to anything. Life cannot be given or taken away.

Q [Another visitor]: So when this body decomposes, some of them turn to different variety of microbes and some turn to gases...

K: Yeah. So don't burn yourself, don't be stingy, give yourself to the worms. They have a party after you die. A big party! Who cares what happens with that what is in vibration and then changes into something else? Transforming and transforming – in this relative transformation.

Q: With death, does the idea of phantom disappear?

K: No. The phantom is still there, the spirit is still there. It does not disappear; the perceiver is still there – as perceived. The experience of a perceiver is still there, which is not – That. It just shifts from the body thing to the space. That's why as per the Tibetan book of the dead, someone sits for forty eight days saying 'Don't go back into that information system. Stay where you are'. Otherwise you immediately jump into the next. This energy has total tendency of jumping into – where there are two liquids meeting and then something else is created again.

– The Song Of Irrelevance p64

Q: The moment my mother died, there seemed to be an incredible energy that came and then it just lifted away like a butterfly on the flower and there was an incredible feeling. What was that?

K: Every time when I was young – butchering a pig, it was the same. It's like a cramp of energy released into the air.

Q: Is that like the bliss?

K: No. It's not like bliss. This little something is entrapped, cramped into a 'me'. Then you cannot hold it anymore and the cramp relaxes and the whole energy opens up.

Q: Isn't it opening up into that...

K: Nothing. It's just opening up into nothing. It doesn't open up in any ocean.

Q: Does it open up into the ocean as you said previously?

K: No. I just said there's an ocean of suffering and you cannot stop it.

Q: So it goes back to the ocean of suffering...

K: No. You don't go into it. There's no 'one' in it, there's just suffering. There's no one going into it.

Q: So, in this suffering there is a freedom from...

K: There's no freedom from anything. You cannot free yourself from the ocean of realization. And you always realize yourself in separation, in the ocean of discomfort. The presence is always discomfort and then in this discomfort, there is more or less discomfort. Then more intense discomfort is being a person and opening up is less discomfortable. But it's still discomfort – more or less discomfort. You can make levels of discomfort.

– *The Song Of Irrelevance p144*

न घटो न घटाकाशो न जीवो न जीवविग्रहः ।
केवलं ब्रह्म संविद्धि वेद्यवेदकवर्जितम् ॥ ३२॥

There is neither a pot, nor the space contained in the pot;
Neither the individual self, nor the body of any individual self;
Know that – All that is, is nothing but Brahman;
Devoid of knowable and knower. [1:32]

Q: My brother-in-law died few days back and I was thinking if you subscribe to the idea that a soul is reincarnated?

K: Maybe. Just like you take your soul to the next morning. It's the same. You go to bed in the deep-deep absence. Then in the morning the soul wakes up again. It's like a reincarnation. It seems like a similar functioning that a 'me' wakes up again. Maybe it's the same when death happens. Maybe it's like a deep-deep sleep night and then waking up in another form. Who knows?

But that doesn't mean that there's one who's incarnated now. You can say it's like a genetic cluster that's incarnated in something else. But right now I wouldn't say that is an incarnation of a 'you'. It's just a label or a mask of a genetic functioning of a past that just continues in something else. Like the Dalai Lama, fourteen times now – can happen. Why not? Everything is possible in this dream. But still there's no one incarnated. No one is ever born.

But this genetic cluster and energy can go on. It seems like a memory cluster of something and then it goes into the next form. That I can see. Sometimes I talk to someone and I see many forms in front of me, changing faces. Just like a cluster of memory effects presenting itself in that form. But I wouldn't say it's now a reincarnation from whatever. But sometimes you see all the faces in front of you – always shifting. Doesn't mean there's one who's incarnated. It's just consciousness showing lineage of memories and not one individual soul, that's incarnated again and again.

Doesn't happen.

It's always the Absolute soul that shows itself in different forms. Sometimes in lineages and sometimes random. Everything is possible. So, there's reincarnation, but not for any 'one'. It's always a reincarnation of consciousness in forms – again and again. As I said, sometimes in lineages a functioning happens again in similar tendencies waking up in that particular form.

– *Worry And Be Happy p201*

सर्वत्र सर्वदा सर्वमात्मानं सततं ध्रुवम् ।
सर्वं शून्यमशून्यं च तन्मां विद्धि न संशयः ॥ ३३॥

Know me to be the Self which is everything and everywhere at all times; That which is eternal, steady, the All, the non-existent and the existent; There is no doubt about this. [1:33]

K: This absolute "no way out," this absolute helplessness, that is paradise. That is being almighty, because that helplessness means there is no control from inside or outside. For That which you are, nothing ever happened, and no one else can control what you are. And no circumstance can change you, or do anything to you, as all the circumstances are because of you, but you are not because of anything. You are causelessness itself. Whatever has a cause is not what you are. So that objective and sensational life, or not life, can never touch that eternal life you are. So be It. There is no practical advice to become that.

– *Eight Days in Tiruvannamalai p181*

Q: So, our perception of time is just an extension of the blink?

K: You just have to experience yourself in all relative ways and all absolute ways. The relative way is that you have a dream of coming and going. That this moment comes and goes, but in coming it doesn't come, because it's already there and in going, it doesn't go. It's just like a frame of movie which is infinite. The frame does not go by going and not come by coming. You just experience one aspect of yourself – moment by moment, but the aspects are never born and never die. They're not created, so they cannot be destroyed.

All of That is what-you-are. Every single aspect, every single moment is infinite in its nature – infinite life – eternal life. Experiencing eternal life moment by moment as every moment in its nature is eternal life – never created, never can be destroyed. The dream is that in coming something comes and in going something goes. In birth nothing is born and in dying nothing dies. That's all!

So, as this moment is never born, it cannot die. It's like – frame by frame, you have to experience yourself – dream fragment by dream fragment. But it doesn't mean fragments are coming or going.

Q: So, is it just that the illusory 'I' that is moving across the panorama?

K: You are the unmovable spectator – the Absolute 'I' – the Absolute seer, who's experiencing itself frame by frame coming from illusionary future and going into an illusionary past. But you are not moving. The frames are coming and going in front of your eyes. Then you make a movie out of it, with an imaginary movement.

You're not moving in it. Never! It's an imaginary movement of frames – moments coming and going. But even to know all of that, you better know yourself – what-you-are in nature – That never needs to know the mechanics. It's magic in a way! Just enjoy your show – by being That what is trying or not trying anything – just to realize yourself.

– Worry And Be Happy p66

वेदा न लोका न सुरा न यज्ञा
वर्णाश्रमो नैव कुलं न जातिः ।
न धूममार्गो न च दीप्तिमार्गो
ब्रह्मैकरूपं परमार्थतत्त्वम् ॥ ३४॥

There are no Vedas or dimensions of worlds,
neither gods nor sacrifices;
No classes or stages of life, neither race nor caste;
Neither the way of smoke nor path of the flame;
The highest Reality alone manifests as Brahman. [1:34]

K: Look, it never stops. Yoga Vashista, King Rama, so many books, the Mahabharata, and Arjuna, and Yudhishthir going to hell and accepting and blah, blah, blah. And look - the story continues, as if nothing ever happened. All these fantastic stories of realization. In spite of Ramana, in spite of Buddha, in spite of Jesus, in spite of all of that holy, holy bogus, nothing happens.

– May It Be As It Is p200

व्याप्यव्यापकनिर्मुक्तः त्वमेकः सफलं यदि ।
प्रत्यक्षं चापरोक्षं च ह्यात्मानं मन्यसे कथम् ॥ ३५॥

If you are free of the pervaded and the pervader,
if you are One and fulfilled;
How, then, can you know the Self to be itself or the
other?![1:35]

Q: Have you ever wondered why this experience is localized there and not anywhere else? Or everywhere else?

K: Yes, I tried. It's like a camera who is wondering why the camera is not everywhere. The perception is not different in anyone. The perceiver is different. The perceived perceiver is different, that's the reference point. But perception is not different. Can you find a difference in perception? Absolutely not. You can only find differences in perceivers, which are reference points of camera positions, perceiving from different positions. But perception still is perception. Having infinite camera points, infinite reference points, looking at whatever, is not different. You cannot make it different at all. And being perception, which is prior to a perceiver, that's all. The perceiver is already perceived. But you cannot find anyone who is perceiving. You can just say there is perception. That's why they call it the absolute Seer, where there is no Seer. And the Seer you can experience is already experienced. And that comes and goes. But that what is, is never-never. So in that sense you call it 'in-no-sense'. That's the innocence of your Nature. And whatever the innocence is sensing is not different from it, but is not that innocence.

So your Nature is absolute innocence. Senselessness. Whatever comes from there can be sensed. And the first sense is the sensor. And then the sensing what can be sensed. But already the sensor is sensed. By what? You will never know what it is, but that is maybe what you are. The absolute Dreamer which is already prior to the dreamer you can dream. The dreamer can be dreamed, the dreaming and what can be dreamed, but who can dream the dreamer?

So you cannot find that dreamer you are in the dream. Whatever you find is only a dream. And whatever you can count is not the counter. You can count the counter, the counting, what can be counted. But that one who is counting the counter, the counting, what can be counted, cannot be counted. As there is no one who counts anyway. That's the tenth man. You always only count what you can count, but you never count the counter. And the counter is never-never. But you are not an accountant. Who makes a story about some precious insights, precious spiritual events or understandings?

– May It Be As It Is p88

Q: Is there no reason?

K: I didn't say there is no reason. I just said it comes anyway – with or without reason. And the next picture doesn't have to make sense as the picture before never needed to make sense. It's an expression of senselessness. The innocence sensing itself in a chain of events – personal or impersonal or anything. All sensations are sensed by That 'in-no-sense' (innocence). Your very nature is the in-no-sense, realizing itself in senses. There's a sensor, sensing what can be sensed – all that is sensed by what-you-are – without any censorship and not censoring what is sensed. The sensor is sensing what can be sensed.

It's the nature of the sensor to censor. Then there's a story of censorship. It wants to make it a special sense. Like Constans wants to make a special sense of real life, because he has a censorship up here. This cannot be it, so it has to be something better, something more. You make a censorship – comparison. This is not it, there has to be something what is more real – that's called censorship. That's called mind and the nature of mind is always censoring – judging how it is. That's one way of realizing yourself. Does it make you more or less? Or does it matter?

You cannot change it. The so-called creator wants to make a better creation. It's always good intention. There are seven billion Gods and everyone wants to censor and know better how existence has to realize itself. This is only the humans and not counting the elephants or the animal world. They all know better – how it should be. Everyone knows better than existence. And everyone is comparing and everyone thinks this cannot be it. There has to be something more. This cannot be all.

No. This is all there is.

– Worry And Be Happy p128

अद्वैतं केचिदिच्छन्ति द्वैतमिच्छन्ति चापरे ।
समं तत्त्वं न विन्दन्ति द्वैताद्वैतविवर्जितम् ॥ ३६॥

Some seek non-duality others seek duality;
They do not know the Truth, which is the same at all times,
everywhere; That which is devoid of both duality and non-
duality. [1:36]

Q: So absolute ease is only in the Self?

K: Only the Absolute which is the Absolute but doesn't know any Absolute. Just by being Absolute and there is no idea of even a second, because there is not even one.

Q: So it is that ease which doesn't need that ease?

K: Yes. That ease which never needs to be at ease. Never. It doesn't even know ease.

Q: And doesn't need any proof of it.

K: No. It never needs to improve or prove anything. And that what needs to improve and always needs to prove, that's called ghost. And the ghost always needs a proof to exist. Only a ghost needs a proof of existence. Existence itself never needs to prove itself.

Q: Doesn't even need to exist.

K: Doesn't even need to exist to exist. So that is the end of Vedanta. Because that what doesn't even have to exist to exist, that breaks all of what you can imagine to know or not know. That what is beyond all imaginary ideas.

Q: Existence is also an imaginary idea?

K: Absolutely. Only in relative existence there is an idea of existence. There is a new book on Zen; it says 'Zen, the biggest lie ever'. I like this. Like 'Advaita, the biggest lie ever'. Even to call it non-duality - you can only call it non-duality in duality. When there is non-duality, there is duality. So, even that is no way out. And who needs to go out of what one is? Who is imprisoned? By whom? So what to do?

– May It Be As It Is p85

K: It's like a spider whose nature is spinning. What can you do against the nature of a spider? Try to make it not spin? The mind has to think. That's his bloody nature – minding the mind, moment-by-moment. So, what's the problem with it? Only when you create a second mind, a second opinion. Then you compare which one is a better mind. Then mind says, I would be a better mind with no-mind – says the mind. Then it says nothing would be better than something. I would be better-off if I would be nobody... blah, blah, blah. Always making concepts because without making concepts, it cannot survive as the first concept. It always needs to be surrounded by concepts of past, present and future, blah, blah, blah.

Then there are others, other masters and other people. Then defining how they are and the bullshit that they say. Why do they do that? Blah, blah, blah. Why? Why? Why? Always why? Why is he enlightened and not me? Why he woke up and not me? I was much more interested and I would fit much better in that chair. [Laughter] Some already buy a dress and imagine how it would be to sit there and get all the attention from everybody. They are all posters in front of the mirror every morning. [Laughter] There are even training camps – preparation for advaita teachers.

Q [Another visitor]: Yeah, he even does it online! [Laughter]

K: Non-duality camps! In Moscow there are many enlightened

ones. Every day a new one pops-up. [Laughter] It's all a theatre. It's all a big circus of bullshit. But what to do? You cannot get rid of it, because it's your bloody circus. Complaining – it's fun, but does it help? No.

– *Worry And Be Happy p157*

श्वेतादिवर्णरहितं शब्दादिगुणवर्जितम् ।
कथयन्ति कथं तत्त्वं मनोवाचामगोचरम् ॥ ३७॥

How can they describe the Truth,
Which is beyond the mind and words,
Which is devoid of white and other colors,
Which is devoid of sound and other qualities?! [1:37]

Q: Can you see someone stuck in samadhi?

K: Yeah. Sometimes people come as awareness and the whole space is filled with light. It's quite energetic. When I see them it's all golden light. Some come with silver light as I Amness. The whole space becomes silver.

Q: What do you do then?

K: I don't have to do anything. I just ask them – Why do you come to me?

Q: Is it good to have a golden light?

K: From a personal point of view you can say there's an evolution from a personal body to spirit and to the awareness. So, from the personal point of view, it's better than this body. But it needs one who discriminates. Yes, it's better in a relative world and if you are interested in that, by all means go for it but leave me alone.

Q: Is it necessary to go through samadhi?

K: If you want to go through that, yes. If you listen to me, maybe not.

— *Worry And Be Happy p214*

यदाऽनृतमिदं सर्वं देहादिगगनोपमम् ।
तदा हि ब्रह्म संवेत्ति न ते द्वैतपरम्परा ॥ ३८॥

When all these appear to you as false;
When bodies and so on appear to you like space;
Then alone is Brahman truly known;
For there the lineage of duality ends. [1:38]

Q: And how to remove the world?

K: By being as you are. If there is Self and nothing but Self then there is no world anymore. That is the only way out: to see that there was never any such thing as world, that world in its essence is consciousness, and consciousness is all that there is. Consciousness is your absolute realization, but you are not your realization. You are that which is realizing itself through consciousness. So you are the very source of consciousness. It is not even consciousness, but consciousness is your infinite body, or your infinite realization. Then there was never any world, mind or obstacles at all because at this realization everything collapses. That is the only realization that I know: to see that the Self is ever realized. And for this there is nothing to do or not to do. Simply be That, which is Self.

— *Interview*

Q: So you might call some maniac or mass murderer…

K: Yeah, you are that. You are that! By you thinking you are alive, you are creating six billion others, and by making them alive, you are killing yourself. You are the mass murderer by saying there are six billion people. You are the biggest mass murderer I know. Simply by your thinking you're alive, you're killing six billion.

Q: I don't think so…

K: You create them! By you creating them, you kill them.

Q: Then how to uncreate them?

K: You don't have to uncreate them; just stop creating. Be what you are, and there is no one left.

Q: And how to be what you are?

K: How? There is no "how."

– *Eight Days in Tiruvannamalai p328*

परेण सहजात्मापि ह्यभिन्नः प्रतिभाति मे ।
व्योमाकारं तथैवैकं ध्याता ध्यानं कथं भवेत् ॥ ३९॥

My natural self also appears not different from the Supreme Self;
It appears to be one and like space;
How, then, can there be meditator and meditation?! [1:39]

K: You want to understand meditation and by that you become a meditator. This is the nature of meditation. You are the question and the answer – Am I? - I Am! That's all. You are the nature of the question and you're the nature of the answer. You yourself are the answer to all your questions. In the main question Am I? – I Am! Just stay in that – that's all. That's the nature of meditation – Am I – I Am.

You are the question and you're the answer permanently. There is nothing to get out of it because you are That what you gain by that question – The answer you already are! Am I – I Am. So it's fantastic!

It's an instant fulfillment. You want to be satisfied and you are instantly satisfied by being what is satisfaction.

– Heaven And Hell p35

K: That's why I'm always hammering, even divine love. All these answers mean nothing. They will simply make a history out of it. Whatever answer you give, it's history. It's time-bound. It's framed. Only that mystery, that total question mark, that absolute absence of anything — Sometimes it sounds very beautiful, blah, blah, blah. But it's still blah, blah, blah. Because only that absolute "no answer"— that's the only answer. This is annihilating the questioner.

Twenty-four hours a day, three hundred sixty-five days a year, whatever second there exists, this question should be That which you are. This question is meditation itself—meditating about the meditator himself and not getting an answer. And then you will see there will be no expectation after a while. There is nothing to expect.

In meditation, there is "I am" meditating about what is "I am," but without expectation of an answer. Without that answer, there is only meditation but no meditator. That is meditation. Everything else—whatever is doing something for an answer, where there is expectation of getting something out if it—is not meditation.

– Eight Days in Tiruvannamalai p34

यत्करोमि यदश्नामि यज्जुहोमि ददामि यत् ।
एतत्सर्वं न मे किंचिद्विशुद्धोऽहमजोऽव्ययः ॥ ४० ॥

What I do, what I eat, what I sacrifice and what I give away;
none of it belongs to me.
I am pure, unborn and imperishable. [1:40]

K: To be what you are nothing has to go. You don't have to renounce anything. That I like about

Ramana – the renunciation of renunciation is what you are. You cannot renounce what you are. So you renounce renunciation and just be that what you are. You devote devotion, because there is

nothing you have to devote to anyone. Who can devote something to himself? And who needs that? So if you ask me, Ramana for me is like as I am, That. But to make him a role model I destroy him

right away. So I have to call him Ramana banana. And only for the monkey mind it is so appealing. Let the monkey mind be busy. Always making role models and all of that holy- holy business. He

needs a holy business, because he is unholy. He is insane, so he creates an idea of sanity. So any moment there is something holy, you create the unholy, in the same instant. Holy shit!

– May It Be As It Is p109

सर्वं जगद्विद्धि निराकृतीदं
सर्वं जगद्विद्धि विकारहीनम् ।
सर्वं जगद्विद्धि विशुद्धदेहं
सर्वं जगद्विद्धि शिवैकरूपम् ॥ ४१॥

Know the universe to be formless;
Know the universe to be changeless;
Know the universe to be devoid of impurity;
Know the universe to be simply of the nature of the Absolute.
[1:41]

Q: You said yesterday that Parabrahman creates the universe...

K: It's dreaming this universe, it's not creating it.

Q: But it dreamt the universe in one instant?

K: In one instant – the dreamer, the dreaming and what can be dreamt are there – in a blink of an eye. When the Absolute eye wakes up, everything is there in a blink of an eye. Out of the Absolute potential wakes up, in a blink of an eye, all is there – whatever can be. Out of the Absolute potential as a Parabrahman, as the Absolute potential of all existence, in that waking up, the whole potential wakes up – as final.

All possibilities, all events are there – instantly, because they were already there in the potential of Parabrahman. As they're already there, it's unchangeable.

Q: If every possibility is there, in a pre-determined way, isn't there a choice between possibilities?

K: No. That's the nature of Parabrahman because there's no second; he cannot control himself because for control or making a decision, it needs two. Then the decider has to be different from that what he's deciding. But in absolute absence of a decider, the definer, there's no one who can decide anything. There's not even a possibility of deciding anything.

But when he wakes up, everything already is final – finished. So, there's no decision, nothing to do anymore, everything is already done. And it's too late to change it because it's impossible to change that what's finished.

Q: So, our perception of time is just an extension of the blink?

K: You just have to experience yourself in all relative ways and all absolute ways. The relative way is that you have a dream of coming and going. That this moment comes and goes, but in coming it doesn't come, because it's already there and in going, it doesn't go. It's just like a frame of movie which is infinite. The frame does not go by going and not come by coming. You just experience one aspect of yourself – moment by moment, but the aspects are never born and never die. They're not created, so they cannot be destroyed.

All of that is what-you-are. Every single aspect, every single moment is infinite in its nature – infinite life – eternal life. Experiencing eternal life moment by moment as every moment in its nature is eternal life – never created, never can be destroyed. The dream is that in coming something comes and in going something goes. In birth nothing is born and in dying nothing dies. That's all!

So, as this moment is never born, it cannot die. It's like – frame by frame, you have to experience yourself – dream fragment by dream fragment. But it doesn't mean fragments are coming or going.

— *Worry And Be Happy p65*

तत्त्वं त्वं न हि सन्देहः किं जानाम्यथवा पुनः ।
असंवेद्यं स्वसंवेद्यमात्मानं मन्यसे कथम् ॥ ४२॥

Reality you are, there is no doubt!
Is there anything to understand? That which cannot be known
and that which itself is self-evident is Self; How, then, can you
understand that?! [1:42]

K: Every word is the living words of totality. It's by total demand of that what is giving light which is making this bulb shining. That energy which is running the whole universe is running this loudspeaker and every word that comes out is a vibration of that what is. That is called the living words; it's the same life that runs the whole show. I can just point to it and you are That what is That.

You are the zero of the zero, the one of the one and the eight of the eight and you are That.

So when there is zero, you are zero, when there is one you are That what is the one, when you are the infinite you are the infinite. But you are not the infinite, you are not finite and you are not the zero. You are That what is realizing itself as the zero, as one and eight and that's a never ending story. There was never any story that could end, nothing in store. No Self-storage, Self cannot be stored.

– Am I – I Am p207

K: Even the doubtlessness is already too much. You can say that the doubtlessness or the wishlessness is the purest form, but the purest is not pure enough, because you can make it different from something else. The wishlessness is different from wish and no-wish.

So even the origin is not the origin. The origin of whatever you can imagine or not imagine is not the origin. It's not original.

– Heaven And Hell p93

मायाऽमाया कथं तात छायाऽछाया न विद्यते ।
तत्त्वमेकमिदं सर्वं व्योमाकारं निरञ्जनम् ॥ ४३ ॥

My child, how can there be illusion and non-illusion, shadow and lack of shadow?
Reality is one. It is all this. It is all-pervading like space, without imperfections. [1:43]

Q: Sometimes, like with some Masters, it seems like the Self is taking the shape of the ego also in the Master...

K: The Self takes never any shape.

Q: So, what are these shapes?

K: All shapes are merely reflections or fleeting shadows in time, but not the Self. They are shadows of the Self. And this shadow of what you are cannot go, because you are that what makes the shadow. Because you are what you are, the shadows are. So, to say, the shadows must go so that I can be, what stupidity is this? Because you are, the shadows are. And if you want the shadows to go, you want yourself to go. This is a way of suicide. This is a suicidal attempt of the Self, so it's Self-suicide. If you want any shadow of what you are to go, you want yourself to go. The shadows are there because you are. And there is no way out. As long you are, the shadows are there.

Q: And when you are not?

K: Then there is no question. Because there is no questioner and there is no light and no shadow.

Q: But there can be still ego there...

K: No. The ego itself is a shadow of what you are, but not what you are. So as long as you take a shadow as real.

Q: Merely shadows...

K: And as long as you want the shadow to go, as your ego, you want yourself to go. Because, the shadow is there because you are. So whatever you want to go, you want yourself to go.

Q: So that's the situation of the seekers...

K: The seeker looks for a way out, looks for the shadow to go. And as long as something has to go, for you to be what you are, this is a suicidal attempt. You want to kill yourself. As long as you want the ego to go, you want to kill yourself; you're looking for a way out.

– *Interview*

K: I am talking to that what is darkness, to itself. So I am talking to the Light which never knows the Light. There is only Self! There is only that what never knows itself. And now in action, in light, and now in vibration, and now it falls in love with some reflection of it, with some shadow of it. And now it became a shadow. What can I do to what I am, believing to be a shadow? Even believing in awareness is a shadow. What can I do? I can just slap it: 'Come on! Wake up from this waking up business!' 'Wake up from waking up!' 'Wake up from being awake!' Because what you are is never-never awake. And there is never any experience of awakeness – what you call awakeness. It's not even awakeness.

– *May It Be As It Is p26*

आदिमध्यान्तमुक्तोऽहं न बद्धोऽहं कदाचन ।
स्वभावनिर्मलः शुद्ध इति मे निश्चिता मतिः ॥ ४४॥

I have no beginning, no middle and no end;
I never was and will never be bound;
I have no imperfections in nature;
I am Purity itself, This I know with certainty. [1:44]

K: The truth that has to be true, cannot be true, because it's a depending truth. The truth which depends on truth, cannot be true. The nature of peace doesn't need any peace to be peace and the truth that needs to be true, cannot be true. Freedom that needs to be free, is not freedom. You will never be free from yourself. So, freedom doesn't know any freedom and freedom is what-is because there's a freedom from a second. But there's no possible way that the freedom can be free. From what? How can you be free? From what? You are That. How can you be free from That?

Freedom is just a pointer that there's no second, that you can be bound to. You cannot be connected to someone or anything because there's no two. That's the freedom of two. But you cannot be free 'from' anything because you are whatever-is and is-not. How can you be free from yourself? Freedom doesn't need any freedom, but 'me' always wants to be free.

– *The Song Of Irrelevance p182*

महदादि जगत्सर्वं न किंचित्प्रतिभाति मे ।
ब्रह्मैव केवलं सर्वं कथं वर्णाश्रमस्थितिः ॥ ४५॥

Nothing of the universe including the primary principle
of cosmic intelligence appears to me; All is indeed Brahman
alone; How, then, can there be any caste or stage in life for me?!
[1:45]

Q: You mentioned some reality prior to Shiva.

K: Prior to the light of Shiva.

Q: Not prior to Shiva?

K: No. Shiva is Self, Shiva is Parabrahman. That what is Shiva is

Shiva. But the light of Shiva, Shiva becoming aware of Shiva, then he becomes relative. A relative experience of light. He becomes aware of himself. Becoming aware of himself, being awake, that's the light of Shiva. But the light of Shiva is not Shiva. It's the light of Shiva. And then comes the space of Shiva and then the whole universe of Shiva. But that trinity, which is realization, is not Reality. It's not different. That's the way Shiva is realizing himself. But it's not that what is realizing itself. So it starts realizing itself as the light of Shiva. As being aware. And then 'I am'. And then whatever comes.

Q: So the light of Shiva is something like creation?

K: It's the first phenomenal experience.

Q: The first stage of creation.

K: The first stage of creation.

Q: Creation of time and space.

K: That's the beginning.

Q: So Reality is before that?

K: That what never starts and never ends, is prior, during, and beyond that experience. Prior simply means it is in spite of it. In spite of the presence of light, Reality is. In spite of it, not because. So the cause never needs any even being awake, or aware of itself.

So it's not different. I don't say there is a difference in it. It's just that your reality is already there before one who is realizing is there. So before an experiencer is there, that what is the experiencer is already there.

— *May It Be As It Is p51*

Q: It is said that you need to have a human body in order to...

K: Who said that? One having a human body who claims that he made it. Who else would claim that?

Q: Shankaracharya...

K: Maybe he meant that you have to realize yourself even as a human – worse as it is. It's the worst incarnation, being a human. Nothing is worse than the fact that you have to be a human. That you have to reflect and need to have a history and you have to remember your childhood. Is that an evolution? Look at a fly, that's the end of evolution – one day life. You wake up in morning and by night – bye, bye. That's the whole lifetime of a fly.

What did humanity reach? Electricity? Computers? Television?

– *Worry And Be Happy p197*

जानामि सर्वथा सर्वमहमेको निरन्तरम् ।
निरालम्बमशून्यं च शून्यं व्योमादिपञ्चकम् ॥ ४६॥

I know always, in every way that I am one,
indivisible and self-sustained;
I am the non-void, void, the five elements,
space and so on...[1:46]

K: The absolute seer is imagining a relative seer. So, out of the absolute seer, the Parabrahman, he imagines brahman. And already brahman is an imagination of Parabrahman and only the Parabrahman is real. The Parabrahman not knowing reality and that's the nature of reality. For reality, there is no reality. There is not even an idea of reality and only in unreal; there are ideas of reality – of real and unreal. In reality, there is no such thing as real or unreal. It doesn't even know itself.

So, Parabrahman is brahman not knowing itself, in its absolute nature. But the moment he knows himself, he becomes relative –

relative creator, creating relative ideas of imaginary events and worlds and universes.

— *Worry And Be Happy p94*

K: I am pointing to that what is with and without. You are with the dream and you are without the dream. That's all. There is no before and after.

— *May It Be As It Is p134*

न षण्ढो न पुमान्न स्त्री न बोधो नैव कल्पना ।
सानन्दो वा निरानन्दमात्मानं मन्यसे कथम् ॥ ४७॥

> *The Self is neither eunuch nor man nor woman;*
> *Is neither intellect nor imagination;*
> *How, then, can you imagine the Self to be blissful or without bliss?!* [1:47]

K: Don't call it anything. Just forget Brahma, underwear or anything. You can call it whatever, call it a piece of plastic underwear. Any word is good enough or not good enough. I call it Para-ox. The ox which has no balls.

You always think that the paradox, the Parabrahman has balls, as if it could do something. But he has no balls, that is why he is a para-ox. He is not a macho up there who can change the world, who is in power. He is the omnipotent but absolutely impotent in this dream. That you cannot get because you think that what is Almighty, that what is omnipotent can change something here. He is impotent in his dream – Absolutely impotent!

— *Heaven And Hell p67*

षडङ्गयोगान्न तु नैव शुद्धं
मनोविनाशान्न तु नैव शुद्धम् ।
गुरूपदेशान्न तु नैव शुद्धं
स्वयं च तत्त्वं स्वयमेव बुद्धम् ॥ ४८ ॥

The Self certainly does not become pure through the practice of six-limbed yoga; It certainly is not purified by the destruction of the mind; Nor is it purified by the instruction of gurus; Being the Truth itself, it is self-illuminated. [1:48]

Q: These practices are somehow working on the mind. Would you say it is a prerequisite that the mind should become quiet, sattvic?

K: No. There will be no mind sattvic enough to become that which is Self. The very idea that the Self has to purify itself is dirty. This word 'purification' in itself is dirty because it implies that the Self is dirty and has to be purified, and the Self would need some purification to be the Self.

It is simply an idea that is coming out of the survival system of 'me', who wants to survive. By having the idea that I have to be purified and by knowing that I cannot be pure enough to be that which is the Self means I can stay as I am, as a little 'me'. It is a trick of this 'me' to stay as a 'me'. Whatever comes out of this 'I' thought is a survival system of this 'I' thought, and you cannot annihilate that which is the 'I' thought.

Only the grace of the Self becoming aware of the absoluteness of what Self is continues this automatic annihilation of that which is not Self ... but not because the 'I' thought wants something. That is what is called grace, and only by the grace of the Self will the Self rest in the Self. But not by any idea of what comes out of an idea.

Q: Are you saying that no practice makes any difference, there are no prerequisites?

K: In spite of all the practices it will happen. There is no way out, and the Self will rest again in what is the Self, but not because of what that which is not Self has done or not done. It is totally blind to what is done or not done because in that which is the Self nothing is ever done and nothing ever happens. So no happening can make what is Self because Self is not part of the happening. The Self dropping out of the idea of existence is a divine accident and cannot be caused by any wanting to have an accident, like driving into something. No. As it all spontaneously comes out of the Self then it all spontaneously goes back to the Self and not because of but in spite of all that happens in time or no time.

As I see it, and I don't say that this is true, this Self is uncaused and can never be caused by anything, otherwise it would not be that freedom which is freedom itself. It doesn't need any freedom of mind or freedom of any circumstance. This freedom is independent of any circumstances, and no circumstance can create that which is Self.

– Interview

न हि पञ्चात्मको देहो विदेहो वर्तते न हि ।
आत्मैव केवलं सर्वं तुरीयं च क्षयं कथम् ॥ ४९॥

There is no five elemental gross body, nor any dis-embodied subtle body; All is verily the Self. How, then, can there be the fourth# or the other three-states?! [1:49]*

---

*Three states (of consciousness) – The waking state, the dream state and the deep sleep (dreamless) state.

#Fourth state (of consciousness) – The turiya state is the background that underlies and transcends the above mentioned three states of consciousness. It is like deep-deep sleep and is one of the closest objective pointer to the Absolute.

K: All this pops up like this. [holds up his thumb, index finger, and then middle finger, and then draws them back into a fist, over and over in cycles, to symbolize the coming and going of different states of awareness] Out of this awareness as "I" [thumb], come "I am" [thumb and index finger] and then form [thumb, index, and middle fingers]. At night, these drop together [tucks in his index and middle fingers], and this remains as deep sleep state [thumb]. But even prior to that, is this [holds up fist to symbolize Heart]. So, as this is prior to awareness, it's prior to "I am"-ness and prior to "I am so"-ness. In whatever state, this [fist] is without any state. There is statelessness.

The first notion, the first experience of light, the first Om or sound, is "I." Out of that "I"-thought comes "I am"-ness and "I am so"-ness. But this [fist] is always what is realizing itself as "I" [thumb] "am" [thumb and index finger] "the world" [thumb, index, and middle fingers]. This [fist] you never lose; this you never left. So whether you go from this state [thumb, index, and middle fingers] to this state [thumb and index finger] to that state [thumb], it cannot make you this [fist], as you are this [fist] in any state. Simply this, Heart itself, not knowing what is Heart and what is not Heart.

– *Eight Days in Tiruvannamalai p95*

Q: Few days back you were making a distinction of Brahman and Parabrahman. What was that?

K: Parabrahman is Brahman not knowing Brahman, not having any idea of being or not being. That is the nature of Parabrahman. When Parabrahman knows itself it becomes Brahman. The creator, then it is awareness. In Christianity that would be the father. Then out of the father comes the spirit, I Amness and then comes the body consciousness, this trinity.

Q: What is awareness, then I Amness and then body consciousness?

K: The purest notion is awareness, then the space experience of spirit and then the matter. But the only Reality is Parabrahman. Reality not knowing Reality, that is the only Reality. Reality not having any idea of what is and what is not Reality that is the nature of Reality. That is the nature of Parabrahman which is Reality. The Absolute dreamer not knowing any dreamer. The first he knows is being a dreamer, the awareness, the purest I. There is an experience of a dreamer sometimes personal sometimes impersonal. When it's personal then the creator is different from its creation when its impersonal the creator is not different from what it is creating. There is oneness and there is separation, both are there. When he is lucky, he is realizing himself as an impersonal realizer.

So you can say the Parabrahman in its Absolute absence of any presence of any experience, is that what he is in its nature and is never losing its nature. Then it starts dreaming itself in a dream-like realization of seven possible ways. But in none of them it can get found or lost, that is all. But try to find yourself in one of the seven states, in the presence or absence or personal or impersonal makes you relative. Even the impersonal states are relative states. Natural state doesn't know any state. Your natural state is being what you are, neither knowing nor not knowing what you are. There is no Absolute knower or not knower present or absent. There is knowledge without even being aware of knowledge. That knowledge doesn't even need to be aware of knowledge or conscious of knowledge or anything. From there which is knowledge is realizing itself as a personal knower or an impersonal knower. Then there is a knower who knows or an impersonal knower in knowing what can be known in the oneness experience. Only separation experience, where the knower is different from what he knows or where the knower is different from what he knows.

– Am I – I Am p64

न बद्धो नैव मुक्तोऽहं न चाहं ब्रह्मणः पृथक् ।
न कर्ता न च भोक्ताहं व्याप्यव्यापकवर्जितः ॥ ५० ॥

I am neither bound nor am I liberated;
I am none other than Brahman;
I am neither the doer nor am I the enjoyer;
I am devoid of distinctions,
of the pervader and the pervaded. [1:50]

K: You are attracted to freedom – That never needs to be free. But because you want to become it, you are not it. Since you want to own it, you cannot get it. You want to have it and you cannot have it – I tell you. There was never anyone who got it. You can 'be' it – that's the easiest – because you 'are' it. But you can never attain it. You will never have it. It will never be yours.

Never ever was there any ownership in freedom. What kind of freedom would it be that could be owned by Constans? Constans's freedom. You can have it forever and no one wants it – Constans's freedom. [Laughter] Maybe you want to sell it afterwards? Maybe you write a book about freedom.

As I say, would this bloody freedom make you more or less? Would you gain anything by freedom? Or with truth? What would you do with truth if you get it?

Q: That's why I asked – Why is it so attractive?

K: Because you just imagine it. Because you imagine it would be better. It's pure imagination. It's like carrots in front of the donkey and the donkey thinks – if I ever get the carrot I would not be hungry any more. So, you may run after the carrot. Even if you don't run after the carrot, that's another carrot.

The question is, why should you be better off than the Self? Look at the Self. I'm always pointing out to the helplessness of the

Self, of reality that has to realize itself – if it likes it or not. But you want to be a special self who wants to stop this realization. Isn't that fantastic? Crazy! As if life can stop living life. What an idea!

You are That what is life and life has to live life – in whatever possible way. Sometimes is not attractive the way you live life. But still you have to live life in that way. What is the problem? You will never be free. How can one become free? There was never anyone who was born. What is there to be free from?

– *Worry And Be Happy p130*

यथा जलं जले न्यस्तं सलिलं भेदवर्जितम् ।
प्रकृतिं पुरुषं तद्वदभिन्नं प्रतिभाति मे ॥ ५१॥

*When water merged with water remains as
inseparable water itself;*
*Likewise purusha (noumenon) and prakriti (phenomenon)
appear indistinct to me. [1:51]*

K: The first awareness – lingam, God knowing himself, like a penis. Then comes yoni, the infinite vagina, the space. The light itself, the lingam, vibrating awareness. Then comes yoni, as infinite space of non-vibration, the absence of time, the absence of vibration. In that infinite space, the lingam starts to vibrate. The penis penetrates space and by penetrating the space, it creates the whole universe – just by vibrating in the non-vibrating.

This is all the vibration of the light you are. Imagine! The Indian mythology is very clear in it. The nature of the first penis is to penetrate whatever is there. So you always try to penetrate yourself by whatever means, by whatever possibility.

At first you penetrate the space, the yoni, the cosmic vagina you penetrate and try to find the end of light in that infinite space. And you cannot find the end of light but you vibrate in infinite ways to fill up that space. By that you fill up the whole universe, the whole milky ways, whatever is there, is you trying to penetrate yourself and you trying to find yourself in that infinite space.

All is absolute. The absolute light, the absolute space and the absolute possibilities of all possible vibrations of that light. All of that is what-you-are. So being what-you-cannot-not-be is being That and that is Nisargadatta's 'I Am That'. And through That, there is no second. And you cannot not be what-you-are. That is the way you are living yourself.

You are light living in all possible ways of light vibrating in all ways. Vibrating and non-vibrating, knowing and not knowing, all whatever is! But by none of that you will know your nature. You cannot know your nature. In any relative whatever you do or not do, whatever knowing or not knowing. It is a realization of what-you-are but not that what-you-are. So what to do?

Now I take another approach and show you why you experience this whole dream, the dream of your realization. But maybe it's not even a dream. The pointer is always you cannot leave what-you-are. And that never came and it will never go. There is only silence, the silence of nothing ever happened. Nothing ever came and nothing will ever go.

By all the movements, by all the imaginary coming and going, nothing ever came and nothing will ever go. Nothing was ever born and nothing will ever die. There is no birth in birth and no death in death. The only thing that can die is the idea of death. What is there that is born? What is there to be afraid of? So what to do?

– Heaven And Hell p115

यदि नाम न मुक्तोऽसि न बद्धोऽसि कदाचन ।
साकारं च निराकारमात्मानं मन्यसे कथम् ॥ ५२॥

If indeed, you are neither bound nor liberated;
How, then, can you think of yourself to be with form or
formless?! [1:52]

Q: Sri Ramana says, 'He who is thus endowed with the mind that has become subtle and who has the experience of the Self is called a jivan-mukta.' Is this the state that can be called Self realized?

K: The fourth state. What Sri Ramana meant by the fourth state is the natural state of the Self. It is selflessness where the Self doesn't know if it is or not, and there is an absolute absence of any sense of existence or non-existence. This is the freedom from the idea of freedom and the absence of any idea of bondage or anything, even the absence of the idea of existence.

So this absolute existence, which is or is not aware of anything, is what Sri Ramana would call jivan-mukta or the fourth state. It is not a state any more. Actually, it is statelessness.

– *Interview*

K: The one who wants to control you, you control them by letting them control you. The controller is controlled by that what he wants to control. What you try to control, controls you if you like it or not. That's hell. But you want to be free; you want freedom so freedom controls you. You are a slave of freedom. Freedom is your master, and then you are a slave.

If truth is your master, then you are a slave of truth. If Self is your master then you are a slave of the Self. Whatever you make higher or an icon you become a slave. Love makes you a slave of love. But why not?

Not to be a slave, you become a slave of not being a slave. No way out. You will always be in Self-service.

Q: Some puppets have me convinced that they are more free…

K: Just look at them being enslaved by freedom. Just tell them, you are bloody slaves [laughter].

— *Am I – I Am p212*

Q: The realization is that there is a lie, that everything is formless…

K: But even that goes away too. Everything is formless, is that a truth?

Q: That there is no form…

K: Is that truth? Whatever you can pronounce and find out, would be covered again. Whatever you say now is separation because the non-form is different from form and formlessness. Then you make another level – emptiness. Then you say I realized that emptiness can never get more or less. Sounds good! Then the opposite of emptiness would not be true.

— *Worry And Be Happy p24*

जानामि ते परं रूपं प्रत्यक्षं गगनोपमम् ।
यथा परं हि रूपं यन्मरीचिजलसन्निभम् ॥ ५३ ॥

I know your absolute form intimately, as it extends everywhere like space;
And appearances of all forms other than that to be illusory like water in a mirage. [1:53]

Q: So, there is no way to stabilize in That?

K: No. It's just another way of experiencing yourself, it's just different. It's less discomfort. Then awareness is lesser discomfort. It's like going into the awareness samadhi where there is not even no-time. Then you are in the third state – time, no-time and then you are the screen where time and no-time, form and formless appear. Then you are awareness – even better – superior consciousness. The most pure – like a screen where all the projections, space and all of that appear but you are always okie-dokie. So, KO (Knock-out, first state), OK (second state), and okie-dokie (third state).

But just as you land there, you have to depart sooner or later. You have to go from no-time to the state of timelessness, to the samadhi of pure awareness. But the moment you come back here, you are as thirsty as before. It's just another way of experiencing yourself. Then you even go prior to that – being inspite of presence and absence of awareness. But then you wake up again. You cannot stop realizing yourself.

Q: Endless process?

K: Endless jumping from one reference point to the other – shift, shift, shift. You are like a sailor that is shipping all the dimensions of the universe and cannot land anywhere. All the dimensions are only there because 'you-are'. And you are discovering nothing new because it was already there. And wherever you land, you depart again.

If you cannot be in this hell of separation what-you-are, you will not become it in any dimension. This is the worse – I agree. Nothing is worse than being a relative human being in a relative time having a story. If you cannot be in this circumstance what-you-are, what is it worth to be what-you-are?

– *Worry And Be Happy* p36

Q: So, you don't have a story?

K: The phantom always has a story, but who cares if the phantom has a nice story or a bad story? It was always a phantom that was unrealized and whatever the phantom realizes, is a phantom realization. It's called fun-tom – have fun with it because it's a never ending story of a phantom who believes in himself and then believes in being realized or not realized. Who cares about an enlightened phantom? Only the other phantoms. It always needs a community of ignorant ideas and one of them maybe is a master-ignorant. The master of ignorance! There are no masters of knowledge. How can there be a master of knowledge? How can there be a master of Heart? You can only be a master of shit.

– Worry And Be Happy p26

न गुरुर्नोपदेशश्च न चोपाधिर्न मे क्रिया ।
विदेहं गगनं विद्धि विशुद्धोऽहं स्वभावतः ॥ ५४ ॥

There is no teacher, no teaching, nothing to condition nor any duty for me; Know me to be pure, bodiless, like the sky. [1:54]

Q: Did you have a teacher? Is it important to have a teacher / Guru? What is the relationship between teacher and disciple? Do you have disciples?

K: No, I didn't have a personal teacher. And for that which is not in time to become aware of itself, nothing is required which is in time. It is always a spontaneous awakening, out of no necessity. It is also called the divine accident. It cognizes itself, not because of, but in spite of everything which comes and goes. The question about important or unimportant is therefore obliterated.

The Self is the only Master I know. It realizes itself in losing and in finding. In this sense it is teacher and disciple and always gives itself absolute lessons.

The Self reveals itself to itself, in its Omnipresence, in the eternal Now. A disciple co-appears with a teacher like a question implies its answer. Out of desirelessness a desire arises in time and dissolves itself in its fulfillment, just as every question finds redemption through an answer. This is the karmic law of consciousness. So, no teacher and no students, only questions and answers.

– *Interview*

विशुद्धोऽस्य शरीरोऽसि न ते चित्तं परात्परम् ।
अहं चात्मा परं तत्त्वमिति वक्तुं न लज्जसे ॥ ५५॥

You are pure, without a body;
You are not the mind, you are higher than the highest;
You need not be ashamed to say, 'I am the Self
– The Supreme Reality'. [1:55]

K: I Am That – what is the presence and I Am That – what is the absence – as That what I Am. But I'm not the presence and I'm not the absence. So I'm not the presence who is different from the absence. But the moment the absence is better for you than the presence, then you become the little one. The first preference!

The moment you are here as a 'me', you meditate to go away. Then any moment you exist, is unbearable, because not to exist is better than to exist. Then you want to become nothing. All your understanding tries to make you understand that you are nothing. Not a thing. I'm not a thing. Everyone makes it like I'm not a thing; I'm no-'thing'. These are 'things' and I'm no-'thing'.

You separate yourself again because the no-thing is separate from everything, from something. But that is better than this one. Then you have to stay in that nothing, in the absence – all the time.

So your happiness is depending on your absence, not the presence. What kind of happiness is that which is depending that it has to be absent? That you have to be absent, that there can be happiness. A relative one again.

I make the picture really black, black, black, no way out. Any presence will be an experience of misery and any absence will be experience of no-misery. But that is what-you-are. What can you do? Can you take that?

No, as a relative 'me', you cannot take it. As what-you-are, no problem, because you are That. In that sense, I like to make it unbearable.

– *Heaven And Hell p88*

कथं रोदिषि रे चित्त ह्यात्मैवात्मात्मना भव ।
पिब वत्स कलातीतमद्वैतं परमामृतम् ॥ ५६॥

O mind! Why do you weep?
Do you, The Self, become the Self by means of the Self?
Drink, my child, the supreme nectar of Non-duality and
transcend all divisions. [1:56]

Q: We're playing here, pretending...

K: Yeah. Generally you try to do something else, take it easy. Have a glass of wine or talk about the bloody tourists standing around and no one needs them.

But here you are confronted. This is a concentration camp. This is a concentration camp – you know that. If you concentrate on That what-you-are, the nature shows itself as a never ending story of 'I' and for that phantom, it becomes very angry. It gets angry and then self-pity – poor me – and all what comes with it. Because anger and self-pity come together. Why did that guy do it? Fuck you all. Maybe you're confronted that there was never anything you controlled and your impotence becomes obvious. Then you become angry.

You know that. When people become old, they have less energy and they become really angry – if they get helpless, if they cannot drive the car any more. My father gets the car out of a garage and bumps into someone and starts shouting – Why did you park your car there? You bloody asshole. It was not me – it was you. Always blaming someone else.

What do I say? I always say, it was bad, it is bad and it will be bad – and there's no way out. It's bad.

Q: I prefer to know That truth, whether it's beautiful or not...

K: That's why in Taoism they say – beautiful words are not real and the reality is never beautiful. It shows you the ocean of pain which you cannot avoid. You have to be what-you-are in the presence of the ocean of pain, because that is compassion. This ocean is an ocean of pain and ocean of humanity and ocean of existence is existence of pain – and you cannot stop it. It will always be there. This is the way you realize yourself – in the ocean of discomfort, dislike. There will never be an end of it.

As absolute is your comfort, as absolute is your discomfort. As absolute your knowledge, as absolute is your ignorance. You can only realize yourself in ignorance, in discomfort. This is like Yudhishtir in Mahabharata, Krishna puts him into hell and asks – Can you take it? And he was lucky enough that there was no tendency of avoidance left in it. In that instant his reaction was – Okay, May It Be As It Is. You are That what is realizing itself, so how can you suffer about yourself? So there was never any sufferer. There is no possibility of a sufferer but there still is an experience of discomfort, but no one has this experience.

– Worry And Be Happy p99

नैव बोधो न चाबोधो न बोधाबोध एव च ।
यस्येदृशः सदा बोधः स बोधो नान्यथा भवेत् ॥ ५७॥

*There is neither knowledge, nor ignorance nor knowledge
combined with ignorance;
He who is forever in such knowledge, is Knowledge himself;
and not otherwise. [1:57]*

K: Chit can never be known, you cannot give any name to what is knowledge. But whatever you can name, whatever you can frame, whatever you can – is relative. All the seven states are relative compared to what you are. And only That is the Absolute not knowing the Absolute. Whatever can be known compared to that what is the nature of peace – is war or shit. Knowledge is shit.

– Am I – I Am p68

K: The moment you pronounce chit it becomes shit, that's the problem. Even to pronounce knowledge, it becomes ignorance. Whatever can be pronounced, even to call it knowledge is ignorance.

Q: [Another visitor]: Even Neti-neti, if used as a tool is…

K: If you use it as a tool of advantage, it's shit. It's the closest but thank God it doesn't work – never needs to work. It will never work and that is fine. And whatever works is shit. And only shit works, and only shit happens.

– Heaven And Hell p172

ज्ञानं न तर्को न समाधियोगो
न देशकालौ न गुरूपदेशः ।
स्वभावसंवित्तरहं च तत्त्व-
माकाशकल्पं सहजं ध्रुवं च ॥ ५८॥

There is no need of knowledge or reasoning or space or time;
Neither any instruction from a guru nor attainment of samadhi;
I am That what is Consciousness itself – The Ultimate Reality;
Like the sky, I am spontaneously changing and ever steady.
[1:58]

K: I'm more from the tradition of Ramana, he never took any disciple. He destroyed relationships from the beginning including the master-disciple relationship. He said that's impossible. How can there be two? How can there be one who knows and other one who doesn't?

Just call it good company. In good company, there's no master and no disciple. In good company, there's only Self, there's 'I' to 'I'. So, there's no master and no slave and no one knows more than the other.

Q: When you say good company, you are making a concession to the language...

K: I just say what Ramana or Nisargadatta would say. I would not even call it good company. You can say bad company is where there are levels, there's one who knows more than the other – relative more or less. In good company, there's 'I' to 'I' – the Absolute to the Absolute – Self talks. So, it's not that you are less than me or I know more than you and I have reached a level of awareness and you have to reach there or I can show you the way. There is no way, nothing to gain.

– *Worry And Be Happy p23*

न जातोऽहं मृतो वापि न मे कर्म शुभाशुभम् ।
विशुद्धं निर्गुणं ब्रह्म बन्धो मुक्तिः कथं मम ॥ ५९॥

I was not born nor do I have death. I have no action,
good or bad; I am Brahman, pure and without attributes;
How, then, can there be bondage or liberation for me?! [1:59]

K: Simply see that whatever is, is already there. Nothing comes and nothing goes. When nothing comes and nothing goes, when there is no birth and death, whatever comes and goes is not coming and not going. So then who is there who has to control something that's not even there?

Maybe here, now, the only thing that can die is the idea of "birth"—which includes ideas of coming and going, of dying, of mortality and immortality, of infinite and finite—these all die at that split second that you see that nothing is ever born, so nothing will ever die.

But no one can take that. Because in that split second, you are gone. That person is living out of that idea that it was born and may die. But in that split second, you see that nothing has ever happened to what you are, or will happen, and you see that you are not born so there is no death for you. Because existence never comes and never goes. What then? That's Zen. No, Zazen.

– *Eight Days in Tiruvannamalai p54*

यदि सर्वगतो देवः स्थिरः पूर्णो निरन्तरः ।
अन्तरं हि न पश्यामि स बाह्याभ्यन्तरः कथम् ॥ ६०॥

If God pervades all, if God is stable, whole and perpetual, and no division is seen; How, then, can He be regarded as outside or inside?! [1:60]

K: To say, "there is no one," there's still one. If you say, "there's no inside and outside," there's still an inside and outside, because it needs one to say that there is no inside and outside, and that one is still making an inside and outside, even by saying it. There is no escape.

This is still part of that understanding. It is still ignorance. Whatever you define, it's ignorance. Any definition comes out of a definer, and that definer is a liar anyway, so whatever lie comes out of that definer himself is a lie. The first definer, "I," already is a lie, as it's an image, it's not what you are, as you are prior to that liar. Out of that lie, only lies come.

– *Eight Days in Tiruvannamalai*

K: You are That what you're looking for – already. Your nature was never outside of you or inside of you. You're that what you're looking for. And what can I do? I can only take what can be taken away. All your just-in-case ideas. And I even tell you that just-in-case will always be there. This is the way the dream happens – call it whatever.

And you have to be what-you-are inspite of that just-in-case, tra...la...la... And you are that, anyway! You are That, you were That and you will be That what-you-cannot-not-be. That is not depending on whatever happened or didn't happen or the idea or no-idea. All of that is only because you are! And you cannot not realize yourself. So what to do?

And there is no why in it. It's just – you realize yourself. And you are That. So what to do? There will always be all differences and all whatever ways of just in cases. But still you are the comfort itself.

– Heaven And Hell p40

K: Do you look at a piece of shit on the street and ask 'what should I do with it?' And you look at a piece of shit inside and you ask yourself because you take it more personal. 'My bloody insight' But it is like a piece of dog shit on the street. The dog looking at his own shit; outside and inside shit. 'What to do with it?'

– May It Be As It Is p228

स्फुरत्येव जगत्कृत्स्नमखण्डितनिरन्तरम् ।
अहो मायामहामोहो द्वैताद्वैतविकल्पना ॥ ६१॥

The whole universe shines eternally without respite;
Oh maya, the great delusion – Just an imagination of duality and non-duality! [1:61]

Q: When you use the phrase 'Realization of the Self', would it be the same as maya?

K: Maya is only when 'you' want to realize yourself in that realization – that's the maya. The dream is only when you set to find yourself in the realization – that's the maya.

Q: When the Self is realizing itself...that's not maya?

K: No. Maya is the illusion that you can find yourself in that realization – that you are something that can be found in that realization. That is what I would call as maya. That you are the realizer different from what is realized – that is maya.

So when you found yourself in realization, if you are an object of realization, that's the maya. Otherwise there is no maya, there is only the Self.

Q: In that sense, you are what is the maya...

K: You are That what is the maya but not knowing any maya. That what is ignorance not knowing any ignorance. But when you are in the maya then you are someone who knows maya and then there is maya. It needs one who defines maya.

Q: 'Knowing' maya is maya...

K: Yeah. And there is a knower, knowing or not knowing – that's maya. When the definer is there defining something – that's maya. Otherwise there is no maya. There's not even Self.

Q: In that sense, there is no realizing of the Self other than the Self...

K: There is not even realization.

Q: Does not need to realize...

K: In that absence of anyone who defines anything, there is no real and no realization.

Q: Neither knowing nor not knowing...

K: Neither-neither. Neti-neti.

– Heaven And Hell p14

साकारं च निराकारं नेति नेतीति सर्वदा ।
भेदाभेदविनिर्मुक्तो वर्तते केवलः शिवः ॥ ६२॥

Forever – 'neither this nor that';
To both the form and the formless;
Truly, only Shiva is – devoid of distinction and identity. [1:62]

K: You don't have to remember, you are That anyway. Don't try to remember, just be That. Don't make it a concept, I just point to something. When I say – you're the absence of the presence, I just point to the fact that you cannot be found in any presence. You cannot find what-you-are, because you are the absence of the presence. And in the absence, you have not lost yourself because your presence cannot be lost in the absence.

But now in the presence, you're the presence which cannot be found in the presence. By whatever present moment, you cannot find yourself. If you can find yourself, you could be something that could be found and that already is hell. Now you found yourself. You claim that you're a human, you know yourself and that already is hell.

So, you better be the absence of any idea of what-you-are. Because what you can find are ideas, concepts, sensational images and all kinds of experiences. But in all those experiences, you cannot be found. You cannot find yourself in the experiencer, experiencing, what can be experienced. If you really look for yourself, you cannot find yourself anywhere. No way to find yourself. You pretend that you're in the experiencer, but if you really look for it, you cannot find yourself.

That's actually Nisargadatta's Ultimate Medicine – look for the seeker and you cannot find that. By not having found who-you-are, you just remain in the absence of – what? You're not even a loser. Because if you would have been a loser, you could have found yourself. As you could not lose yourself, you're neither the loser nor the finder. You're just – who knows? Who needs to know? But still you are! The laziest you can be, which has never done anything. Never active or inactive, neither doing nor not doing – neither.

That's the famous neti-neti, you are neither that nor That and That never needs to have any idea about acceptance or tolerance. Acceptance, tolerance only applies to the phantom concept world. Love, hate, all needs someone who calls something – something and has an idea about something. And that's the root thought 'I' – that always creates problems which would not be there without it. That's called mind.

– *Worry And Be Happy p75*

K: You don't have to be, to be – That's what-you-are. That what has to be, to be, is already too late. It's depending on being. You are when you are and you are not when you are not. You're the presence and you're the absence. But you're not the presence or the absence. But you're the presence when there's presence and you're the absence when there's absence. But you're not the presence and you're not the absence.

You will never know what you are. You are That! You are That, when there's presence, you are the presence. You're the absence when there's the absence. But you're not the presence and you're not the absence. Because if you would be the presence, you would not be the absence. And if you would be the absence, you would not be the presence.

Undecided! Yes and no. In presence, yes, I Am That. In absence, yes, I Am That – but neither. This is absolute neti-neti – neither the presence nor the absence – you-are. Stay in That what-you-cannot-not-be because you are That which is in the presence and in the absence what-it-is. You don't need a presence to be what-you-are. And you don't need an absence to be what-you-are.

– *The Song Of Irrelevance p133*

न ते च माता च पिता च बन्धुः
न ते च पत्नी न सुतश्च मित्रम् ।
न पक्षपाती न विपक्षपातः
कथं हि संतप्तिरियं हि चित्ते ॥ ६३॥

You have no mother, no father, no brother;
You have no wife, no son, no friend;
You have no likes or dislikes;
Why, then, is there anguish in your mind?! [1:63]

K: Normally you are happy when your children leave the home because they found out that the children could not give the happiness that they are looking for. They are just doing their duty because the conditioning of the surrounding makes them do that – like mother Mary. She realized her Self by seeing her son die. Then the love of a mother was broken and she saw no hope and could not bear it. Then a limit was crossed and she became the black Madonna. Then she was realized as that which was never born and never had any son, but there are always limits and degrees where this can happen.

So, even the love of the mother would break – sooner or later. It has to break. It's just a technique of consciousness to create circumstances of imaginary heart-breaks, the imaginary love affair with someone else. The Bible says – You shouldn't love anyone more than your self. And if you do, you would suffer!

– *Worry And Be Happy p168*

K: Nothing gives you satisfaction. All is empty. No drinking, no friends, no family, no work. All of that becomes [blowing in the wind] – empty! Like a void. No hope anymore in anything. No comfort you can find in any little thing. Before you were in the ashram and you were so happy with the energy and the shakti bullshit. Now it's so empty. Even this light bullshit, the kundalini – who bloody needs it? All of that becomes completely empty and that's called grace.

Q [Another visitor]: And then?

K: Nothing then. You're just crucified to what-you-are – that's all. You get pierced by the spear of destiny. Your destiny is that you have to face yourself infinitely. There's no 'then'. There will always be Zen and Zen and Zen – the infinite Zen – the hope that there will be an end – drops, but there's no end to it. So, in the end, there's no end.

– *The Song Of Irrelevance p172*

स्वभावसंवित्तरहं च तत्त्व-
माकाशकल्पं सहजं ध्रुवं च ॥ ५८॥

O mind, you have no day or night;
There is neither sunrise nor sunset for you;
How, then, can the wise imagine formlessness to be affected by form?! [1:64]

K: What makes the world turn? What brings the sunset? The sunrise? What creates the whole universe? No one will ever know. But That what-is, by that whole universe is, brings you here to listen to that. You can say the absolute dreamer, dreaming the whole existence, makes you sit there and me sit here. There is maybe a why in it, but it's just why not? If it just has to be like this, why not?

– *Heaven And Hell p150*

Q: So every concept...

K: There is no concept! Show me a concept? Where is a concept?

Q: As long as I say...

K: There is no 'as long'! Who says 'as long'?

Q: Nobody says...

K: Nobody says? Who is this nobody?

Q: I am the nobody...'

K: It's amazing! Whatever she says she goes deeper and deeper into the shit! You are like swimming in shit and then you try to keep your mouth above the shit. But the shit is what you are! And you think you have to keep your head on top of the shit. Everyone who puts his head out of the shit I cut!

Q: Good analogy!

K: Because that what is shit is chit. There is no difference between chit and shit. But you wanting to be on top of shit, you are the master of shit. So any moment you want to master yourself, control yourself, you are the master of shit. A shit master. Shit happens. And only shit happens. Because what you are never happens. But even to recognize that is too much, is shit. Fantastic!

– May It Be As It Is p25

नाविभक्तं विभक्तं च न हि दुःखसुखादि च ।
न हि सर्वमसर्वं च विद्धि चात्मानमव्ययम् ॥ ६५॥

The Self is neither divided nor undivided;
Experiences neither pleasure, nor pain, nor anything else;
It is neither universal nor particular;
Know the Self to be the immutable One. [1:65]

Q: Everyone is walking around pretending to be happy. Is that what is happening?

K: It's all pretending. They are pretending to be happy and pretending to be unhappy. If you just stop pretending and be-what-you-cannot-not-be – that's all, Then you are neither. Then there's neti-neti – neither happy nor unhappy, because you don't even know what you are and how you are. And you don't have to know how you are and what you are. That what needs to know what-it-is and gives it a name for sure is a definer and nothing is fine enough for that definer. He always wants to find himself and he is always pro-found. [Laughter]

Q: That's why you say – They are happy and I want to be like them...

K: They just want to make you jealous. They are bad! [Laughter] They are nasty people. [Laughter] Shoot them! Be generous and show the other people that you are not happy. [Laughter] That makes them feel good – maybe. If you show them how happy you are – it's like a war – Look you asshole, I can be happy!

Q [Another visitor]: So, it's about showing that you are unhappy?

K: It's the same. It's a competition between the two, who is more unhappy or happy. It's always a competition. Who is more beautiful or more ugly? Who is more realized than the other one? Competition on every level – everywhere. My master is better than yours. And if you have the same master, then you say my master loves me more than you.

Q [Joking]: I see him more...

K: I see under him. [Laughter] I am closer to his underwear, you just see his trousers. [Laughter] I am more aware as I see his underwear.

It's amazing, the competition never stops. The moment you wake up, even when there is no one around, you compete with yourself. There is already a competition, who is ruling today? The one who wants to wake up quickly or the one who wants to stay in bed? There are many definers waking up in the morning and everyone wants to be the main definer today, and has a concept of what is better for today – What to do? Competition! Who rules today? My mother or my father or me? My genes or my understanding? Out of what should I live today? Out of that – I am not? Or out of that – I am? What is my basis today? Then you start your baseball.

At first you have to remember what-you-are, a man or a woman. That's already a big decision every morning. [Laughter]

– *Worry And Be Happy p30*

नाहं कर्ता न भोक्ता च न मे कर्म पुराऽधुना ।
न मे देहो विदेहो वा निर्ममेति ममेति किम् ॥ ६६॥

I am neither the doer nor the enjoyer;
I have no karma (action) either present, past or future;
There is neither a body for me, nor am I bodiless;
What could be 'mine' or not mine to me?! [1:66]

K: Your nature is helpnessness because you are not part of the dream and the dream is already dreamt, you cannot change your own dream. How can you change a dream which is already dreamt? You are not part of the dream and that what is part of the dream has no power. That would have the power of dreaming has no interest because for what you are it has no interest. Never makes any difference. That for what makes a difference has no power. The 'me' has no power because its already part of the dream. That what is dreaming everything the Almighty is not part of the dream and cannot interfere. There is no interference. No control. That is the non-doership, there was never any doership or controllership in anything.

That Absolute is Absolute and has never done anything. Whatever is done and can be done is part of the dream. But that what can do something has no power of changing anything. That what could change has no interest. No need. So, no bridge. That what you are never needs, and that what needs cannot. That what could, need not.

– Am I – I Am p43

न मे रागादिको दोषो दुःखं देहादिकं न मे ।
आत्मानं विद्धि मामेकं विशालं गगनोपमम् ॥ ६७॥

I have no faults such as attachment;
Nor do I have suffering arising due to the body;
Know me to be the one Self, vast as the sky. [1:67]

K: The one that needs to accept, is a phantom and you may become a phantom that's closer to acceptance. But it's still – shit! Relative acceptance from a relative 'one' who accepts.

Q: So, Absolute acceptance?

K: Doesn't exist. No one can have it. So, what you cannot have, you should not be interested in. It's bad. Then they say you say all is shit and it's bad and then I see you and I don't see a person who is unhappy. I tell them, if you don't know happiness, that's just fine. You don't need to know anything and in that happiness, is just seen as another bullshit. If you don't have to be happy, it's not so bad. You don't have to be good, you always will be bad.

Q [Another visitor]: So, it's always going to be lonely...

K: It's always going to be lonely as there's no second. You will always be alone. [pointing to a sleeping visitor] No hope, nothing that can be done, he went straight to sleep. [Laughter] He's exercising as a corpse, already.

– *Worry And Be Happy p21*

K: I Am what I Am – the absence and whatever you try to do, to attack me [Laughing] – try harder. I like everything [Laughter] only because I don't need it. I like everything only because I don't need to like it. There's no demand That I have to like it, but I like the dislike as much as I like the like – don't get it wrong. But I hate you all! [Laughter] Unconditionally. Whatever you do, I hate you anyway. Then you can do whatever you like.

That's the beauty of hate. You can do whatever, you can hate them anyway. For love, you always have to work and find a reason to love somebody. But hate is natural. You even hate that you exist. And then there's someone else that you hate equally. That's the nature of presence – hate. It's fun.

And if everything is hate, it's unconditional hate. So, in nature it's absolute, but if there's hate and love, that's hell.

–*Worry And Be Happy p62*

सखे मनः किं बहुजल्पितेन
सखे मनः सर्वमिदं वितर्क्यम् ।
यत्सारभूतं कथितं मया ते
त्वमेव तत्त्वं गगनोपमोऽसि ॥ ६८॥

O Mind, my friend, what use is much vain talk?
O Mind, my friend, all this is mere conjecture;
The core essence, I have already told you;
You are the ultimate Reality, unbounded like the sky. [1:68]

Q: You're just pointing to the uselessness of words and concepts to try and communicate what you're pointing towards...

K: No. I'm just pointing to the entertainment. [Laughter] It's entertaining, it's not useless.

Q: I'm talking about the words...

K: The words are very entertaining because they have no meaning.

Q: [Another visitor]: It may be useless for you...

K: You had said it right, you cannot catch me. I'm always jumping from one branch to other and I don't mind going from one concept to another because one is as good or bad as the other one. They are all false anyway. I make a false statement here and I make a false statement there. False, false, false, false. Whatever can be said, whatever can be pronounced.

Q: [Another visitor]: The feeling of 'I Amness' is also false?

K: Absolutely. Whatever we can talk about is false. That's the entertainment. If there would be one Truth in it that would be hell. If Truth could really be pronounced, if it really could be presented... Thank God it cannot be presented and never be known by anyone.

Q: So this state which cannot be pronounced...

K: There is no state. Even the unpronounceable state is just false. Even the unpronounced is false.

– *Heaven And Hell p75*

येन केनापि भावेन यत्र कुत्र मृता अपि ।
योगिनस्तत्र लीयन्ते घटाकाशमिवाम्बरे ॥ ६९॥

It does not matter where a yogi dies, It does not matter how he
dies; He merges with the Absolute;
Just as space within a jar merges with space outside,
when the jar is destroyed. [1:69]

K: The biggest teaching of Yogi Ramsuratkumar was there when he was in a coma. Hanging on machines, being on strings, and then when somebody came, he lifted the arm. He was like in a glass house. People could come and see him being in that room, hanging on the machines, totally depending. And on the auspicious day of Shivaratri three years ago, they turned it off. Just to make it auspicious.

That's the biggest teaching you can get. The helplessness itself. He was known as one of the biggest siddhi masters, but that teaching was the greatest I ever saw—being that total acceptance, not changing anything, hanging on machines, simply saying "Okay, what comes, comes. Let be what can be. So what?"

– *Eight Days in Tiruvannamalai p157*

तीर्थे चान्त्यजगेहे वा नष्टस्मृतिरपि त्यजन् ।
समकाले तनुं मुक्तः कैवल्यव्यापको भवेत् ॥ ७०॥

Whether he dies in a holy place or in the house of an outcaste;
Even if he loses awareness at death, merges in the Absolute
alone. [1:70]

Q: Ramana just laid down his life when he was fifteen...

K: He imagined what it would be to die. But he didn't die. He went through all the experiences of dying but in none of those experiences what-he-was could die. The body could die; the ideas of spirit could die. All what you can imagine could die but still you are what-you-are. You are Absolute, without all of that you can experience – even without the experiencer you-are. And that cannot die because That was never born. That's what he experienced.

Your nature is inspite of everything what-it-is. That's the death experience. Everything can die but what-you-are cannot by any means die by any experience. As you are not born in the experience of birth because you are already there before the two liquids meet, you are already there before you have a mask, a persona. You would be afterwards what-you-are. There's no one who's born. How can there be someone to die when in the first place there was no one born?

Find first who's born now. Can you show me anyone who's born? Show me one. You can show me pieces of meat but you cannot show me what-you-are. It cannot be found in anything. Flesh comes in a flash and in a flash it goes. Nothing is lost when someone dies. Nothing is gained if a baby is born. Life doesn't become more or less when there's more or less – something more or less. Seven billion people now. But what does it mean? Infinite supply - never enough.

— *Worry And Be Happy p203*

धर्मार्थकाममोक्षांश्च द्विपदादिचराचरम् ।
मन्यन्ते योगिनः सर्वं मरीचिजलसन्निभम् ॥ ७१ ॥

Duties in life, wealth, enjoyments,
liberation and everything animate;
Such as men and inanimate objects – everything;
In the eyes of a yogi, is like water in a mirage. [1:71]

K: I always ask people if they want to switch and take my job, no one wants it. There is no advantage that you have to talk everyday about what no one wants to know. Everyone wants to have some tools for happiness and I can only repeat that I am not here to make you happy. And the functioning of your daily life will not be different afterwards.

The only thing that may happen, when what-you-are what-you-cannot-not-be, for you there is no daily life any more. There never was and there never will be. And that what has the daily life, there will be the next bullshit.

Q: That's a huge advantage, that's like you are out of the jail, beautiful!

K: But that is what-you-are. Why do you want to make a functioning in this bloody world?

Q: Because right now I'm stuck in this bloody world, when I get out of it, I wouldn't worry about it...

K: The one who wants to get out of it, will never get out of it. And that what-you-are was never in it. So for what-you-are there will be no difference and for that what has a difference, it's always not good enough. The misery will not stop. Why should it stop?

There will always be a 'me' and where there is a 'me', there is a misery.

– *Heaven And Hell p82*

Q: Why are you giving these talks?

K: They are part or aspect of being. No-one is talking and no-one is listening. Without sense and reason. For the question of why there is only one answer: why not?

Q: How can we integrate this in our daily life?

K: That which is requires no integration. And that which is not, will never be integrated.

Recognize the perfect realization of Reality and be what you are. Everything is exactly the way it is, because Being has manifested itself this way and not otherwise.

– *Interview*

अतीतानागतं कर्म वर्तमानं तथैव च ।
न करोमि न भुञ्जामि इति मे निश्चला मतिः ॥ ७२॥

There is no karma (action), either present, past or future;
Which has been performed or enjoyed by me;
This I know without a doubt! [1:72]

K: You may say there's a karmic consciousness, like an action-reaction chain, that you can see. When there is an action, there's a reaction. But That which is acting and That which is reacting are no different. And there is no intention in action, and there is no reaction in reaction. There is meditation of "I am"-ness as consciousness meditating. This is like realization of That which is Self. But there is no intention in anything.

All this is Self-experience or Self-realization; there is nothing that is not. The Self cannot decide how to realize. That helplessness is what is your nature. You are in a total helplessness or hopelessness.

That Selflessness, which has no direction, can never decide what comes next.

– Eight Days in Tiruvannamalai 39

K: Your nature never did any action, never did it nor did not; neither it's the source nor not the source. You can never know what you have done or not done, neither you have done anything nor not done.

No intellect, no mind, no sage can grasp what one is – never ever. This great mystery always remains the absolute mystery. That is the closest pointer to that, but even calling it a mystery is already too much, then whatever you come up to describe it is too much or too less. No way, you will always fail and that is the joy of failing. You will never know yourself or not know yourself. You will never know yourself in any relative way, in any description, in any definition. But still you have to be what you are, that you can call knowledge but that knowledge never needs to know itself to be what it is. That what needs to know what it is, for sure, is not that.

What you are in nature never needs to know nature, neither it knows nature nor it doesn't know nature, it is nature but there is absolute absence of any idea of nature or no-nature. That you can call nature, but no whatever happening in this artificial dream will ever lead you to your nature, which you never left.

– Am I – I Am p148

K: Thank God that what you are can never be reached, not even by yourself. As it cannot be reached, it cannot be affected. By anything. So there is no cause and no effect in what you are. And that's Advaita, because Advaita means there is no second. And when there is no second, there is no effect from anyone. Who can be affected by what? It needs two for being affected. And effects are only in the dream. So only dream objects are affected by other dream objects. And that continues, like a chain of reactions. Effects,

effects, effects.

But you cannot find the cause. The action you cannot find. Energy cannot be found. You can only experience the effects of energy. And not by one of these effects can energy be controlled. Only effects controlling effects. Very effective sometimes, but who cares? So when I say you have to know yourself in the absolute absence of any presence of anyone who knows or doesn't know, that you do every night. So it's nothing new for you. You know yourself in the absolute absence of any presence of any absence of any knower or not knower in deep-deep sleep. To know yourself as that what never needs to know or not to know itself - that is ease.

– May It Be As It Is p59

शून्यागारे समरसपूत-
स्तिष्ठत्येकः सुखमवधूतः ।
चरति हि नग्नस्त्यक्त्वा गर्वं
विन्दति केवलमात्मनि सर्वम् ॥ ७३ ॥

The Avadhut, alone, living in an empty dwelling;
Abides in contentment, pure and equanamous;
Having renounced all, depending on nothing, he moves about naked; Perceiving Self in all and within. [1:73]

Q: So I'm going away empty...

K: For That which is you as absolute Heart, you are absolutely empty of any idea of what you are and are not, even the idea of "emptiness," being even empty of the idea of "emptiness," which no one can be. So you may come, but no one goes. An idea came, but as an idea never came, you never go again. As you never arrived, you cannot leave anymore. So the ghost is gone. The image, the phantom, is seen as it is.

Q: And also there's no bottle...

K: You're right. There's neither inside nor outside—but there is. If you say there is none, there's still is one.

Q: One?

K: To say, "there is no one," there's still one. If you say, "there's no inside and outside," there's still an inside and outside, because it needs one to say that there is no inside and outside, and that one is still making an inside and outside, even by saying it. There is no escape.

This is still part of that understanding. It is still ignorance. Whatever you define, it's ignorance. Any definition comes out of a definer, and that definer is a liar anyway, so whatever lie comes out of that definer himself is a lie. The first definer, "I," already is a lie, as it's an image, it's not what you are, as you are prior to that liar. Out of that lie, only lies come.

– *Eight Days in Tiruvannamalai p118*

K: Jesus said you can only come as the naked existence. No owner can ever go through the eye of a needle. You cannot join me until you are totally naked, naked of any idea of what you are and what you are not—naked existence itself.

In that nakedness, there is paradise. Because there is no one left who can be happy or unhappy, lucky or unlucky, knowing or not knowing. All that—taking that as real, as one who does exist, as "me"— is dream-like, you make a dream real, and then you are trapped in those images and objects and you become an object. But you are That which is Heart. And you have never left it, so you cannot gain it back. By any technique or understanding, you cannot become what you are.

This understanding is not an understanding; This understanding is actually the total dropping of the one who understands. But this cannot be done by that one. It happens by itself. As it came by itself, that falling in love with that image, it drops out of love the same way, by itself, and not by any understanding or any technique or whatever that meditator has done.

– *Eight Days in Tiruvannamalai p153*

त्रितयतुरीयं नहि नहि यत्र
विन्दति केवलमात्मनि तत्र ।
धर्माधर्मौ नहि नहि यत्र
बद्धो मुक्तः कथमिह तत्र ॥ ७४॥

Where there are neither the three states nor the fourth;
Where everything is experienced as the Self alone;
Where neither virtue nor vice exists;
How, then, can there be one who is bound or one who is liberated?! [1:74]

K: Scientists have found that anti-matter and matter are running the universe that is form and non-form together. When enlightenment takes place there is a fusion of this form and non-form, and in this fusion the light of awareness remains. The scientists say that out of this fusion comes pure light. They can now produce anti-matter and make it fuse with matter, and out comes light, the primal source of both form and non-form.

This is what we would call enlightenment – this experience of coming out of the form and non-form and becoming that which is light, the primal light of awareness, that which is called Arunachala. But then to see that even this light of awareness, this first notion of existence without time or no-time, even that is not what you are. Realization is turning to face that which is prior to this first notion of existence.

So that first light as a primal source is not even that which you are; even that definition is not what you are. Out of this 'I', this primal light as awareness, comes 'I am' and then 'I am so and so.' But all these three states are the dream of the dreamer himself.

So even the first dream or experience of 'I' as awareness is a sensation already; it's a phenomenon. But the phenomenon of that which is Self is in all phenomenal states, so it can never be changed. The fourth state is that state of being the Self without even knowing that there is a Self or not. This is a total non-knowing, the total absence of the knower or non-knower. That is the turiya.

* Q: What is 'transcendental turiya'?

K: It is to transcend the experience of primal light as cosmic consciousness and to be that which is prior to that, to be that which is consciousness, in essence. This is the realization that what you are is ever realized. This is nothing new or old; this is your very nature and nothing has to be done or not done for it. It all comes out of this; this is the very source of whatever is and is not, and without this nothing would be or not be. And you are that, that's all.

– *Interview*

K: This body is molecules, but this is like an "in-form-ation" in what dream? There are not even molecules that are building something. Where are the molecules you're built of? You go back and back and you can't even find anything.

The whole scientific world, for centuries, they want to find matter, but they haven't found any matter up until now. So it doesn't matter. [group laughs] So first find something that has incarnated and then we can talk about what that is. But as they never found anything that is incarnated, it doesn't matter.

–*Eight Days in Tiruvannamalai p252*

विन्दति विन्दति नहि नहि मन्त्रं
छन्दोलक्षणं नहि नहि तन्त्रम् ।
समरसमग्नो भावितपूतः
प्रलपितमेतत्परमवधूतः ॥ ७५॥

Neither rejoicing in mantras;
Nor rejoicing in the rhyme of tantras;
As the all-pervasive essence, absorbed in not-knowingness;
The Avadhut merely speaks the Truth. [1:77]

Q: Are there any practices that can take you to enlightenment?

K: Every practice will take you to that which you are, but no special practice. Whatever one is doing is the very best he can do, and what he is doing came from that which is the source, the Self. There is no question that whatever is done is done by Self to become that which is Self. As soon there is consciousness, consciousness is Self-enquiry. This Self-enquiry for sure will lead to that which is prior to consciousness. But there is no special technique to it.

So the technique of Sri Ramana of 'Who am I?' is just a pointer. This is not a technique; it is simply reversing what came out as 'I am so-and-so' to become 'Who am I?' which then leads to this unknown openness of existence. But it will happen in spite of the technique, not because of it, because the Self has no cause and cannot be controlled or caused by any technique.

Q: For example, there are some common practices like meditation, mantras, chanting and so on.

K: Yes, all wonderful, and they all come out of the very same source, but all the mantras and meditation cannot make the Self be the Self. You cannot become that which you are through anything.

Q: Because you already are that?

K: Yes. And if this could be controlled by any technique or mantra, sadhana or tapas then the Self could be controlled – and this Self I do not know, because the Self that can be controlled needs a second Self to be controlled by. There is simply no second Self who can control the first Self, so actually I don't know. It's all okay. But in spite of all the techniques and doings, that which can never be done 'is'.

–Interview

सर्वशून्यमशून्यं च सत्यासत्यं न विद्यते ।
स्वभावभावतः प्रोक्तं शास्त्रसंवित्तिपूर्वकम् ॥ ७६ ॥

There exists neither complete void nor voidlessness;
neither truth nor untruth;
The Avadhut, having realized the essence of scriptures;
Has uttered this spontaneously, naturally. [1:76]

Q: Do you ever meditate?

K: I never stop. What am I doing here? I am presenting you a talking meditation. Talking the living words and don't expect anything to come out of it. That's talking meditation, the living words, there is no intention, no expectation in that what is living word. There is no need of any result or any goal. It's like there is no teaching, nothing to learn, this intentionlessness is just living words. This what we are doing here is meditation.

– Am I – I Am p13

K: As an idea, a pointer. But the Self doesn't know any Self. There is only "Selflessness," you may call it, "lovelessness," "existencelessness." I am pointing to that "idea-lessness," where all the icons—of divinity, of God—are gone. This Godlessness I'm talking about. You are That which is God, but God doesn't know any God, no second or whatever. That which cannot be talked about or defined—that's what I'm talking about.

This paradox cannot be solved. We talk about something that cannot be talked about. So we can talk about it, but it makes no difference. It's just pointing out that it makes no difference whether you talk or not.

For That which you are, it never makes any difference, whatever you say, whatever you define or don't define. There is nothing more or less. There is no quantity in it, of whatever idea of "divine" or anything. All this is gone. This is freedom which has no idea about freedom.

Q: Emptiness?

K: Not even emptiness. Even emptiness is too much. This is That which is emptiness, and this is That which is fullness, and this is That which is whatever you name, but it has no name.

– *Eight Days in Tiruvannamalai p37*

Chapter Two

बालस्य वा विषयभोगरतस्य वापि
मूर्खस्य सेवकजनस्य गृहस्थितस्य ।
एतद्दुरोः किमपि नैव न चिन्तनीयं
रत्नं कथं त्यजति कोऽप्यशुचौ प्रविष्टम् ॥ १॥

The teacher, even if young, unlearned,
or addicted to the enjoyment of sense objects;
Whether a servant or householder;
Should not be rejected on these grounds;
Just as a gem fallen in dirt is not discarded. [2:1]

Q: What about the habits that you get over time?

K: I have so many bad habits, I watch too much television. How can I change it? I watch too many movies too and really bad ones. That is a really big part of the discussion between me and my girlfriend, she wants to watch a love story and I want to watch a crime story. It's really hell for her and it's hell for me to watch love stories [laughter].

Q: But they are both stories, why one over the other?

K: It's my tendency. These are like two main tendencies, wisdom which wants to destroy everything: the body is not true, the world is not true, destroying everything. Then the other one is Heart which tells you love is the solution but both are lying. None of them is a solution.

Q: They are both just habits…

K: Yes and if it happens that my tendency goes towards there, what shall I do? I tried many times to watch love stories but it didn't function, it's still pain.

Nisargadatta said on one side there is love which tells me – I'm everything and on the other side there is wisdom that tells me I'm nothing and both are empty promises. Between the both 'I Am' flows, both are empty, both promise something and tell you something and both tell you lies. The heart tells you something and the intellect tells you something and both are liars. None of them can deliver what they promise.

One promises you peace by being everything the other promises you peace by being nothing and both are lies. Peace is what you are already and it cannot be delivered by wisdom or by Heart. And both are empty vessels.

Q: And if you take both of them together, then you have got two empty vessels…

K: Then you have two bullshits. People say you should have an open heart and an open spirit both together, and then you are complete. Who needs to be complete? That's the question, who bloody needs to be complete to be what one is?

Again me wants to be complete, having a total intellect. Then on the other side an open heart [sarcastically]. Then walking on these two legs, you are complete as what you are. Hallelujah.

– Am I – I Am p171

नैवाल काव्यगुण एव तु चिन्तनीयो
ग्राह्यः परं गुणवता खलु सार एव ।
सिन्दूरचित्ररहिता भुवि रूपशून्या
पारं न किं नयति नौरिह गन्तुकामान् ॥ २॥

*The teacher's worth is not to be measured by his
scholarly and literary merits;
A seeker of Truth should pursue the essence of Truth alone;
Does not a boat devoid of beauty and attractive paint;
Ferry its occupants across?! [2:2]*

Q: How to transcribe it into the book?

K: Yeah, you can write brmm... brmm.... [Laughter].

For me it would be the same as the high, profound or brmm... brmm.... There's no difference. Makes no difference. All the day brmm...... is no different than talking all the day about the substratum and the absolute and the highest of the highest. And all the levels of the underlying truth. All the blah, blah, blah, brmm... brmm... brmm... The resonance would be no different. Different resonance but that what is resonating to itself would not be different in nature. It would be just resonating to itself in the absolute resonance to that what is That. It never needs this high – tra...laa...laa... Of this abstraction of abstraction.

But it's fun too. You can talk very high and very profound and then [making sounds of trumpet] the entire spectrum of all the bullshit you can do and none of them makes you more or less as you are. You can be professors and professors of Upanishads with Yoga-vashishta up and down. And you can go to the zoo and play with the monkey. As you play with yourself, or you press an ant between your fingers.

– *Heaven And Hell p159*

Q: So the way you look at the spiritual...

K: Business?

Q: Business. The people who are so-called enlightened, all the scriptures, all the philosophers...

K: I like it all! I love it!

Q: Yes, but you have an approach to that, like a destructive one, or de-constructive.

K: Yes, I kill it by loving it.

Q: What the Western philosophers call deconstruction.

K: No, I even go so far to destruct the destructor.

– May It Be As It Is p156

प्रयत्नेन विना येन निश्वलेन चलाचलम् ।
ग्रस्तं स्वभावतः शान्तं चैतन्यं गगनोपमम् ॥ ३ ॥

Effortless and unmoving, the Self is all that is
moving and not-moving;
It is pure consciousness, naturally calm, like the sky. [2:3]

Q: So, is it just that the illusory 'I' that is moving across the panorama?

K: You are the unmovable spectator – the Absolute 'I' – the Absolute seer, who's experiencing itself frame by frame coming from illusionary future and going into an illusionary past. But you're not moving. The frames are coming and going in front of your eyes. Then you make a movie out of it, with an imaginary movement.

You're not moving in it. Never! It's an imaginary movement of frames – moments coming and going. But even to know all of that, you better know yourself what-you-are in nature – That never needs to know the mechanics. It's magic in a way! Just enjoy your show – by being That what is trying or not trying anything – just to realize yourself.

This is one aspect of realizing yourself in a personal camera position. When you're the space, there's already no reference point. And then you experience yourself as awareness, there's not even space or time. Even that is a fragment of what-you-are and then the experience of beyond is another movie – an absence of a movie – it's part of the movie. And the impersonal awareness which comes, then the personal being a human. All the seven different levels of the movie are permanently there. You just shift between all those possibilities which are already there and never come and never go. There are seven different variations of dreaming yourself or experiencing yourself.

And none of them is better than the other.

– *Worry And Be Happy p67*

अयत्नाछालयेद्यस्तु एकमेव चराचरम् ।
सर्वगं तत्कथं भिन्नमद्वैतं वर्तते मम ॥ ४॥

How can That which is One and All-pervading;
That, which effortlessly moves all things
– movable and immovable, be differentiated?
To me, That is non-dual. [2:4]

K: The Self always enjoying itself, by being the Self. So that what is Self enjoys even the un-enjoyment of that what is not Self. Absolutely, you can never disturb the perfect happiness of the Self. This cannot be disturbed by anything. And that what can be disturbed is not the Self, that's all. And the Self never cares about that what is not

Self. The Self is not the caretaker of that what is the unfolding of the Self. The Self is pure Self, and this is absolute perfect happiness itself. The absence of any idea of what the Self is not, or what the Self is. That is the perfect happiness and perfection of the Self. And this cannot be disturbed or erased or be done anything with it, because this is not an object in time that you can move or not move. So it always comes back to the point, be prior to that what is time and space. Just see that that what you are cannot be touched by that what is sensational or phenomenal.

– *Interview*

अहमेव परं यस्मात्सारात्सारतरं शिवम् ।
गमागमविनिर्मुक्तं निर्विकल्पं निराकुलम् ॥ ५॥

I am verily the Supreme as I am Shivam (Absolute principle);
I am the substantial and the insubstantial;
Neither do I come, nor do I go;
I have no movement; I have no form. [2:5]

K: What would be there without that definer that defines coming and going and birth and death? Changes. That is called the devil, the master of time, the master of hell, of differences. Without the me there are no differences. It needs a definer of a 'tree' to differentiate between 'water' and other things. As a baby you don't know these differences. It's a conditioning of the me that came to you to make differences between things and you learnt it and what you learnt will be gone one day and again you will be without that system of differences.

It came and it will be gone sooner or later. As it will be gone, it's already not there. Why do you care about something that will be gone by itself? It came by itself it will be gone by itself. Why do you worry about it? You want to make it earlier? That you seek to make it earlier?

– Am I – I Am p26

Q: Many seekers are looking for enlightenment as if it is an experience. What is enlightenment?

K: Enlightenment is to see that which is the Self is ever enlightened and that which is not the Self will never be enlightened, and then to be that which is the Self. Then there is no before and no after.

Q: Could you unfold that a little bit?

K: The simple dropping out of time or no time; the dropping of that 'me', which was simply a false Self. This is an absolute dropping of any sense of existence. The very first notion of existence dropped by the simple recognition of that which one is, prior to the very first notion of existence. But not knowing it then by any experience, just seeing that this first experience of the notion of existence is not what you are. So in this non-experience of that which you are, in the experience of whatever you can experience is not what you are, you simply rest. This is not something big or small; it is simply a little 'Aha!' It's nothing special. It is like a split second, and everything is done.

– Interview

सर्वावयवनिर्मुक्तं तथाहं त्रिदशार्चितम् ।
संपूर्णत्वान्न गृह्णामि विभागं त्रिदशादिकम् ॥ ६॥

Thus I, unaffected by my constituent elements, remain as Myself; Though worshipped by gods, being perfect wholeness itself; I see no distinctions such as gods and otherwise. [2:6]

K: You are trying to give a name to that which has no name. Many million years ago there was no idea of Shiva or Durga or Parvati and still existence was existence. All that came will be gone. All the stories of gods and religions and all of that. It's just a glimpse of an eye. It's just God lifting his eyebrow and story of the entire humanity and stories of all of that are created.

It sounds so important, all the tradition and everything. But if you see in the total picture, it's a grain of sand on the beach. The whole story of India, the whole whatever, the whole story of Shiva and Parvati, it's not even there.

– *Heaven And Hell p167*

K: If you really go towards that dimension of absolute, it really becomes like [blowing in the wind]. But otherwise if you break your finger nail, it's like the whole universe is breaking. [Laughter] And if you have a little understanding, you think that the whole universe understands. And you are right! The whole existence in that moment understands it and the whole existence is breaking the finger nail.

It has the same importance as sipping the next sip of coffee or breaking a finger nail or the whole universe collapsing in one instant. In the quality, there is no difference. The quality is that what-you-are is experiencing itself in the smallest and in the biggest. But then making it a story of Shiva or Parvati and Ganga is wonderful, but in totality it's just a fraction.

But in that moment you are involved in your puja, it becomes a total reality for what-you-are. The smallest thing and the biggest thing. And there is a never ending story of it. You go from the smallest to the biggest and all the frequencies and all the possibilities, in that you realize yourself. In whatever possible way. None of them is more or less, that's the beauty of it.

The next sip of coffee, the next taste of nothing, has the same quality of what-you-are as the totality of blissful background traa-laa-laa.

– Heaven And Hell p168

प्रमादेन न सन्देहः किं करिष्यामि वृत्तिमान् ।
उत्पद्यन्ते विलीयन्ते बुद्बुदाश्व यथा जले ॥ ७॥

Neither doubt nor ignorance, cause a slightest ripple in me;
Let occurrences of modifications of the mind continue;
They arise and dissolve like the bubbles in water. [2:7]

Q: So in your own experience there was some moment of 'Aha!' Did you find then that Karl's vasanas, Karl's stuff would come up?

K: Even more.

Q: Even more?

K: In this fire it really comes up. There is no attachment so you just look and see this stuff coming up? Yes; you just see.

Q: And by the seeing, it is destroyed?

K: By that acceptance 'you are'. With this acceptance there is no control system running any more. The control system is armour around you, and this armour, what you would call the personal consciousness, gets destroyed. Without the control system of this 'me' being in control, without the attention of whatever this 'me' or this 'I'-thought is, the energy really becomes alive again. Consciousness comes into fire and whatever was there as memory pops up in the hell-fire of awareness, which is simply the source. This body-mind memory, even the whole memory of the universe comes with it. It is not only 'my history'; it has to be the history of all mankind and even further, the history of the whole universe that gets burned in this awareness. So the whole of time gets burned out. All the ideas that came with time have to be burned out in this timelessness, in this acceptance of being 'that what is', and in this emptiness you are.

– *Interview*

महदादीनि भूतानि समाप्यैवं सदैव हि ।
मृदुद्रव्येषु तीक्ष्णेषु गुडेषु कटुकेषु च ॥ ८॥

*Thus I ever pervade entire existence beginning
with cosmic intelligence
– pervade all things soft and hard,
tasteful and tasteless. [2:8]*

K: All this collection of precious understandings and deep insights is what? Not worth more than a fart in the wind, for what you are? It stinks for a while but then it's gone. So this little me is like a fart, coming out of the Absolute. And the fart stinks for a while, maybe for 50 years, 80 years, whatever, but the stinker, which is just like a little smell, will be gone one day. But the Tastelessness, the Smell-lessness of your Nature, which is the origin of all the little smells, stinking stinkers, this Tastelessness can never be tasted in that. So your Nature is tastelessness, you cannot taste what you are. So you are Tastelessness. And whatever you taste, the taster, is already a taste. And whatever the taster is tasting is tasting is bitter, compared to what you are.

That's why they say you are the Sweetness itself. Whatever the taster is tasting is bitter compared to the Tastelessness you are, which can never be tasted by itself. So that absolute Tastelessness, the absolute Taste, of any absence of anyone who tastes or doesn't taste anything, that's the Sweetness of your Nature. That's the Sweetness itself. But you can never experience it, because whatever you experience is second hand. It's just a bitterness. It's bitter compared to what you are. Because all of that is bitter-field, the whole realization is bitter compared to the Sweetness you are. Any moment of experience, like every sip of coffee, whatever, a sunset, is not beauty, it is a reflection of beauty. It's not different from it, but the Beauty you are, thank God, can never be experienced in any reflection of it. So enjoy it. Enjoy that you don't have to enjoy yourself in anything. And the joy you are cannot be found or lost in any experience.

– *May It Be As It Is p32*

कटुत्वं चैव शैत्यत्वं मृदुत्वं च यथा जले ।
प्रकृतिः पुरुषस्तद्वदभिन्नं प्रतिभाति मे ॥ ९॥

As pungency, coolness and softness being the nature of water,
are non-different from water itself;
Likewise, prakriti and purusha being my nature
are no different from me. [2:9]

K: The doubtful existence will always out of the doubtful existence doubt itself and by doubting itself trying to get rid of the doubt. And trying to get rid of the doubt, trying to become real or knowing what is. Because that what it would be would be not doubtful. But trying to become it will always be a doubtful attempt. It goes on and on and on. Never ending story. It's like Shiva creates his own puppet house, and then playing with the puppets he becomes a puppet himself. And then trying not to be a puppet, he stays a puppet. And that's the nature of Shiva, becoming a Jiva. Playing around with himself. Creating images of himself, and after a while he believes in his own image. So he cannot even blame anyone else. He is stupid enough to play with himself. And then he becomes this real play. And then trying to get out of the play because he gets bored with the play, is impossible. Because he was never in the play.

— *May It Be As It Is p235*

सर्वाख्यारहितं यद्वत्सूक्ष्मात्सूक्ष्मतरं परम् ।
मनोबुद्धीन्द्रियातीतमकलङ्कं जगत्पतिम् ॥ १०॥

Devoid of all names
— subtlest of the subtle and highest of the highest;
Devoid of mind, intellect and beyond the senses;
Is the stainless Lord of the universe. [2:10]

K: That's why they call it Para-brahman or Parama-atman, because they don't want to name it. They don't want to fix it; they don't want to make an object out of it, because already out of awareness you can make an object. Because you can name it. You can define it.

So, and "I" as awareness is not "I am" as cosmic consciousness, or "I am this" as identified consciousness, so there would be a separation between awareness, cosmic consciousness and the identified consciousness. So there is still separation. So if you would call it awareness, it would be separated from "I am Karl". But the "I am Karl is not different from the Self. The awareness is not different, the "I am" is not different, and the "I am Karl" is not different. So if you would call it awareness it would be different from the "I am".

— *Interview*

K: You are that what is the I am. But that what is the I am doesn't know any I am. So if God would pronounce that what is God, he would maybe say - I don't agree, because what is God doesn't even know any God who could say something - but if, just imaging, like a pointer, he would say 'I am that I am'.

Q: That is what is in the bible.

K: Yes, that's why an imaginary God would say, by understanding that he is an imagination; he would say 'I am that I am'. This is like the most consciousness can realize. Which is already a dream. Because consciousness is Vedanta. That what is - there is no consciousness. Consciousness is dream. Consciousness is already the realization of Reality. It's not different from Reality, but that what is Knowledge is neither conscious nor unconscious. It doesn't even know consciousness, never needs consciousness. It never needs to be to be.

Q: And it is written that the question was 'What is your name?' not what you are. 'I am what I am' is the name of God. It points to the duality already.

K: If God would define that what God is, he would say 'I am that what is the definer, but I am not the definer'. If he would say that. So that what is the definer is not the definer. 'I am that what is the I am'. Amazing. It's never finished.

— *May It Be As It Is p33*

ईदृशं सहजं यत्र अहं तत्र कथं भवेत् ।
त्वमेव हि कथं तत्र कथं तत्र चराचरम् ॥ ११॥

In the natural state of Self,
how can an 'I' continue?!
How could there still be a 'you' or a 'world',
sentient or insentient?! [2:11]

Q: Splitting the second is splitting the other...

K: Yeah. In splitting the second, it's just being what-you-are, being what-is. That's splitting the second. There's no me and no you. That's splitting the second. It's not in a split second.

Q: Splitting the sense of separation...

K: The book of Papaji about split second is not about moment in time where you have an insight. No! Splitting the second happens every night, by being what-you-are. And by being what-you-are, there's no second – you are That! And That is maximum culpa. You're the absolute owner of what-is – you are That! You are That what is realization. But you're not the one who's realizing itself.

But you are sitting here to get minimized to be maximized.

– *The Song Of Irrelevance p125*

K: If you see that there was never anyone who was enlightened, that just takes that one away who is unenlightened, that's all. Very simple. It is not something that is a big deal. It's just a split second. You split all these ideas of gaining something in the dream just by being what you are, by just seeing there wasn't even anyone here. So if this is gone, where are all the others? There are only others because there is one here. No one here, no one there.

– *May It Be As It Is p119*

गगनोपमं तु यत्प्रोक्तं तदेव गगनोपमम् ।
चैतन्यं दोषहीनं च सर्वज्ञं पूर्णमेव च ॥ १२॥

The Self expounded to be like the sky indeed is the sky itself;
It is pure Consciousness, defectless, omniscient
and ever complete. [2:12]

K: As you are in the absence what-you-are, you are now in the presence what-you-are. Whatever happens now in the presence cannot make – anything. There is no consequence for you because when this [pointing to the body] will be gone, you still are the absence of what-you-are.

So whatever happens in this presence of life, however it is, does not have a slightest impact for what-you-are. Whatever you gain as knowledge or understanding is all … [blowing in the wind]… comes and goes. It will be gone, it's already gone. Whatever comes now is already gone. It's all dead.

All the coming, all the fleeting shadows, experiences, sensations of deepest understandings and whatever, it's all… [Blowing in the wind] Entertainment! Just for fun.

– *Heaven And Hell p108*

पृथिव्यां चरितं नैव मारुतेन च वाहितम् ।
वरिणा पिहितं नैव तेजोमध्ये व्यवस्थितम् ॥ १३ ॥

Despite taking forms of earth, fire, air and water;
It remains unaffected by these,
remaining always the same.[2:13]

Q: This movement that you want to get somewhere or you want to get something like enlightenment or the dissolution of the search is totally non-sense. It's hopeless...

K: That's the beauty of it.

Q: I'm fed up with it...

K: Even that is beautiful. You are playing 'fed-up' looking for yourself. For how long? And then you start again and even by being fed-up, you look for yourself because you think that maybe by being fed-up, you find something.

– *The Song Of Irrelevance p15*

आकाशं तेन संव्याप्तं न तद्व्याप्तं च केनचित् ।
स बाह्याभ्यन्तरं तिष्ठत्यवच्छिन्नं निरन्तरम् ॥ १४ ॥

Space is pervaded by It, but It is not pervaded by anything;
It exists as both – within and without;
It is indivisible, perpetual and unlimited. [2:14]

K: You are even inspite of awareness. In spite of the light of Shiva, you are That what-you-are. That you can call Parabrahman – the Absolute dreamer – which is with and without the dream. The dream starts with awareness and space and whatever comes out of That space. But inspite of it, with and without the experience of awareness – you are. This omnipresence, which is in the absence or presence of anything what-it-is, That is the Absolute because there's no second to That.

That you can call Reality that starts to realize itself as a realizer, as awareness. It becomes a creator, creating what can be created. But with and without the creator – you are. So, you are not the creator, not the creation and there's nothing to create. That you can never know, but you are – That. That is not something you can attain by awareness. How can you attain that by awareness which is already there without the awareness? What an idea!

– *Worry And Be Happy p209*

K: Whatever idea cannot touch what you are. So even the idea of identified consciousness, cosmic consciousness, awareness, these are merely ideas in time and space. That what is in time and space cannot touch what is prior to time and space. And that is what you are, without naming it.

— *Interview*

सूक्ष्मत्वात्तदृश्यत्वान्निर्गुणत्वाच्च योगिभिः ।
आलम्बनादि यत्प्रोक्तं क्रमादालम्बनं भवेत् ॥ १५॥

Its extreme suitability and qualitylessness make it imperceptible;
The yogis call it the source of all qualities;
That which was sought as an object;
Is found to be the substratum itself. [2:15]

Q: Are you saying that Am I – I Am is a way in the dream, that you can remind yourself what-you-cannot-not-be?

K: No, No. If you could just stay in the Am I – I Am, after whatever time, you don't exist as what you think any more. It would erase all your story. If it has to happen, it will erase all your story. And it has to be 24 by 7 by 365, not only two hours a day. Not just when you remember.

That's the beauty of Am I – I Am; it becomes your very nature. Without any effort, Am I – I Am! You don't even have to pronounce it in your brain. It's just a natural state of being, Am I – I Am!

Q: This is just like a sublime, non-verbal…

K: It's a state of being. It's not like you question yourself Am I? – I Am. It starts like it – try it. Try it for one hour Am I – I Am. After whatever time, you don't even have to pronounce it, inside or outside any more. It becomes like a stream of presence. It's not an effort.

It may start with remembering Am I – I Am. But if you do it 24 by 7, then it becomes like a presence. An effortlessness of presence, in the presence.

Q: [Another visitor]: Self-remembrance?

K: No, there is no remembrance. There is no need for memorizing it. The Self doesn't need to remember itself. It's not a memory. It's just to be what-you-are. It's not memorizing something. It's called self-abidance. Abiding in that what is Am I – I Am! It's Nisargadatta's stay in 'I Amness'.

And how to stay in the 'I Amness' is Am I – I Am. Just stay in that question first, then automatically the questioner and the answerer disappear. And even the question disappears and even the answer disappears in that – Self-Abidance.

That's what Ramana calls the natural state – in the presence. Being the presence, not knowing any presence. In that presence here-now, there is 'I Amness'. But there is no one who is in the 'I Amness'.

– *Heaven And Hell p218*

सतताऽभ्यासयुक्तस्तु निरालम्बो यदा भवेत् ।
तल्लयाल्लीयते नान्तर्गुणदोषविवर्जितः ॥ १६॥

Through ceaseless pursuit, when meditation becomes objectless;
Transcending merits and demerits, total dissolution occurs;
By the dissolution of the object of meditation itself. [2:16]

Q: Yesterday you were talking about the meditation, that 'am I, I am'. I didn't understand.

K: That would be self-inquiry. The answer to 'am I' is 'I am',

Q: 'Am I?' There is a question mark?

K: There is no question mark. You just pronounce 'Am I' and then out of 'am I' you don't know where it starts any more, it just becomes 'I am'. So the question is the answer. But the question 'who am I?' - it's always like it becomes a special answer. But if the question becomes the answer, it becomes a stream of existence in the presence. So the 'am I' becomes the presence of 'I am'. And in that there is just what you are. If you want to do something, self-inquiry, that is the question which is the answer. So there is no questioner and no answerer in it. So in that question there is no questioner. In the answer there is no answerer. So the question is the answer. It becomes like a stream of presence. And that you have to do 24/7/365.

Q: Only 24/7/365? That's all?

K: If you do it uninterrupted, even silently, you don't even have to pronounce it. You just stay in the 'am I, I am, am I', it just becomes like a sound of Om, like a light and sound, permanent stream of existence. That is like when Ramana said that sound remained, the Shruti in Indian music, this basic sound of a vibration of existence. And the rest of all the other sounds are just like notes on a screen of that. But the basic sound is uninterrupted. So all the other information's are varying, but this is uninterrupted that.

And if you can just stay in that, I promise you after whatever time there will be no me any more. Simply staying in that, being that, there is a total annihilation of any idea of any relative I. If you can do that. But you cannot do it. If it will happen it will happen by itself. Because your pressure will be so high or your so-called 'earnesty' – it's a false translation of Nisargadatta – it needs that unavoidable demand of existence which presses you into that sound, to give your attention only to that what is attention. A permanent stream of what you are. And that is like being depressed 10 meters under water, not getting any air any more for the me. And then automatically by being what you are it becomes a total ease. But without that you will always try to get a personal comfort, more advantage. So all the other meditation, whatever you try otherwise, yoga and all of that, is all for a personal advantage. But this is like a total demand of existence itself which is pressing you into that concentration camp of that uninterrupted 'am I, I am'. It becomes like a holocaust for the I. You will be burned out by just that. But if that happens, it's in spite of what you have done or not done in your whole existence at all.

– May It Be As It Is p221

विषविश्वस्य रौद्रस्य मोहमूर्च्छाप्रदस्य च ।
एकमेव विनाशाय ह्यमोघं सहजामृतम् ॥१७॥

For the destruction of the dreadfully poisonous universe –
The source of delusion;
There is but one infallible antidote
– the nectar of naturalness. [2:17]

K: The total annihilation of the sufferer is, when you are what you are, when you are that what is without beginning and without end. And the absolute Self-cognition, the Self-realisation, is when the Self is absolutely the Self. And how can the Self not be absolutely the Self? And when there is only Self this is the absolute annihilation of separation, that there is a separate self.

Q: But that means, this idea of separate self collapses, it just vanishes at some point.

K: That what is spontaneously arising, as an "I am" idea of I-thought, can only spontaneously disappear. Because the Self itself has no necessity that something gets annihilated, because the Self only knows the Self by being the Self. And that what is part of the realisation of the Self, if this comes and goes, who cares? First there must be one who cares about whether something has to come or to go. Find the one who cares.

– *Interview*

K: When you are the desirer, the desiring and the desired, then you are That what-you-are. There's no desire any more, there's no ownership of desire. There's still desire but – you are That – the desirer, desiring what can be desired. Then there's no harm in it, you cannot suffer about it when there's no separation in separation. Then there's an experience of separation but in nature there's no separation. Yes there is, but there's not. This is the end of suffering.

– *Worry And Be Happy p190*

भावगम्यं निराकारं साकारं दृष्टिगोचरम् ।
भावाभावविनिर्मुक्तमन्तरालं तदुच्यते ॥ १८ ॥

Form is perceptible to the eye,
the formless is perceived mentally;
The Self is indescribable,
either as being or non-being. [2:18]

K: You have to see the form and the non-form in the same moment. You see that That which is form is formless and you are That which is seeing that form—you are the Source of both. You are emptiness and fullness, or That which is form and non-form, as both are there as what you are, space-like and That which isn't even form. But you are not form and you are not even space.

– *Eight Days in Tiruvannamalai p49*

K: Be what is quiet and see. You are the Absolute seer and you cannot not see. You see, when there is seeing what can be seen and even if there is nothing to see, you experience the absence. What you are is always experiencing itself, in presence and in the absence. In the seen and in the not seen, you are that what is the Absolute seer. Call it the Absolute Dreamer; my preference is to call it the seer. There is like a perception. You are that what is perception and perception perceiving the presence and perceiving the absence is still perception.

So you can call it the Absolute seer or the non-seer seeing. Call it whatever, just be that what can never be seen in anything, or not seen. There can only be a seen or non-seen, being or not being because you are. But you are not because there is being as you are also in the non-being what you are. Your nature doesn't demand the presence of being to be or the absence of being. You are in the presence and in the absence of whatever you imagine what you are.

–Am I – I Am p81

बाह्यभावं भवेद्विश्वमन्तः प्रकृतिरुच्यते ।
अन्तरादन्तरं ज्ञेयं नारिकेलफलाम्बुवत् ॥ १९॥

The external aspect is referred to as the universe;
The internal aspect is referred to as nature;
Know That to be the innermost of the inner;
Like sweet water at the core of the coconut. [2:19]

Q: When Sri Ramana was asked, 'When will realisation of the Self be gained?' he replied, 'When the world, which is what is seen, has been removed there will be realisation of the Self, which is the Seer.' What is the true understanding of the world?

K: The world is there the moment the 'I' appears. Out of this 'I' the spider creates the world surrounded by creation, then the 'I am' as formless consciousness. Then the creative force of the 'I am' creates all this information, which we call world. So this information of universe or world is consciousness in form, coming out of the non-form of formless consciousness.

Consciousness creates by simply getting into form. That which is world is actually consciousness in action, like Shiva dancing with himself and creating this universe out of his dance. The essence of everything that is form and non-form is consciousness. All there is, is consciousness, as cosmic consciousness.

— *Interview*

भ्रान्तिज्ञानं स्थितं बाह्यं सम्यग्ज्ञानं च मध्यगम् ।
मध्यान्मध्यतरं ज्ञेयं नारिकेलफलाम्बुवत् ॥ २०॥

Illusory knowledge relates to what is outside,
Subtler knowledge to what is inside;
Know That which is more interior than the inside;
That which is like sweet water within the core of the coconut.
[2:20]

K: Whatever you realize, however profound, however deep, your nature never demanded that. It's just a part of the story of one realizing something. Even becoming cosmic consciousness is still stupid. From the beginning till the end, whatever happens in this presence – is ignorance. Even the absence is ignorance. These are the two sides of knowledge – experiencing itself in the presence of ignorance and the absence of ignorance. The absence of ignorance seems more comfortable and the presence of ignorance is discomfortable. But what to do? You cannot not realize yourself.

And if one realizes himself as whatever, what about the consciousness in other cases? One is realized and the others are stupid as hell. How can that happen?

–Worry And Be Happy p25

Q: You have been saying that the moment you start speaking everything is a lie.

K: The Nature of every word is true. But not the word you understand. But the Essence of everything, whatever vibration is Energy, that what is. So they are real lies. So even the lies are real. To call that 'Lila', one wants to be detached from something. It's another goal. Then it's a personal advantage. 'I am detached now because I see everything as Lila'. No! You are that what is Reality and this is your realization. And there is no one who can escape it.

Q: So these are the real lies?

K: Yes, these are real lies, and you experience yourself in real lies. And the experiencer and what can be experienced are real lies in experiences. But not in their Nature. The Nature of the world is what you are; the Nature of the universe is what you are. You are the Nature itself. But there is no second nature. That's all. But that one who says 'this universe is all a lie', he wants to claim that he is real. Ha, ha, ha, ha.

So everyone who understands something wants to understand 'everything is false, but not me'. All a misunderstanding, from the beginning. Missed-understanding. Missed in action.

– May It Be As It Is p219

पौर्णमास्यां यथा चन्द्र एक एवातिनिर्मलः ।
तेन तत्सदृशं पश्येदुद्विधादृष्टिर्विपर्ययः ॥ २१॥

On the full-moon night, just as the moon is seen;
By un-flawed eyes clearly as one, alone;
The one Reality too should be seen with such clarity;
Know sight to be flawed when two (duality) are seen. [2:21]

Q: Consciousness is always duality.

K: The idea of consciousness creates duality. God knowing himself there is consciousness. He is conscious to exist, there is consciousness. Already there is duality.

Q: And the root is the desire.

K: Out of that duality, the doubtful God, comes the doubter. And out of the doubter comes all the doubting and what can be doubted. The false is already there, that God can know himself. God can be conscious about that what is consciousness. Or God. There is two. Consciousness being conscious about consciousness is two consciousnesses. Already the dream starts. So consciousness waking up, becoming aware to be conscious, or to be the purest consciousness, already is separation.

– *May It Be As It Is p41*

K: A concept, a ghost needs a reference point. The 'me' always needs a reference point which is relative because when there would be no relative there would be no 'me' any more. The 'me' survives in only relative experiences. It always needs a reference to something else. It always needs duality, it lives by duality. If there would be no duality it could not exist.

So what it is doing, even trying to get enlightened, he confirms that there is one who is unenlightened. He trying to wake up confirms the one who is unawake! He tries to realize himself and confirms the one who is unrealized. So whatever is coming from that doer or non-doer is trying to survive.

The ghost, the doubtful me always needs doubtful actions to survive as that what is a doubtful me. Even claiming, I am so sincere, I am honest, I only live for truth or whatever. Just doing it confirms the one who needs it. Fantastic! Even doing it you confirm the one who survives by that. That will never stop. That is the way you realize yourself.

Neti-Neti is the best, was always the best and always will be the best. The deep-deep sleep pointer is always good. The deep-deep sleep means in deep-deep sleep there is total absence of anyone who is or is not and still what you are is what it is. From there comes the presence.

But to know yourself as presence as that what doesn't need the presence to be That what it is. That is what you are.

– Am I – I Am p96

अनेनैव प्रकारेण बुद्धिभेदो न सर्वगः ।
दाता च धीरतामेति गीयते नामकोटिभिः ॥ २२॥

In this way the intelligence seems divided
but actually is not;
He who teaches this is truly great;
He deserves a million praises. [2:22]

Q: About singing the glory of forms...
K: That's what I say; I'm singing the glory of forms. You can enjoy

them because you're not part of it. You like everything because you don't need it. That is the singing of songs of glory of informations that give you pure joy, because you don't need it. Because they cannot bring you joy. That's the joy of emptiness of forms.

Your nature, which you can say is the joy that doesn't need joy, is enjoying all informations of... And no one needs them. It's a dance of information which is pure joy because there is no need for it. It's a pure entertainment of life, but it doesn't need to make sense or anything. You don't get more or less by any of this information. So, they're pure beauty.

Q: So, there is in a sense natural information of That coming from there [closing his fist] to rejoicing beauty...

K: It never stops. It's not rejoicing because the absence never dies and the presence is permanently dying and is re-born. So, this moment dies so that the next moment can be born. Because this moment died into the absence, into the hidden and something else comes into the front. So, there is death and birth – permanently, but what-you-are is not gone by something going and doesn't come by something coming. It's a permanent death and birth experience. It's a total construction and destruction. It's like Vishnu and Shiva in persona. There is no difference.

Q: When you were saying that sat-chit-ananda, it's all shit...

K: Yeah, but that's the beauty of it. Shit or emptiness or that it cannot bring you anything, for me it's the same. If one would not be shit, then you really make something shit. All is shit, all is equally shit – empty, cannot bring anything. Then it's fine. Then there's not even shit because you who sees everything is shit, is part of the shit. You're That what you see.

So, everything without exception, there is nothing what is not shit – including the seer. The seer, the seeing, what can be seen is chit or shit – doesn't matter. The shit is only there when the seer is different and not shit, seeing shit. There is no exclusion and then shit doesn't know shit and there is sat-chit-ananda. That's the happiness of shit – not knowing happiness and not needing it.

– *Worry And Be Happy p77*

गुरुप्रज्ञाप्रसादेन मूर्खो वा यदि पण्डितः ।
यस्तु संबुध्यते तत्त्वं विरक्तो भवसागरात् ॥ २३॥

*On receiving the gift of wisdom by the guru's grace;
Whether one is foolish or wise, Truth is apperceived;
Leading to detachment
from the ocean of bondage. [2:23]*

Q: Are there any qualifications for enlightenment?

K: To be the Self, yes.

Q: For example, are there any practices that can take you to enlightenment?

K: Every practice will take you to that which you are, but no special practice. Whatever one is doing is the very best he can do, and what he is doing came from that which is the source, the Self. There is no question that whatever is done is done by Self to become that which is Self. As soon there is consciousness, consciousness is Self-enquiry. This Self-enquiry for sure will lead to that which is prior to consciousness. But there is no special technique to it.

So the technique of Sri Ramana of 'Who am I?' is just a pointer. This is not a technique; it is simply reversing what came out as 'I am so-and-so' to become 'Who am I?' which then leads to this unknown openness of existence. But it will happen in spite of the technique, not because of it, because the Self has no cause and cannot be controlled or caused by any technique.

– *Interview*

K: Isn't it fun? Just for sport. This big tiger plays with you like a little mouse and it's not even hungry. It just plays around with you. This idea that there's grace that takes care of you – awfully bullshit bah, bah, bah. [Mocking] A baba that takes care.

Q: But everything is grace...

K: No. Grace is bullshit. [Laughter] You can say your nature is grace. But grace doesn't need grace. There's no grace for what-you-are. There's no self for what-you-are. There's no God, there's no bliss, there's nothing what you talk about. It's all imaginary bullshit from an imaginary phantom, having an imaginary truth or imaginary grace – out of fear.

It's really amazing. All for fun. Unbelievable! All my precious insights, all my precious things and all what I have done and suffered – all for nothing. [Mocking] Does it really have to be for nothing? I went through all those nights of not sleeping and fucking with my mind about who I am. All for nothing!

– *Worry And Be Happy* 171

रागद्वेषविनिर्मुक्तः सर्वभूतहिते रतः ।
दृढबोधश्च धीरश्च स गच्छेत्परमं पदम् ॥ २४॥

He who is free of attachment and hatred,
devoted to the good of all;
Firm in knowledge and steady of mind
shall attain the supreme state. [2:24]

K: Out of an "okay" always comes a "not okay" again. You have to live with it. Even to call it "predestination" is trying to control it, because by understanding it as predestination, that freedom or that peace that comes by that that understanding of predestination.

You cannot step out of it. No way out.

That detachment is so totally attached to that detachment. When I am asked what you do, I say – Be totally attached to what you are, be that absolute being, as you cannot not be attached to what you are, being that attachment itself. You cannot leave what you are. In absolute identification, there is no separate identification any more, and the separate one is simply dropping—but that cannot be done. That absolute identification that you are That cannot be done—you have to be it! But not by any understanding, not by choice, not by anything, as you are That anyway, as you cannot not be It, that's all! So be It!

– Eight Days in Tiruvannamalai p79

Q: Even Vivekanandji used to say, to realize the Self, help the poor and needy...

K: Help yourself because you are the poor and needy. [Laughter] Look in the mirror and you will see one. [Laughter] If you want to see a beggar in your eyes, you look at the mirror in the morning and watch your eyes. Then you will see a beggar who is poor and needy. So, help yourself.

Q: So you think he was also getting rid of people?

K: Of course. If you see one is not ripe like an apple, you don't try to make it ripe. You just say come next time. See you next time, and then maybe. You don't pull the grass so that it grows faster. If you see that in that moment it's not working, okay come next time. And in the meanwhile you can cook, make something useful. But don't bother me.

What did Nisargadatta do when someone was there for eight days? He said if you didn't get it in eight days, you will not get it in eighty years here. Go home and come back when, whatever...

– Heaven And Hell p100

घटे भिन्ने घटाकाश आकाशे लीयते यथा ।
देहाभावे तथा योगी स्वरूपे परमात्मनि ॥ २५॥

As space within a pot merges in the universal space
when the pot is broken;
A yogi, when his identification with the
body-mind perishes, merges into Self;
Which is his Original Supreme state. [2:25]

Q [Another visitor]: Ramana just laid down his life when he was fifteen...

K: He imagined what it would be to die. But he didn't die. He went through all the experiences of dying but in none of those experiences what-he-was could die. The body could die, the ideas of spirit could die. All what you can imagine could die but still you are what-you-are. You are Absolute, without all of that you can experience – even without the experiencer you-are. And that cannot die because That was never born. That's what he experienced.

K: That what you are is an open front and open back. The next moment comes. Welcome, well-go. There is no advantage in keeping anything, or disadvantage. Sometimes something stays for a bit longer. But even that goes sooner or later. So the front door and back door are always open. And in the middle there is a collector functioning, collecting something he likes or doesn't like. And there is a collection of a his-story. But this will be gone sooner or later. When this body dies it will just go through the open back door, as everything. In German we say 'The last shirt has no pockets'. So you cannot take anything away from this collection of whatever deep insights, deep realizations. It will all be gone with this...

– May It Be As It Is p126

उक्तेयं कर्मयुक्तानां मतिर्यान्तेऽपि सा गतिः ।
न चोक्ता योगयुक्तानां मतिर्यान्तेऽपि सा गतिः ॥ २६॥

The destiny of those devoted to action;
Is a consequence of their thought at the moment of their death;
But the destiny of a yogi established in Yoga (Unicity);
Is not determined by his thought at the end. [2:26]

K: I'm talking about peace – silence. Nothing can happen any more because everything happened already. So, why do you fear? Even the fear you cannot avoid because even the fear is necessary. If you cannot get rid of the fear or anything, what to do?

Just be what-you-cannot-not-be, the next sip of coffee, the next thought. The next is unavoidable – So what? It's simply the next realization of what-you-are which is absolutely fixed. Even you as the almighty self cannot change the destiny of the next moment. Whatever you experience is – destiny, destiny, destiny. And no one made any choice for that. No one could ever change it.

So, the Absolute reality cannot change the next moment of realization.

– *Worry And Be Happy p174*

या गतिः कर्मयुक्तानां सा च वागिन्द्रियाद्भवेत् ।
योगिनां या गतिः क्वापि ह्वकथ्या भवतोर्जिता ॥ २७॥

One may speak about the destiny of those devoted to actions;
The same cannot be said of yogis – motionlessness itself;
Here the idea of destiny cannot survive. [2:27]

Q: So, what do you think about the future?

K: There's a future which is already there and the past is not gone.

Q: So, it has already happened?

K: Nothing happens. All the experiences of the future, you will experience them again and again. This moment is infinite and you've already experienced it infinite times. And last time, you had the same question actually and I gave you the same answer. It's a déjà vu – again and again. Nothing comes, nothing goes. You will end up here, again and again. You don't even move from this moment.

Nothing moves, nothing comes, and nothing goes. No coming in coming, no going in going. You're stuck eternally to what-you-are. [Laughing] You are the absolute addict to That what-you-are. And you cannot stop being addicted to That what-is, because you are That!

But you have to experience yourself as a junkie for That. But it's junk. The idea of Self is junk, you know That. Whatever you can gain is junk and if you expect something that comes from junk, you become a junkie. A junkie means you're looking for the key of heaven, but even heaven is a junk, compared to what-you-are.

– *Worry And Be Happy p70*

K: When there is infinite, there is finite. When there is eternal, there is no-eternal. When there is this, then there is that. You always make polarities. And for what-you-are, there is neither.

– *Heaven And Hell p174*

एवं ज्ञात्वा त्वमुं मार्गं योगिनां नैव कल्पितम् ।
विकल्पवर्जनं तेषां स्वयं सिद्धिः प्रवर्तते ॥ २८॥

A yogi has no particular path;
Simply the renunciation of imagination
Leads to realisation
which occurs naturally. [2:28]

K: I'm looking in to your nature and That is always quality itself and the rest is fiction anyway and to That – no way leads. That is the absolute no-way of Buddha. No way! Whatever is in the way is a phantom and the phantom can only be advanced or dis-advanced.

– *The Song Of Irrelevance p18*

Q: It appears that it gets better and better as you walk on this path, whatever path it is you are walking. I mean, that's how I experience this journey. It gets better and better.

K: But what can get better, can get worse again. That idea of "better" is already quite worse.

– *Eight Days in Tiruvannamalai p269*

तीर्थे वान्त्यजगेहे वा यत्र कुत्र मृतोऽपि वा ।
न योगी पश्यते गर्भं परे ब्रह्मणि लीयते ॥ २९॥

Wherever a yogi may die, besides a holy river or in
the house of an outcaste;
Is never again the product of a mother's womb;
He merges in the supreme Brahman. [2:29]

Q: So this collection is...

K: It's an analogy of a soul who collects little pearls of events and calls it my story. It's a relative soul of a collector, collecting relative events like pearls hanging around his neck, and calling it 'my story'. And it begins with my birth, and ends with my death. And in between there are bigger and smaller events and maybe a very big one would be enlightenment. And then he puts all the other ones into his back, that no one sees them, and only the enlightenment stone is in front. And then he shows it: 'Look how enlightened I am! This event on September 9, 1993, look at it, since then I am sharing that'.

Q: But event, after death, it goes out the back door...

K: Whatever enlightenment creates an enlightened one is bullshit. In one instant it's gone.

Q: But the energy cannot be destroyed...

K: Energy cannot be destroyed. But the phenomenal expressions of energy will be destroyed anyway, just by the next moment. So whatever comes is already gone. So what now comes as the next moment is already gone. By coming it's already gone. But what is the absolute Experiencer is not coming in these experiences of coming and not going in these experiences of going. So in going nothing is going and in coming nothing is coming. So an 'I am' came, and an 'I am' will be gone. And you still will be what you are, as you are now what you are. And to be that is Effortlessness. Efforts are only in dream.

– May It Be As It Is p127

सहजमजमचिन्त्यं यस्तु पश्येत्स्वरूपं
घटति यदि यथेष्टं लिप्यते नैव दोषैः ।
सकृदपि तदभावात्कर्म किंचिन्नकुर्यात्
तदपि न च विबद्धः संयमी वा तपस्वी ॥ ३०॥

He who has realized the unborn, incomprehensible natural state;
Is not tainted, though enjoying the fruits of his desires;
Ever free of taint, ever action-less;
The ascetic, concentrated on the Self, is never bound. [2:30]

K: If Ramana would have been twenty when it happened and if he had fucked girls before, he would have been a house holder for the rest of his life and not sit on a mountain. You never know. But since he didn't have sex, the whole thing was gone for him. Now they say you have to be a celibate. But I tell you if Ramana had a good sex life before, he would just have continued – like eating. How does it make a difference, having kids or not?

– *Worry And Be Happy p170*

Q: No way to put the devils away?

K: No.

Q: Shit! [Laughter]

K: I would say, little bit of mind-fuck is not so bad. Let there be sex – let the mind-fuck itself. The body will always have the tendencies of fighting and doing things. It's part of the system – tendencies fighting against tendencies. It's phantoms fighting against phantoms, shadows fighting shadows. What to do?

– *The Song Of Irrelevance p126*

निरामयं निश्रितिमं निराकृतिं
निराश्रयं निर्वपुषं निराशिषम् ।
निर्द्वन्द्वनिर्मोहमलुप्तशक्तिकं
तमीशमात्मानमुपैति शाश्वतम् ॥ ३१॥

He attains the supreme Self;
Who is eternal, pure, devoid of fear, form and support;
Who is devoid of body, desire and beyond the pairs of opposites;
Who is free from illusion and has inexhaustive power. [2:31]

K: In knowing and not knowing, you are what you are. I'm talking about that absolute freedom from dependency on knowing or not knowing. I'm not talking about some knowledge of myself, because that would still be dependency. In spite of knowing and not knowing, I am what I am, not because.

Q: Okay.

K: I'm always talking about that. In spite of individuality, of personal and impersonal experiences, I am what I am.

Q: And in spite of attachment, in spite of desire, I am what I am. Regardless.

K: That's what God was saying when he was asked who he is. "I am that I am." In spite of whatever. So who needs this drop of individuality?

– *Eight Days in Tiruvannamalai p222*

K: The fearlessness, the carelessness is so attractive that maybe by that attraction you drop whatever can be dropped because there is no fear for it. But when you are alone at home the fear is so overwhelming that you never dare to go to that place of sadness for instance, of loneliness.

But in that fearlessness, the loneliness becomes more attractive. The sadness becomes an attractive place and when you are in sadness you can call it as a natural melting away in sadness. Then in sadness you suddenly realize that there was never any sadness for you because the sadness is your natural being. This loneliness is so natural, why did you fear that? How to fear what you are? Loneliness is what you are – there is no second. Any experience is loneliness and suddenly there is loneliness and there is no one who is lonely any more.

Only fearing that what you are makes you separated from what you are. In fearlessness, in that company it may be easier to happen, this so called fearlessness gets created so that you can face and drop all the faces and face that what is never needed and drop that and you still are what you are. So face-off.

– Am I – I Am p205

वेदो न दीक्षा न च मुण्डनक्रिया
गुरुर्न शिष्यो न च यन्त्रसम्पदः ।
मुद्रादिकं चापि न यत्र भासते
तमीशमात्मानमुपैति शाश्वतम् ॥ ३२॥

Neither through the study of Vedas,
nor initiations nor a tonsure;
Neither through the guru-disciple relationship nor wealth;
Nor through perfection of mudras (hand postures);
His perfection is inspite of these activities. [2:32]

K: It all depends on the first thought. Go to the "I"-thought, directly, and simply in that question "Who am I?" annihilate that "I"-thought, rooting it out totally by that question. That "I"-thought is the idea of being born, of existence at all. When that is really rooted out, totally up-rooted, then there is no way back. But as long as this first card is there in that card-house of your concepts, that first card will always make another concept. The house will build again.

You may cut some branches, but it means nothing, because the tree will grow back even further. So controlling the mind is making it grow even more. You have to go to the root of the mind, that "I"- thought. Without rooting that out totally, it always will grow again even more, even making a religion out of it.

Then comes a religion out of experiences of whatever spiritual kind, but the "I"- thought is still there, and it makes a personal history of religious experiences. There are many enlightenments and awakenings and experiences, but they are taken personally. And then comes a religion out of it, or a technique, or even a Yoga technique, of cutting some branches.

Ramana was very radical, in a sense, to go directly to what is the root-thought. Because without that root-thought, there is no tree any more—never was, never will be. That's the meaning of that supreme Yoga, which is the direct path to annihilating the first thought, the first card of your card-house of concepts. The first card of the idea even of "existence," the first notion of existence as "I," which is awareness, the "I"-awareness—already that is a phantom.

Out of that awareness—as the Father, Source—always comes "I am" and "I am so-and-so." By seeing the first awareness, "I," already as a mirror and not what you are, not Heart which is prior to that "I"-thought, you stay in That which is prior, the mystery of That which is Heart. Being totally empty of any idea of what you are and what you are not, there's an absolute emptiness which is freedom of ideas of a second, of whatever.

– Eight Days in Tiruvannamalai p135

K: You can only be ready for some relative truth. Maybe high energy or intense experiences or something, but never for yourself. The Self never asks you to be ready for what you are. There is no need for readiness. So you cannot mix it. That's why I ask: what is your goal? If your goal is having a light body, being in a super natural 'Aurobingo' state, wonderful, then you can prepare yourself by whatever learning, by yoga techniques, by whatever. And then there are many teachers who can teach you how to do that. Whole Poona is full of it. The whole world is full of it. But there is no way that you get ready enough for that what you are. But still you have to try. So in a relative sense, to have a healthy body, a healthy ego, you can do something. That you can function in the world perfectly, in harmony with your surroundings, all of that can happen. But you can never prepare yourself for That.

— *May It Be As It Is p14*

न शाम्भवं शाक्तिकमानवं न वा
पिण्डं च रूपं च पदादिकं न वा ।
आरम्भनिष्पत्तिघटादिकं च नो
तमीशमात्मानमुपैति शाश्वतम् ॥ ३३॥

Where there is neither the form of Shiva nor Shakti;
Where there is neither light nor the feet of God;
Where there is neither form, nor content
nor any entities such as a filled jar;
Such is the eternal supreme state he attains. [2:33]

Q: Are there any practices that can take you to enlightenment?

K: Every practice will take you to that which you are, but no special practice. Whatever one is doing is the very best he can do, and what he is doing came from that which is the source, the Self. There is no question that whatever is done is done by Self to become that which is Self. As soon there is consciousness, consciousness is Self-enquiry. This Self-enquiry for sure will lead to that which is prior to consciousness. But there is no special technique to it.

So the technique of Sri Ramana of 'Who am I?' is just a pointer. This is not a technique; it is simply reversing what came out as 'I am so-and-so' to become 'Who am I?', which then leads to this unknown openness of existence. But it will happen in spite of the technique, not because of it, because the Self has no cause and cannot be controlled or caused by any technique.

Q: For example, there are some common practices like meditation, mantras, chanting and so on.

K: Yes, all wonderful, and they all come out of the very same source, but all the mantras and meditation cannot make the Self be the Self. You cannot become that which you are through anything.

– *Interview*

यस्य स्वरूपात्सचराचरं जग-
दुत्पद्यते तिष्ठति लीयतेऽपि वा ।
पयोविकारादिव फेनबुद्बुदा-
स्तमीशमात्मानमुपैति शाश्वतम् ॥ ३४॥

That, from which the universe of the sentient and insentient,
is born, maintained and destroyed;
Like bubbles created, floated and destroyed
in the foam of the ocean;
Such Supremeness is attained by the yogi. [2:34]

K: When you are what-you-are, there is instantly, there was never and there will never be whatever you imagine. The moment you are something what you imagine, all that imagining is as real as you are. What an almighty energy you are! By whatever the almighty takes himself as real, becomes real. If you take the body as real, the body becomes real. Fantastic!

What an almighty dreamer you are! By whatever the almighty dreamer takes as real, it becomes real. By being a body, you are a real body beyond real bodies. What an amazing energy! By giving attention to the body, it becomes real and then the entire universe is real and all the bodies whatever comes with it. But all this is by making [pointing to his body] this real, giving attention to it.

Then Ramana comes and says, give attention to that what is attention – by being attention. But by whatever you give attention to, is what?

– Heaven And Hell p19

K: That's why I say there is a split second with absolutely no before or after. This [holds up his fist to symbolize Heart] is in spite. There is no awakening. From what? There is simply no way out. Absolutely no way out. But even that is not there. You just have another coffee, because nothing has changed.

There is simply "Aha." Because That which is awareness, or That which is perception itself, was always as pure as at that moment, because in that split second, you go to eternal existence. Back to Adam and Eve, or whatever. And you see, there was always that perception, pure as it was, in no sense. Always in no sense. There are sensations coming and going, and whatever ideas, but that was, is, as it was. There was no time and even non-time.

Q: So I am watching a movie now?

K: You are the movie!

– Eight Days in Tiruvannamalai p59

नासानिरोधो न च दृष्टिरासनं
बोधोऽप्यबोधोऽपि न यत्र भासते ।
नाडीप्रचारोऽपि न यत्र किञ्चि-
त्तमीशमात्मानमुपैति शाश्वतम् ॥ ३५॥

He attains That eternal supreme Self;
Where there is no need of breath control nor fixed-stares;
Nor is there need for any yogic postures or regulation of nerves;
Where nothing is to be learned or unlearned. [2:35]

K: Absolute ignorance means knowledge being absolutely ignorant of being what you are and what you are not. That's nature of knowledge. So the nature of knowledge is ignorance.

But out of the nature of ignorance, knowing yourself is knowledge. There is only knowledge, by being knowledge – it is ignorant about itself, by knowing itself it is ignorant about itself, but it's still knowledge. There is only knowledge as ignorance or as knowledge. It's never-never. There is no two.

For me it's not a negative, actually the Neti-Neti is the most positive because negative times negative means absolute positive. No-No means yes, it's a no to no. It's an absolute yes, but by pronouncing it, you create an opposite of no. But saying no-no is an absolute unpronounced yes. You have an absolute no to no, then it's yes but you don't have to pronounce it.

So, Neti-Neti means absolute no-no. Are you? No-No. That would be the answer because then the unpronounced remains as that what is the absolute positive. But the positive doesn't know any positive. But the pointer to that is negative-negative, its mathematics. But it doesn't help, Thank God and no one needs to be helped by anyone.

– Am I – I Am p203

K: That what knows everything is false is as false as that one who doesn't know. No exception. But it's absolute false and the pointer is just that the absolute ignorance is as absolute false as that absolute knowledge you are looking for. The absolute is absolute. The absolute is absolute in being what it is, not even knowing what it is and what it is not or in ignorance. It is as Absolute as it can be. It is never not Absolute. When it's absolute false, it's Absolute false.

It's just the nature of what is – Absolute. And Absolute means, there is no second. So, in the Absolute false, there is no second false.

– *Heaven And Hell p78*

नानात्वमेकत्वमुभत्वमन्यता
अणुत्वदीर्घत्वमहत्त्वशून्यता ।
मानत्वमेयत्वसमत्ववर्जितं
तमीशमात्मानमुपैति शाश्वतम् ॥ ३६॥

Devoid of 'many' or 'one' or many-and-oneness;
Devoid of infinitesimal as well as infinite proportion;
Devoid of no-thingness, nor is it a thing that is measurable;
Devoid of knowledge or knowingness;
He attains That incomparable Supreme. [2:36]

K: What is wrong with the "me" being bothered by something else? Only you take yourself as a "me" and something else as a second. Then everything is an enemy.

Out of that first lie that you exist, out of that first "any-me," you are in an enemy situation. At the moment you are, as being born, or whatever, you create six billion others, and these six billion others are enemies. As the first "me" already is an enemy. So by being prior to the first "me," you are prior to those six billion, whatever, images. So they are all living by what you are, but you are not living by them.

What to do then with that first "me" and those six billion other ones, if you cannot get rid of them? As you are that helplessness that cannot not imagine itself as that one and six billion others, as you cannot not wake up to that awareness of "I" and then "I am" and then the world, as you cannot not create by being That which is absolute, That which is the manifestation—what to do?

– *Eight Days in Tiruvannamalai p217*

K: When Nisargadatta was dying in the last moments he said, 'Now with this body, all the tendencies of this body are leaving me. Whatever happened to this body before are leaving now with this body and there's still no one who cares'.

So, that carelessness of its nature is permanent. The caring and the not-caring, the knowing and the not-knowing belongs to this body. Even the vertical knowing belongs to the body. It comes with this body and will leave with this body, but the carelessness is the screen where the caring and not-caring, the knowing and the not-knowing, the discussion, the fucking and the not-fucking happens. It's un-spoiled, there's no spot on it. It's as it was before – spotless.

– *The Song Of Irrelevance p126*

सुसंयमी वा यदि वा न संयमी
सुसंग्रही वा यदि वा न संग्रही ।
निष्कर्मको वा यदि वा सकर्मक-
स्तमीशमात्मानमुपैति शाश्वतम् ॥ ३७॥

He attains That supreme, eternal Self;
Whether he has perfect self-control or not;
Whether he has withdrawn his senses or not;
Whether he has abandoned all actions or not. [2:37]

K: It's not a non-experience. It's the experience that, what is an experiencer and whatever you can experience, you are not. It's an absolute experience of being absolutely independent of whatever you experience, even absolutely independent of that experiencer. It's an absolute experience of That which you may call "freedom," but having no idea of what is and what is not freedom. It's simply being That which can never be touched by any senses or by anything you can sense of objective life.

So you are as That which is ever in no sense. All the senses are there, but you are never in any sense—never was and never will be. And for That which was never in any sense, which was never born and may die, in that moment, the idea of "death" is dying. That's all. You see what you are is never-never.

– *Eight Days in Tiruvannamalai p318*

> मनो न बुद्धिर्न शरीरमिन्द्रियं
> तन्मात्रभूतानि न भूतपञ्चकम् ।
> अहंकृतिश्चापि वियत्स्वरूपकं
> तमीशमात्मानमुपैति शाश्वतम् ॥ ३८॥

He attains that supreme, eternal Self;
Who is neither the body nor the mind;
Who is neither the intellect nor the senses;
Who is neither the subtle nor the five gross elements;
Who is without the 'I' sense or the sense of being space-like.
[2:38]

Q: I want to ask you about the third eye of Shiva.

K: The eye of Shiva is not Shiva; the third eye is like the perception point of Shiva. Neither personal nor impersonal, the third point. But even that perception point, the light of Shiva is not Shiva. It always looks through the persona, the impersonal and then the third eye which is neither personal nor impersonal. But still that is not it.

Q: So that is like transcendence?

K: It tries to transcend, but that what needs to transcend is still relative. Whatever can be transcended is relative. Really transcending is being that what you cannot not be, which never needs to transcend anything.

The Absolute transcending is – being what you cannot not be which never needs to transcend anything. That what needs to transcend something is a relative – transcending from a relative transcender. Whatever he transcends is not good enough and that what is your nature never needed to transcend anything to be what it is. That what needs to transcend something is still a phantom who woke up, transcended some place, landed somewhere but it's never good enough.

Wherever you land, you have to depart again. Whatever realization you can gain, you have to lose again. That's all the Upanishads, all the Yoga-Vashishta. The Sage was sitting and King Rama comes to him realizing his true nature, that I am not the body, I am not the spirit, I am the absolute Neti-Neti. He was so overwhelmed by his happiness and blissful realization that out of gratitude he took his biggest diamond ring and presented to the sage. What did the sage do? He opened the big urn full of diamond rings; he just put it there and closed it – see you next time.

– Am I – I Am p141

Q: That which is dreaming, when it hears that, it assumes immediately that it needs to transcend...

K: Yes, you have to transcend the transcender.

Q: This is another idea...

K: No, it is not an idea! You absolutely transcend the transcender by being that what is in spite of the transcender transcending or not transcending. That is transcending the transcender. It's the easiest you cannot do. What's the problem? Renouncing the renouncer just by being what-you-are, you do that every night.

– May It Be As It Is p142

विधौ निरोधे परमात्मतां गते
न योगिनश्चेतसि भेदवर्जिते ।
शौचं न वाशौचमलिङ्गभावना
सर्वं विधेयं यदि वा निषिध्यते ॥ ३९॥

Transcending all injunctions, the yogi attains That supreme Self;
His mind freed of thought induced by duality;
There is neither purity nor impurity, nor any distinction of sex;
Fortune and misfortune have no relevance for him. [2:39]

K: You have to laugh about your joke. Because you are the trap and you are stepping into your own trap of wanting to gain something. You are the inventor of religion. Whatever religion there is, is because of you, because you have the idea that some knowledge or whatever can add something to your nature. You create all this religion, all that you can imagine. You are the dharma-keeper himself. You are the inventor of the idea of "purity," so it makes you dirty. You are the inventor of whatever "divine," so it makes you shit. Whatever is, is because of you. If you want to complain, you find the one! [Group laughs] It's fun to complain about yourself, what you have done. So what!

– Eight Days in Tiruvannamalai p60

Q: It is pure existence.

K: Even to call it pure Existence is still doubtful. Whatever you call it, it's not it. 'The Tao you can talk about is not the Tao'. It doesn't have to be pure. What existence has to be pure? Only a relative one. Existence doesn't know Existence. And there is no necessity of being pure. There is not even an idea of anything. All these ideas are in dream. Only in the unreal there are ideas of real or unreal and pure or impure.

– May It Be As It Is p115

मनो वचो यत्र न शक्तमीरितुं
नूनं कथं तत्र गुरूपदेशता ।
इमां कथामुक्तवतो गुरोस्त-
द्युक्तस्य तत्त्वं हि समं प्रकाशते ॥ ४० ॥

If mind and speech are incapable of revealing That;
How can there be any instruction by a guru?
How can a guru reveal in words,
That which is the self-illuminating, all-pervading, Absolute itself.
[2:40]

Q: Do you have a teaching, and which one?

K: Recognize everything as a lie, specially the one who recognizes everything as a lie.

Q: Why are you giving these talks?

K: They are part or aspect of being. No-one is talking and no-one is listening. Without sense and reason. For the question of why there is only one answer: why not?

– Interview

Q: We listen to concepts and feel the understanding, then why do we keep coming back to listen to more? It's like it's not really understanding...

K: Because it's not about understanding. Whatever you understand is a misunderstanding and you cannot otherwise take it personal. And when there is one moment where you cannot take it personal, then there is a carelessness which is always there. But it's not about understanding.

So you have to come again and again to the good company of the carelessness until that is so attractive – that by that attraction you drop all understanding just by being what you are. Ramana and Nisargadatta said the only thing that you can do is be in good company. That is being that which you cannot not be in the company of what you are. In carelessness where there is no need of any understanding and there is no teaching and learning needed.

Then by that attraction you drop everything what was never needed.

– Am I – I Am p205

Chapter Three

गुणविगुणविभागो वर्तते नैव किञ्चित्
रतिविरतिविहीनं निर्मलं निष्प्रपञ्चम् ।
गुणविगुणविहीनं व्यापकं विश्वरूपं
कथमहमिह वन्दे व्योमरूपं शिवं वै ॥ १॥

Quality and absence of quality do not exist in him the least;
How shall I worship Shiva
who is devoid of attachment and detachment?
Who is devoid of qualities good and bad;
Who is formlessness and yet the substance of all forms;
Who is omnipresent like space. [3:1]

K: The quality of your nature is never more or less and can never become what-it-is – by anything. Now that shit happens, so what? It's a happening of shit. So, be it, as it is. And for That, nothing has to be realized – that's the best. You are by nature in the presence of shit and in the absence of shit – what-you-are. And That what-you-are never needs to know That – what-it-is. That what needs to know, is part of the presence and will never know what-it-is and will never know itself.

And whatever it knows is a relative knowledge known by a relative knower. The whole consciousness is relative and ignorance. What-you-are never needs it. You are with and without that consciousness – what-you-are.

– *Worry And Be Happy p33*

K: Whatever you say or don't say – it is not. It has no attribute or no-attribute, neither it has nor it has not. Neither it is nor it is not, it neither exists nor doesn't exist. Whatever you say is false. Whatever you say, whatever you don't say, whatever you hear, think or not think is all false. False, false, false, false, false!

Because whatever you come up with or not come up with needs opposites, needs to exist. Even emptiness needs to exist to be emptiness.

– *Am I – I Am p147*

श्वेतादिवर्णरहितो नियतं शिवश्च
कार्यं हि कारणमिदं हि परं शिवश्च ।
एवं विकल्परहितोऽहमलं शिवश्च
स्वात्मानमात्मनि सुमित्र कथं नमामि ॥ २॥

Shiva is ever devoid of colours – white or any other;
That supreme Shiva is both the cause and the effect.
I am thus the Supreme Shiva, devoid of all doubt;
O beloved friend, by which (my) self do I bow down
to which (other) Self? [3:2]

K: Ramakrishna Parahamsa's basic teaching was that I can doubt myself. But prior to the doubter – that I experience myself as a doubter doubting myself – the doubtlessness of the existence has to be there. Without the doubtlessness of the existence, there is no possibility of the presence of a doubter, doubting to exist or not to exist. That's all.

The doubtlessness is the absolute omnipresence, which is never-never – has to-be before even the imaginary doubter can doubt or not doubt. Even the possibility of one who could or could-not can only be there because the doubtlessness of what-is – has to-be. Prior beyond of all presences and absences – That doubtless is. That there can be a presence or absence at all – That has to-be – and That is what-you-are, That you cannot-not-be, and That is realizing itself as all that whatever doubting or not doubting.

– The Song Of Irrelevance p181

निर्मूलमूलरहितो हि सदोदितोऽहं
निर्धूमधूमरहितो हि सदोदितोऽहम् ।
निर्दीपदीपरहितो हि सदोदितोऽहं
ज्ञानामृतं समरसं गगनोपमोऽहम् ॥ ३॥

I am neither beginningless nor with beginning,
I am ever Manifest;
I am neither concealed nor revealed,
I am ever Manifest;
I am neither illuminated nor un-illuminated,
I am ever Manifest;
I am nectarean Jñana,
the essence in all and all-pervasive like space. [3:3]

Q: You mentioned some reality prior to Shiva.

K: Prior to the light of Shiva.

Q: Not prior to Shiva?

K: No. Shiva is Self, Shiva is Para Brahman. That what is Shiva is Shiva. But the light of Shiva, Shiva becoming aware of Shiva, then he becomes relative. A relative experience of light. He becomes aware of himself. Becoming aware of himself, being awake, that's the light of Shiva. But the light of Shiva is not Shiva. It's the light of Shiva.

And then comes the space of Shiva and then the whole universe of Shiva. But that trinity, which is realization, is not Reality. It's not different. That's the way Shiva is realizing himself. But it's not that what is realizing itself. So it starts realizing itself as the light of Shiva. As being aware. And then 'I am'. And then whatever comes.

– May It Be As It Is p51

K: What you are never had any form, it never manifested in any information, it was always beyond all presence and absence whatever you can imagine. It's only there because you are, but what you are doesn't have to be to be. What has to be to be is already too late, that is the easiest. Splitting the second, splitting even the idea that there is a one who can be lonely, being what you cannot not be because there is neither one nor no one because that what you are doesn't even know to exist. That is the short cut, you cut whatever can be cut, that is the Neti-Neti.

– Am I – I Am p115

निष्कामकाममिह नाम कथं वदामि
निःसङ्गसङ्गमिह नाम कथं वदामि ।
निःसारसाररहितं च कथं वदामि
ज्ञानामृतं समरसं गगनोपमोऽहम् ॥ ४॥

I am the desire in desirelessness; How can it be spoken of?!
I am the attachment in the ever unattached;
How can it be spoken of?!
I have no essence, yet, I am the essence of all;
how can I describe that?!
I am nectarean Jñana,
the essence in all and all-pervasive like space. [3:4]

Q: It's like desiring desirelessness...

K: Yes. It's impossible. There is only a wish because wishlessness is there. So it comes out of what it is, the wish is rising from wishlessness, and will go back to wishlessness. Automatically. Naturally. There is a natural rising and going again. And the wishlessness is uninterrupted what it is. So the realizer starts and whatever is realizing, and then it will be gone one day. But by that dropping of the unrealized one, no one becomes realized. So there is enlightenment, but in enlightenment there is no one who becomes enlightened. There is just a drop of the unenlightend one. Naturally, as it was rising, it will drop again. It is already gone now. It cannot even drop any more. It never rose, that's the problem. So we can talk about realization. Realization may happen. But it never creates any realized one. And then just to be that what-you-cannot-not-be is just the drop of the idea that there could be one or is one at all.

That cannot be done by anyone. You do it any night anyway. It's more than natural. Every night you happily drop the world and the body and whatever can be dropped, just to sleep. And no one fears that something may happen there. And every morning this pops up again. But if you could avoid it you would happily stay there, where no one is.

— May It Be As It Is p92

K: Just by being what you are, which is That, there is a total detachment. But not any relative detachment of one who is detached from something else. That's always like this little misunderstanding that there is one in realizing, creating one who is realized. Never happened. The unenlightened one drops. The little owner drops. Just by you being what you are, which is the absolute owner. But the experience of the relative owner doesn't have to go for that. That's the beauty of your nature: nothing has to be changed. It never asked anything. Never demands anything. Never needs anyone to be different. So there is an absolute acceptance of that what is. Just by being what you are. But not by any achieving any relative acceptance. So it will never be your acceptance.

— May It Be As It Is p110

अद्वैतरूपमखिलं हि कथं वदामि
द्वैतस्वरूपमखिलं हि कथं वदामि ।
नित्यं त्वनित्यमखिलं हि कथं वदामि
ज्ञानामृतं समरसं गगनोपमोऽहम् ॥ ५॥

How shall I speak of That which is non-dual?
How shall I speak of That which is dual?
How shall I speak of That which is eternal and non-eternal?
I am nectarean Jñana, essence in all and all-pervasive like space.
[3:5]

Q: This idea of Wittgenstein was quite appealing to me when he said like whatever you talk about, Reality or whatever, is something you cannot talk about, because any words you use are going to be wrong. So talking about that, talking about Parabrahman, or about Self, is futile...

K: Yes. But that's the fun of it. That's the joy in it. We are sitting here and talking and talking, and maybe in one split second you see it's all bullshit. Whatever can be said, whatever can be not said is all bullshit. It cannot make me more or less as I am. So it was good for something. That it didn't give you anything. That it doesn't give you anything, that's the good thing about it. That nothing comes out of it. That's the good thing about it. So we can talk and talk and talk. But this is the meaning of good company. There is no one who wants to change anything, and still talking like hell – this paradox, this living paradox.

– Heaven And Hell p90

K: As an idea, a pointer. But the Self doesn't know any Self. There is only "Selflessness," you may call it, "lovelessness," "existencelessness." I am pointing to that "idea-lessness," where all the icons—of divinity, of God—are gone. This Godlessness I'm talking about. You are That which is God, but God doesn't know any God, no second or whatever. That which cannot be talked about or defined—that's what I'm talking about.

This paradox cannot be solved. We talk about something that cannot be talked about. So we can talk about it, but it makes no difference. It's just pointing out that it makes no difference whether you talk or not.

For That which you are, it never makes any difference, whatever you say, whatever you define or don't define. There is nothing more or less. There is no quantity in it, of whatever idea of "divine" or anything. All this is gone. This is freedom which has no idea about freedom.

Q: Emptiness?

K: Not even emptiness. Even emptiness is too much. This is That which is emptiness, and this is That which is fullness, and this is That which is whatever you name, but it has no name.

– *Eight Days in Tiruvannamalai p37*

स्थूलं हि नो नहि कृशं न गतागतं हि
आद्यन्तमध्यरहितं न परापरं हि ।
सत्यं वदामि खलु वै परमार्थतत्त्वं
ज्ञानामृतं समरसं गगनोपमोऽहम् ॥ ६॥

It is neither gross nor subtle, It neither comes nor goes;
It is without a beginning, middle or any end.
It is neither high nor low;
I am indeed declaring the ultimate Reality;
I am nectarean Jñana, the essence in all,
all-pervasive like space. [3:6]

Q: I always thought about how could Maharaj perform bhajans?

K: Or Ramana working four hours in the kitchen, trying to feed the disciples. There is nothing more or less important. The next sip of coffee is what-is. Next whatever your attention goes into is Reality, and the next is reality, and the next. The small is not small and the big is not big. There is no difference in quality in anything. What to do?

That is called an ordinary man. When you are man, you are the man. When you are the spirit, you are the spirit. And when you are awareness, you are the awareness. And when you are the absence, you are the absence. And when you are beyond the absence, you are beyond the absence. When you are the highest totality, you are the highest totality.

But when you are here – the man – you are the man. And you are the fingernail and you are all whatever is. It makes no difference in the quality of what-you-are, or in the intensity. It's like the light of Shiva has no beginning and no end. And you will never reach the end in the higher or lower. The highest doesn't know any highest and the lowest doesn't know any lowest and the middle doesn't know any middle. All of that is what-you-are.

– Heaven And Hell p169

K: If you really go towards that dimension of absolute, it really becomes like [blowing in the wind]. But otherwise if you break your finger nail, it's like the whole universe is breaking. [Laughter] And if you have a little understanding, you think that the whole universe understands. And you are right! The whole existence in that moment understands it and the whole existence is breaking the finger nail.

It has the same importance as sipping the next sip of coffee or breaking a finger nail or the whole universe collapsing in one instant. In the quality, there is no difference. The quality is that what-you-are is experiencing itself in the smallest and in the biggest. But then making it a story of Shiva or Parvati and Ganga is wonderful, but in totality it's just a fraction.

But in that moment you are involved in your puja, it becomes a total reality for what-you-are. The smallest thing and the biggest thing. And there is a never ending story of it. You go from the smallest to the biggest and all the frequencies and all the possibilities, in that you realize yourself. In whatever possible way. None of them is more or less, that's the beauty of it.

The next sip of coffee, the next taste of nothing, has the same quality of what-you-are as the totality of blissful background tra-la-la.

– Am I – I Am p70

संविद्धि सर्वकरणानि नभोनिभानि
संविद्धि सर्वविषयांश्च नभोनिभांश्च ।
संविद्धि चैकममलं न हि बन्धमुक्तं
ज्ञानामृतं समरसं गगनोपमोऽहम् ॥ ७॥

Know perception to be intangible like space;
Know the objects of perception to be intangible like space;
Know well, that the pure one is neither bound nor free;
I am nectarean Jñana, the essence in all,
and all-pervasive like space. [3:7]

K: Even if you call it the eye of God – is wrong – for sure. Why should it be less wrong than anything else? I always say that everything I say is wrong. I say so many stupid things the whole day. [Laughter] Just-in-case.

No, it's just so that you rest in that what never needs to rest. And that is prior and inspite and beyond that perceiver you believe to be. That is the only trouble you have. Because when you are the perceiver, the seer, then everything comes out of just-in-case you are. Because it's a doubtful existence. That what is inspite and prior and beyond that perceiver, where the perceiver appears in, which is the first presence. But what you are is in the absence of the perceiver – that's all.

Calling that even perception is not right. You're just with and without – whatever. And you are with the perceiver and you are without the perceiver. You're in the presence and you're in the absence. That's all. But you can never say what that is.

– *Heaven And Hell p36*

K: You want to control the ideas, so the ideas control you. What an idea! Then you control all the ideas and you have a peaceful mind, but then the peaceful mind controls you! It always needs two for control. So, whatever you control, controls you. It's not one side only. If you control the whole universe, the universe controls you. You are imprisoned by control. Prison, prison, prison.

But actually you are longing for moksha and you think for moksha, I have to control the mind. [Mockingly laughing] What an idea! And as much you control the mind, the mind controls you. Crazy!

What an idea that you have to control something for freedom! What kind of freedom would it be – that needs control? What kind of knowledge would it be that needs to know something? Or understand something?

Only relative knowledge, a relative knower or a relative what you call – maya. There is a need, a little 'me' who out of fear wants to control his surroundings. The basic is always fear – control. And this little 'me' will always try to control the 'me' – himself and the surrounding.

– Heaven And Hell p18

दुर्बोधबोधगहनो न भवामि तात
दुर्लक्ष्यलक्ष्यगहनो न भवामि तात ।
आसन्नरूपगहनो न भवामि तात
ज्ञानामृतं समरसं गगनोपमोऽहम् ॥ ८॥

I am not difficult to comprehend
nor can consciousness hide me, my child;
I am not difficult to perceive
as I am not hidden in the perceptible, my child;
I am not hidden in the forms, my child;
I am nectarean Jñana, the essence in all
and all-pervasive like space. [3:8]

Q: You put it in a way like it is very easy...

K: It is more than easy, it is actually absolutely your nature and it's the easiest of the easiest to be what you cannot not be. Everything else is absolute difficult and too heavy. It's more than easy.

Q: But this me doesn't allow the easy things...

K: Who do you think you are? Who is this bloody me who thinks he can prevent the nature of being nature? That you can make nature not the nature? That the nature suffers about you? You really think existence suffers about you?

No one gives a shit if you suffer or not, not even yourself. All your suffering, all your misery are all for nothing. But you want to have a reason, you want to have the dark night of the soul – that the misery makes sense, that there is something in for you. Then you look for examples and UG and someone else and think maybe my suffering is not for nothing, maybe there is a hidden reason in it.

There is no bloody meaning for it, there is just a me needing a meaning and wanting to be special again and trying to make sense – where there is no sense needed. You think otherwise you cannot bear your so-called miserable life because if it's really for nothing you will be in your self-pity. All your crying for nothing, shit!

– Am I – I Am p168

K: It's more than easy to be the ease itself. But you cannot have it. You cannot be at ease. You can never be at ease. That one, who needs to be at ease, is a phantom. You are ease. And nothing is more easy than to be that what you are. And that is never-never that what is ease. And that dis-ease of one who wants to be at ease is a disease. Whoever wants to be healthy must be sick. But you never became sick, how can you be cured?

– May It Be As It Is p48

निष्कर्मदहनो ज्वलनो भवामि
निर्दुःखदुःखदहनो ज्वलनो भवामि ।
निर्देहदेहदहनो ज्वलनो भवामि
ज्ञानामृतं समरसं गगनोपमोऽहम् ॥ ९ ॥

I am the fire that burns the karma
of one who is beyond all karma;
I am the fire that burns the suffering
of one who is beyond all suffering;
I am the fire that burns the body
of one who is bodiless;
I am nectarean Jñana, the essence in all
and all-pervasive like space. [3:9]

K: In India there was a message written on the back of a rickshaw – 'No one remains a virgin, sooner or later everyone gets fucked by existence'. No, you cannot become That what-you-are, you were always that and in the presence you are That consciousness which is the fucker, the fucking and the fucked – you know that. It's the total fuck-tory of presence – consciousness being the penetrator, vibrating in the infinite vibration of the whole universe. Energy reacting to itself in so-called karmic consciousness, never ending karmic consciousness.

The only karma that's here is the karma of consciousness – as a reaction to itself, moment by moment. An absolute reaction to itself. So, did anything happen in that? Did consciousness become more or less? Did any baby come out of it? Or any realized consciousness? Was there any unrealized consciousness? Or consciousness is just pretending to be unrealized and the next step would be to pretend being realized?

– Worry And Be Happy p51

K: How can you fear yourself? Come on. How many times you hear that you are the flame where all the fire comes from. You are the coolest of the coolest. Nothing can burn you because you are the Absolute Dreamer dreaming the dream of hell. That what is dreaming everything can never be touched by the dream, never be affected by all the side effects.

— *Am I – I Am p75*

निष्पापपापदहनो हि हुताशनोऽहं
निर्धर्मधर्मदहनो हि हुताशनोऽहम् ।
निर्बन्धबन्धदहनो हि हुताशनोऽहं
ज्ञानामृतं समरसं गगनोपमोऽहम् ॥ १० ॥

I am the fire that burns the sins
of the one who is sinless;
I am the fire that burns the attributes
of the one without attributes;
I am the fire that burns the bondage
of the one who is without bondage;
I am nectarean Jñana, the essence in all,
and all-pervasive like space. [3:10]

K: You catch yourself by not catching yourself, by being what you are. I am that what I am means you are the fish. Then there is nothing to catch. You are the catcher, the catching and the catched. It's a catch 22 [laughter]. Otherwise it's always like catch me if you can.

It's a trick for sure, as Ramana said you become aware of this and you put the I in the awareness fire and sooner or later the stick is gone. Staying in that Am I-I Am, there is no place you can hide. There is no surviving in it because there is no birth and there is no death in it. There is just That what is That. It's a trick for sure, then it becomes attractive and maybe you try it. By trying it you get into that hell-fire of awareness and this ownership burns out by itself. Maybe, maybe not.

Q: The me may burn?

K: Yes but for me it's the coolest fire ever because that fire is so cool that it never burns anyone. Its inspite of absence or presence of any me what it is and that is the biggest not burning fire because the me would be very lucky if it would burn. Then it's worth to burn – Another fish.

But this is the coolest of the coolest. This never needs to burn anything to be what it is. The guest can stay forever and no one cares. That's the worst for the guest because the guest wants to be kicked out. If existence tries to kick out the guest, the guest becomes real. But the existence doesn't care if the guest is there or not. That is the end of story which never started anyway.

– Am I – I Am p219

K: When I talk about the fire, it is the coolest fire you cannot imagine. That's what burns you because it doesn't have any interest in you. That burns you totally. Because if it really would be a fire and it would want to burn you totally, you would be happy because then you are somebody. There is somebody who needs to be burnt. That makes you happy. But when I tell you, the coolest fire, it doesn't even know you, it doesn't even need to burn you. You can be there forever. It gives you a shit if you are there or not. You are absolute irrelevant if you are burnt or not. Who needs to burn you?

That's the coolest fire I am talking about. If there would be someone whose tendencies need to be burnt you would say – Yes! Take me. I am ready!

– Thailand 2013

निर्भावभावरहितो न भवामि वत्स
निर्योगयोगरहितो न भवामि वत्स ।
निश्चित्तचित्तरहितो न भवामि वत्स
ज्ञानामृतं समरसं गगनोपमोऽहम् ॥ ११॥

My child, I am not devoid of emotion or emotionlessness;
My child, I am not devoid of unity or separateness;
My child, I am not without awareness or awarenesslessness;
I am nectarean Jñana the essence in all,
and all-pervasive, like space. [3:11]

K: There is an experience of separation. But I can only say: by the experience no one is separated. There was never anyone who was separated. It's like the snake looking at it's own tail. It's still the snake. The ignorance is that you take this tail as a different snake. As the world is different from what you are. But now trying to overcome that, you make it more and more real. That's why you better don't know yourself at all, not even as a snake or anything. Just be the snake not knowing a snake. That what is the snake, what is there to fear?

That is what you cannot not be; your natural state is to be that what is Kundalini. But there is no one who has Kundalini. You are energy. But there is no one who has energy. Who is the owner of energy? Show me anyone who has energy. It's the other way around. Energy has you. Energy plays you. Who claims to have energy? A phantom!

– May It Be As It Is p128

K: If at all I'm here, it's for peace you are. That what-you-cannot-not-be, which is your nature. The closest you can say is peace, the peace of no second. The peace of neither existing nor not existing.

The peace of not even knowing if you are or if you are not. The absolute independence of any idea to be or not to be.

This doubtlessness of what-you-are, that peace, is uncomparable to anything you can gain in this so-called life. Of any pleasure or whatever you can experience by understanding. So, compared to what-you-are, all is [blowing in the wind]. Shit!

– Heaven And Hell p83

निर्मोहमोहपदवीति न मे विकल्पो
निःशोकशोकपदवीति न मे विकल्पः ।
निर्लोभलोभपदवीति न मे विकल्पो
ज्ञानामृतं समरसं गगनोपमोऽहम् ॥ १२॥

Not through intention, do I, who am beyond attraction
appear in attraction;
Not through intention, do I who am beyond grief
appear in grief;
Not through intention, do I who am beyond greed
appear in greed;
I am nectarean Jñana the essence in all
and all pervasive like space. [3:12]

Q: Money?

K: Money is fun.

Q: How to balance between too little and too much?

K: There's never enough money. [Laughter] It doesn't harm to have more money. If you have more and more millions, but after the first one it makes no difference. Money is neutral, money is just money. I like money. It doesn't harm, it doesn't bring anything and doesn't take anything. It doesn't bring you happiness and doesn't take away your suffering. It's just money. People always blame it for some reason. It's not the money, it's their greed. The idea of what they can buy with it or how much they need. Money is like oxygen, needed for breathing.

Q: It's just for needs?

K: No. It comes when it comes and when not, it doesn't come. Mostly you have to work for it but some people don't have to work. It comes from heritage. They're even more fucked. [Pointing to a visitor] Like he gets money for not working. [Laughter]

Q [Another visitor]: What about people who need money and don't have enough?

K: Even the richest person doesn't have enough. He will find a reason that he needs more. Even Bill Gates doesn't have enough; he has so many plans of saving the world. He needs more money. It's never enough.

Q: Too much money is harmful...

K: Yeah. Imagine there's enough money then no one would work any more. Everyone would die. You have to create a need so that people do something. That's the trick. You need a pressure or need so that something happens. They think I need that television so I have to work. For the basic things like water and bread there would always be enough.

But for those special needs – what you think makes you happy – the new car, the television, the apartment, sofa, fridge, then you're in trouble. That makes you work hard. Because your neighbour has a new car, you need one or the neighbour's wife has new clothes, your wife needs it too. There's a competition running. It's not the money that's bad; it's the competition between people.

But even that's natural. It's like a sport. Everyone feels insecure and thinks that when I gather this and that, I would be more secure.

More money is more insurance – I don't have to worry so much. It's all about fear, fear that you would not survive without money. All of that is being insecure.

– Worry And Be Happy p198

संसारसन्ततिलता न च मे कदाचित्
सन्तोषसन्ततिसुखो न च मे कदाचित् ।
अज्ञानबन्धनमिदं न च मे कदाचित्
ज्ञानामृतं समरसं गगनोपमोऽहम् ॥ १३॥

The creeper of worldliness does not affect me;
The joy of pleasures do not affect me;
The bondage of ignorance never binds me;
I am nectarean Jñana the essence in all,
and all-pervasive, like space. [3:13]

Q: So the bondage is really the freedom. Because the bondage is the evidence of freedom.

K: Yes, but freedom is just an idea. Freedom is bondage. You will never be free.

– May It Be As It Is p185

K: It's more or less suffering, more or less discomfort. Comfort is your nature and comfort means that there is no one who needs anything. There is a satisfaction itself, Sat itself. There is satisfaction by nature that can never be reached. That is not a state. That is 'what you are'. But every state that you can experience is an experience of discomfort. Comfort can never be experienced and can never be reached; all you can reach is discomfort. That's wonderful!

– Am I – I Am p20

संसारसन्ततिरजो न च मे विकारः
सन्तापसन्ततितमो न च मे विकारः ।
सत्त्वं स्वधर्मजनकं न च मे विकारो
ज्ञानामृतं समरसं गगनोपमोऽहम् ॥ १४॥

The unhappiness produced by rajas (activity)
has no effect on me;
The suffering produced by tamas (inertia)
has no effect on me;
The tranquillity produced by sattva (purity)
has no effect on me;
I am nectarean Jñana, the essence in all,
and all-pervasive like space. [3:14]

K: You need to have a birth certificate and your mother around to remind you that you exist as her daughter. It needed three years to hammer it in to your brain that you are the daughter of your mother, that you have this body. Then the memory effects and the functioning are established. And then you are stupid enough to memorize yourself.

But before – who was born? And who had a bowl? You play with your balls but you don't have one. The ownership starts at three years, before you have no body. You have no body, you have no balls. All the rest always comes later. The whole stories and all the...

– Heaven And Hell p180

K: So, what is there to gain by the next or to lose? That's the main thing. There is nothing to gain or to lose in how it will happen next. No gaining or losing for what I am and whatever, but if you take it personal, then you may have to act now for what you want to prevent in the next. You have to earn the merits.

So, if you believe that you don't want to be reincarnated, just with the wish of not wanting to be re-incarnated any more, you are already incarnated. Because that makes you incarnated now as a 'me' and by not wanting to re-incarnate again, you are already incarnated – as the next 'me'. Never ending story.

— *The Song Of Irrelevance p70*

सन्तापदुःखजनको न विधिः कदाचित्
सन्तापयोगजनितं न मनः कदाचित् ।
यस्मादहङ्कृतिरियं न च मे कदाचित्
ज्ञानामृतं समरसं गगनोपमोऽहम् ॥ १५॥

The action that causes regret or misery does not affect me;
The mind tormented by tortuous yogic effort does not affect me;
Whatever stirs up the ego, does not affect me;
I am nectarean Jñana, the essence in all,
and all pervasive, like space. [3:15]

K: You can call it this energy cluster of what you call me is reacting. What the past created as a cluster of energetic intentions, what is me, reacting to an outside event. Consciousness already is a reaction of that what is, not knowing itself. Consciousness already is a reaction. And in that reaction, reaction happens. As a dream of reaction. All of that is reaction. You cannot find any action in anything. You cannot find energy. You can only experience effects. Reaction. But you cannot find energy. So what is it? What does react? You cannot know what is acting or reacting. You can only experience the effects of it. And effects are ideas. But there is no one who owns them.

– *May It Be as It Is p266*

K: Without the absolute there would be no answer which is already a reaction of the action you are. By that action all the reactions are there. There is no one, neither the absolute nor the relative one answering.

You want to make it relative again and again – putting the absolute in the relative space. You can only experience reaction. God knowing himself is a reaction of what he is. Being reaction, trying to know the action. You hate to be a reaction and not the action. Then you have to react to all the other reactions. Totally dependent and reacting, reacting, reacting.

And every moment you are the reaction, you want to know where the action is.

– *Heaven And Hell p201*

निष्कम्पकम्पनिधनं न विकल्पकल्पं
स्वप्रप्रबोधनिधनं न हिताहितं हि ।
निःसारसारनिधनं न चराचरं हि
ज्ञानामृतं समरसं गगनोपमोऽहम् ॥ १६॥

I am the end of the movement of the unmoving One;
I am neither with intention nor without;
I am the end of dreaming and wakefulness;
I am neither good nor evil, neither moving nor still;
I am neither substance nor insubstantial;
I am nectarean Jñana, the essence in all,
and all-pervasive like space.[3:16]

K: None of these whatever events of the world, of the universe, and the suns and things, never altered your nature. So, you can be stupid as hell – Who cares? It doesn't make you stupid, experiencing yourself as stupid and playing stupid. That what is playing itself as stupid is not stupid by playing stupid. It just plays stupid. You always do 'as-if'.

I don't want to change it. I have no intention to change anything. I can just point – Look at it! Be what-you-cannot-not-be and enjoy the play because this is one way of playing and it's as good or as bad as the other way of playing. Playing this body, playing this life of Karl is as good or as bad as any bloody life of any bloody elephant or ant or any bloody whoever.

It's stupid, but the question is – What to do? You try every possible way to end that bullshit, but trying to end the bullshit is part of the play. So, even that is cheating yourself – but who cares of being cheated by oneself? No one else can cheat you as you can cheat yourself. You are the trapper, the trapping and the trapped – in persona. The Absolute persona trapping itself in a relative persona. Who else can make you believe that you have a bloody body as you can make yourself believe in that bullshit?

— *The Song Of Irrelevance p154*

K: This is actually the experience of Ramana, when he was lying down and having this life experience, because whatever could die, he let die. But life itself was still untouched by it. So life itself cannot be touched by any object or idea which can drop, which comes and goes. So if you let all those dream ideas and concepts, simply drop away, in that substratum which is left over—the total leftover of existence, the total nakedness, what cannot get any more naked—you will see that life itself is ever unborn and never dying and you can never leave it.

Simply see that, what you can experience, you cannot be. So by seeing whatever experience, you drop, you go more and more back to what is the absolute experiencer, as you see the experiencer as part of the experience. It becomes again That which is life itself, which is never coming and never going, which is not part of the phenomena of fleeting shadows of experiences, experiencers and whatever. That's why it's called "dream-like." It's not a dream, but it's dream-like.

– *Eight Days in Tiruvannamalai p174*

नो वेद्यवेदकमिदं न च हेतुतर्क्यं
वाचामगोचरमिदं न मनो न बुद्धिः ।
एवं कथं हि भवतः कथयामि तत्त्वं
ज्ञानामृतं समरसं गगनोपमोऽहम् ॥ १७॥

I am neither the knower, nor the known,
I am beyond reason; Unfathomable by logic,
I am beyond speech, mind and the intellect;
How can the ultimate Reality ever be described by words?
I am nectarean Jñana, the essence in all
and all-pervasive like space. [3:17]

K: The ultimate truth is there's no truth – they say. But even that's too much. You need to listen to [Ludwig] Wittgenstein – What you cannot talk about, you should be quiet. This is being quiet – talking like this. You don't have to stay quiet to be quiet. You can say as much as you like and you still will be quiet as if you haven't said a word. Who needs to be quiet to be quiet? It's not sitting somewhere and not saying anything – that's saying too much. That's talking too loud – someone who's not saying something.

But empty words – this is being quiet. That's the silence in the words, the empty words and not sitting somewhere being especially quiet. This is silence. What else is silence?

— *Worry And Be Happy p126*

निर्भिन्नभिन्नरहितं परमार्थतत्त्व-
मन्तर्बहिर्न हि कथं परमार्थतत्त्वम् ।
प्राक्सम्भवं न च रतं नहि वस्तु किञ्चित्
ज्ञानामृतं समरसं गगनोपमोऽहम् ॥ १८॥

The Self is neither divided nor undivided,
is neither within nor without;
It was never created, nor relishes creation,
Unattached, it is not an object with substance.
I am nectarean Jñana, the essence of all
and all-pervasive like space. [3:18]

K: I don't talk about the truth but because it has to exist to exist, it cannot be real. How can Reality depend on existence? Because it has to exist, it cannot be real. And it has to exist in something else. And what Reality would it be if it has to exist in something else?

Like the body has to be in the universe, the world. And how can That be depending on something be real? What kind of Reality is that? This relative reality which has to exist in something else. Which is depending on something? What kind of dependent Reality would it be? And what kind of Reality is that?

It's a 'maybe' reality. Maybe it is, maybe it is not. You will always have to doubt it. But what kind of Reality you can doubt? Even that you have to ask is the body real or not, it's already doubtful. So it cannot be Reality.

Q: I only asked because after I got into these talks and started hearing Nisargadatta and Ramesh and I heard that body is not real, you are not your body. That's when I also felt, maybe it's not real, that's why I asked...

K: For me it's neither. You will take it in a wrong way anyway. You take it as my body and you want to make it real or unreal. And if it's unreal, you want to make it an unreal body. It's too much. An infinite just-in-case, case. That will never stop.

– *Heaven And Hell p46*

रागादिदोषरहितं त्वहमेव तत्त्वं
दैवादिदोषरहितं त्वहमेव तत्त्वम् ।
संसारशोकरहितं त्वहमेव तत्त्वं
ज्ञानामृतं समरसं गगनोपमोऽहम् ॥ १९ ॥

I am verily the Self, free from the clutches of attachment;
I am verily the Self, free from the clutches of destiny;
I am the verily the Self,
free from the suffering of relative existence;
I am nectarean Jñana, the essence in all
and all pervasive like space. [3:19]

K: That detachment is so totally attached to that detachment. When I am asked what to do, I say – Be totally attached to what you are, be that absolute being, as you cannot not be attached to what you are, being that attachment itself. You cannot leave what you are. In absolute identification, there is no separate identification any more, and the separate one is simply dropping – but that cannot be done. That absolute identification that you are That cannot be done – you have to be it! But not by any understanding, not by choice, not by anything, as you are That anyway, as you cannot

not be It, that's all! So be It!

— Eight Days in Tiruvannamalai

In a total death experience you see that what you are cannot be touched by death. If what you are cannot die then it was never born. Only that which is born can die; so you are not born, that's all. This is not knowing what you are or if you are, but simply that you are not born.

— Interview

स्थानत्रयं यदि च नेति कथं तुरीयं
कालत्रयं यदि च नेति कथं दिशश्च ।
शान्तं पदं हि परमं परमार्थतत्त्वं
ज्ञानामृतं समरसं गगनोपमोऽहम् ॥ २० ॥

If I am not the first three states of mind,
how can I be the fourth?
If I am not any of the three kinds of time,
how can I be the fourth?
I am serenity itself, the absolute Reality;
I am nectarean Jñana, the essence in all
and all-pervasive like space. [3:20]

K: That first light as a primal source is not even that which you are; even that definition is not what you are. Out of this 'I', this primal light as awareness, comes 'I am' and then 'I am so and so.' But all these three states are the dream of the dreamer himself.

So even the first dream or experience of 'I' as awareness is a sensation already; it's a phenomenon. But the phenomenon of that which is Self is in all phenomenal states, so it can never be changed. The fourth state is that state of being the Self without even knowing that there is a Self or not. This is a total non-knowing, the total absence of the knower or non-knower. That is the turiya.

Q: What is 'transcendental turiya'?

K: It is to transcend the experience of primal light as cosmic consciousness and to be that which is prior to that, to be that which is consciousness, in essence. This is the realization that what you are is ever realized. This is nothing new or old; this is your very nature and nothing has to be done or not done for it. It all comes out of this; this is the very source of whatever is and is not, and without this nothing would be or not be. And you are that, that's all.

– Interview

दीर्घो लघुः पुनरितीह नमे विभागो
विस्तारसंकटमितीह न मे विभागः ।
कोणं हि वर्तुलमितीह न मे विभागो
ज्ञानामृतं समरसं गगनोपमोऽहम् ॥ २१॥

I have no division, long or short;
I have no division, wide or narrow;
I have no division, angular or circular;
I am nectarean Jñana, the essence in all
and all-pervasive like space. [3:21]

K: What would be there without that definer that defines coming and going and birth and death? Changes. That is called the devil, the master of time, the master of hell, of differences. Without the me, there are no differences. It needs a definer of a 'tree' to differentiate between 'water' and other things. As a baby you don't know these differences. It's a conditioning of the me that came to you to make differences between things and you learnt it and what you learnt will be gone one day and again you will be without that system of differences.

— *Am I – I Am p25*

K: It makes no difference. There is no discrimination in the "I" or the "I am" or the "I am so-and-so." In all this, even in separation, there is no separation, in oneness there is no oneness, and in "I"-ness there is no "I"-ness. All these [thumb, index, and middle fingers] are ideas. Even the first "I," the first word or sound, already is a reflection of That.

— *Eight Days in Tiruvannamalai*

मातापितादि तनयादि न मे कदाचित्
जातं मृतं न च मनो न च मे कदाचित् ।
निर्व्याकुलं स्थिरमिदं परमार्थतत्त्वं
ज्ञानामृतं समरसं गगनोपमोऽहम् ॥ २२॥

I never had a mother, father, son or the like;
I was never born and never did I die,
nor did I ever have any mind;
I am the Self, unwavering and ever steady;
I am nectarean Jñana, the essence in all
and all-pervasive like space. [3:22]

K: This is really stupid, for the source to look for the source. Because the source is already the source, whether it looks or doesn't look. And if you see, that you already were the source, and always will be, you see, how stupid it was to look for the source, as the source. Because the source has no source. And when Nisargadatta said, you are the child of a barren woman, it means, that what you are has no coming and no going. It never was born and never may die. Because it was not born.

– *Interview*

Q: On what basis do we say that your nature is unborn and uncreated and eternal?

K: Even that unborn is too much. It's a lie. If you would be the unborn, you would still be too much. There is still one who is unborn and then experiencing all this but he is not involved. Then you are in the world but from not the world and all of that. But you are still one too many who is not involved. It's all [blowing in the wind]...

– *Heaven And Hell p109*

शुद्धं विशुद्धमविचारमनन्तरूपं
निर्लेपलेपमविचारमनन्तरूपम् ।
निष्खण्डखण्डमविचारमनन्तरूपं
ज्ञानामृतं समरसं गगनोपमोऽहम् ॥ २३॥

I am purest of the pure, beyond reason,
having infinite forms; I am neither attached nor detached;
I am beyond reason, having
infinite forms; I am neither divided nor undivided;
I am beyond reason, having infinite forms;
I am nectarean Jñana, the essence
in all, and all-pervasive like space. [3:23]

K: Absolute means there is no second. And the absolute can never be attached to something else because there is nothing it can be attached to. So the absolute detachment, there is no one who can be detached from anything. There is not one who sees the world as an illusion and then is detached from the world. Just by being what you are, which is That, there is a total detachment. But not any relative detachment of one who is detached from something else. That's always like this little misunderstanding that there is one in realizing, creating one who is realized. Never happened.

– *May It Be As It Is p110*

Q: You know, today I had the idea, "I understand, so this must be wrong, because it's beyond understanding." [Laughs] So I felt guilty that I understood.

K: Oh, that's good. Doubting whatever you can understand. Totally doubt it. Become that total doubting. Because whatever is new, cannot be it. You are still in spite of whatever understanding, however beautiful it can be. Whatever makes sense or not, in spite of it, you are. It will go again. So don't hang on it. Because the trip is always that you hang on whatever blissful experience you take as understanding, as deep. "And I was never as close as then, to what I am." What an idea?!

– *Eight Days in Tiruvannamalai p246*

ब्रह्मादयः सुरगणाः कथमत्र सन्ति
स्वर्गादयो वसतयः कथमत्र सन्ति ।
यदेकरूपममलं परमार्थतत्त्वं
ज्ञानामृतं समरसं गगनोपमोऽहम् ॥ २४॥

If the Supreme Reality is one and stainless,
How can Brahma and the hosts of gods live there?!
How can there be a heaven and other worlds with all its
people?! I am nectarean Jñana, the essence in all
and all-pervasive like space. [3:24]

Q: Are all the mythological stories fragmentation of the mind?

K: It's all a psychological explanation of how you are, how Shiva works in you. I'm just pointing out that it's all the nature of the Self – different tendencies, patterns of Shiva. So, even when Shiva gets married, he gets jealous like you. In the Bible, there are similar stories of God getting jealous and having revenge. It's everywhere. It's just a pointer to the Self in its different facets of experiencing itself. So, even God himself is not safe. If he exists, he gets the same bullshit as everybody. No way out.

– The Song Of Irrelevance p73

K: It's all just-in-case because you don't know. As I don't know, I'm the believer. That makes you a believer, you are believer of the now and you are believer of later and before. Because you are a believer – just-in-case, praise the Lord and Shiva and whoever is there. Maybe.

I like India, there are so many just-in-case Gods. [Laughter] Hanuman, Vishnu, Brahma, How many just-in-case Gods do you need?

Q: [Another visitor]: You go to mountain, Hanuman is better to pray, if you are in the ocean there is another God, it depends on your situation.

K: Yeah, you always need a special God. In Greece too. In western world there is only one, and he is very pure – very poor. That God is very over worked.

– *Heaven And Hell p23*

निर्नेति नेति विमलो हि कथं वदामि
निःशेषशेषविमलो हि कथं वदामि ।
निर्लिङ्गलिङ्गविमलो हि कथं वदामि
ज्ञानामृतं समरसं गगनोपमोऽहम् ॥ २५॥

How shall I speak of the Self,
which is 'not-this' and not the 'not-this'?
How shall I speak of the Self,
which is infinite and the finite?
How shall I speak of the Self,
which is with gender and is genderless?
I am nectarean Jñana, the essence in all
and all-pervasive like space. [3:25]

K: What can be pronounced, you give names and what cannot be pronounced, you just be quiet about That. Whatever you can name is shit in that way.

So you can make it easy, you can call everything shit. Just to make it easy. Then you don't have to remember. Then whoever you meet – Ah, shit! That's neither-neither. That's neti-neti; you meet the one who neither is, nor is-not. In the morning, the shit song starts. You're only in the universe because you give it names. But if you only have one name for everything, then there is no discrimination of anything. Sounds good but it doesn't help either – but one tries.

— *The Song Of Irrelevance p76*

K: Wittgenstein would say what you cannot talk about you should be quiet about.

Q: That means you can't talk...

K: No, I can talk infinitely about what I am.

Q: No, that what you cannot talk about – better to remain quiet.

K: No. That doesn't help. I say so many words, and have never said anything. This is a paradox.

— *May It Be As It Is p89*

निष्कर्मकर्मपरमं सततं करोमि
निःसङ्गसङ्गरहितं परमं विनोदम् ।
निर्देहदेहरहितं सततं विनोदं
ज्ञानामृतं समरसं गगनोपमोऽहम् ॥ २६॥

Though inactive, I forever perform the absolute action of non-action; Though devoid of attachment and detachment,
I am the supreme joy; I am everlasting bliss devoid of form and formlessness, I am nectarean Jñana, the essence in all and all pervading like space. [3:26]

K: Whatever requires an effort is false. The failure fails even by doing nothing. It's the most lazy bastard you can be by just being what you are – laziness itself. Whatever needs an effort or no-effort is false. The effortlessness of what you are cannot be reached by any effort or no-effort, that's the beauty of it, that's the joy of it. You can make an effort like hell or you make no effort by doing nothing and you think that by doing nothing, by meditating or being quiet you get it.

No, neither by doing any action or non-action you can get it. Thank God and praise the Lord, just in case.

– Am I – I Am p154

K: The "me" is part of the enjoyment. The "me" never did enjoy anything! It's part of That which is enjoyed. That "me" is an idea and cannot enjoy anything. Whatever is experienced is experienced by that experience itself, that Absolute. That Absolute cannot not enjoy itself. It's joy itself, because there is a total absence of anything, of any idea of joy or no joy.

Q: Then how can there be joy?

K: How can there be no joy? It's just a name for something which is joy because there's an absence of whatever. You are a total absence of any idea of one who has joy or no joy, and that is the Absolute enjoying itself by not knowing joy. So that joy doesn't know joy.

– Eight Days in Tiruvannamalai

मायाप्रपञ्चरचना न च मे विकारः ।
कौटिल्यदम्भरचना न च मे विकारः ।
सत्यानृतेति रचना न च मे विकारो
ज्ञानामृतं समरसं गगनोपमोऽहम् ॥ २७॥

The illusory universe is not my image nor does it affect me;
Its deceit and crookedness do not reflect me, nor do they affect
me; Its truths and untruths do not reflect me,
nor do they affect me; I am nectarean Jñana, the essence in all
and all pervasive like space. [3:27]

Q: So, consciousness is creating a picture.

K: Consciousness can't create anything.

Q: Who is creating then?

K: There is no creator, there is no creation. There is only Self and the unfolding of the Self. This is an infinite unfolding. And there is no creation and no creator. All there is, is Self and there is no second Self, that's all. And there is no creator and no creation. That's the main point. There is no separate creator and there is no separate creation. There is no separate God and there is no...

Q: But sometimes you speak of the Creator God.

K: No. I say, out of this unfolding "I" as awareness comes as a thought the "I am", and out of the "I am" comes the "I am an object, in time". And all this is part of the unfolding. But in all this there is no creator and no creation.

– Interview

K: You cannot take truth, you cannot know truth because the moment you look into truth, you are gone. There's no truth, there's no one who can know truth. But when you look at the truth, that one who sees truth – dissolves – instantly. That's called the split-second – you cannot take it. No one could ever take it. When there's truth, there's no one – never was, never will be – because there's no two.

That's what Ramana said to UG [Krishnamurti] when he asked – Can you give it to me? Yes! But can you take it? The moment you look, you're gone. You wouldn't have anything from it. You cannot have it. You cannot claim to have it. And whoever claims that he realized truth, is an asshole. There was never anyone who realized truth. In truth, there's no truth.

– The Song Of Irrelevance p159

सन्ध्यादिकालरहितं न च मे वियोगो-
ह्यन्तः प्रबोधरहितं बधिरो न मूकः ।
एवं विकल्परहितं न च भावशुद्धं
ज्ञानामृतं समरसं गगनोपमोऽहम् ॥ २८ ॥

I am unaffected by divisions created by time nor can I be split in parts; I am never awakened within nor am I ever un-awakened;
I am neither deaf nor mute;
Devoid of the need of intention or purified emotions,
I am nectarean Jñana, the essence in all
and all pervasive like space. [3:28]

K: This is what we would call enlightenment – this experience of coming out of the form and non-form and becoming that which is light, the primal light of awareness, that which is called Arunachala. But then to see that even this light of awareness, this first notion of existence without time or no-time, even that is not what you are. Realisation is turning to face that which is prior to this first notion of existence.

– *Interview*

K: Concept or not concept, I have no idea. I just ask anyone, whoever I meet, to meet myself, be what you cannot not be. And without that there would not even be a doubting, not even a concept could arise. Even the word concept cannot be there. Even that someone sees 'everything is a concept', only a concept can see there is only concept. So I have no idea. Only illusion would claim 'everything is illusion'. For me there is no such thing. But otherwise you can say, out of fear you can say, maybe the idea of God arises.

– *May It Be As It Is p53*

निर्नाथनाथरहितं हि निराकुलं वै
निश्चित्तचित्तविगतं हि निराकुलं वै ।
संविद्धि सर्वविगतं हि निराकुलं वै
ज्ञानामृतं समरसं गगनोपमोऽहम् ॥ २९॥

I am neither with nor am I without the Lord,
I am unperturbed; I am neither the mind nor not the mind,
I am unperturbed; Know me as the transcendental one who
cannot be disturbed, I am unperturbed;
I am nectarean Jñana, the essence in all
and all-pervasive like space. [3:29]

Q: Did you have a teacher? Is it important to have a teacher / Guru? What is the relationship between teacher and disciple? Do you have disciples?

K: No, I didn't have a personal teacher. And for that which is not in time to become aware of itself, nothing is required which is in time. It is always a spontaneous awakening, out of no necessity. It is also called the divine accident. It cognizes itself, not because of, but in spite of everything which comes and goes. The question about important or unimportant is therefore obliterated.

The Self is the only Master I know. It realizes itself in losing and in finding. In this sense it is teacher and disciple and always gives itself absolute lessons.

The Self reveals itself to itself, in its Omnipresence, in the eternal Now. A disciple co-appears with a teacher like a question implies its answer. Out of desirelessness a desire arises in time and dissolves itself in its fulfilment, just as every question finds redemption through an answer. This is the karmic law of consciousness. So, no teacher and no students, only questions and answers.

– Interview

K: When there's absence, you are the absence and that's prior to the presence. When you are presence, you are the presence. You are That what is the absence when there's absence. You are the presence when there's presence. When there's neither absence nor presence, you are That what is neither absence or presence. You are That what is – that-what-is – whatever it is. There's nothing other than you.

– The Song Of Irrelevance p176

कान्तारमन्दिरमिदं हि कथं वदामि
संसिद्धसंशयमिदं हि कथं वदामि ।
एवं निरन्तरसमं हि निराकुलं वै
ज्ञानामृतं समरसं गगनोपमोऽहम् ॥ ३० ॥

How can I call this a forest or a temple?
How can I call this as proven or doubtful?
Remaining forever in and as uninterrupted equilibrium,
undisturbed; I am nectarean Jñana, the essence in all
and all-pervasive like space. [3:30]

Q: So it is that ease which doesn't need that ease?

K: Yes. That ease which never needs to be at ease. Never. It doesn't even know ease.

Q: And doesn't need any proof of it.

K: No. It never needs to improve or prove anything. And that what needs to improve and always needs to prove, that's called ghost. And the ghost always needs a proof to exist. Only a ghost needs a proof of existence. Existence itself never needs to prove itself.

Q: Doesn't even need to exist.

K: Doesn't even need to exist to exist. So that is the end of Vedanta. Because that what doesn't even have to exist to exist, that breaks all of what you can imagine to know or not know. That what is beyond all imaginary ideas.

– *May It Be As It Is p85*

निर्जीवजीवरहितं सततं विभाति
निर्बीजबीजरहितं सततं विभाति ।
निर्वाणबन्धरहितं सततं विभाति
ज्ञानामृतं समरसं गगनोपमोऽहम् ॥ ३१॥

Devoid of life and lifelessness,
the Self illuminates forever;
Devoid of seed (cause) and seedlessness (causelessness),
the Self illuminates forever;
Devoid of bondage and liberation
(nirvana), the Self illuminates forever;
I am nectarean Jñana, the essence in all
and all-pervasive like space. [3:31]

K: It's unbelievable. The idea of happiness, especially of the happy end, creates all the unhappy beginnings. All that bloody suffering. Whatever is bloody, whatever has blood in his whatever, is a bloody suffering. And for sure not life. Because life doesn't need any blood to be life. And that what needs blood to be alive is a bloody suffering. So now you got it. Your precious body. Eckhart Tolle calls it 'pain body'. You pay every day. It's a paying body.

– *May It Be As It Is p237*

Q: That's why you say that there's no truth...

K: The truth that has to be true, cannot be true, because it's a depending truth. The truth which depends on truth, cannot be true. The nature of peace doesn't need any peace to be peace and the truth that needs to be true, cannot be true. Freedom that needs to be free, is not freedom. You will never be free from yourself. So, freedom doesn't know any freedom and freedom is what-is because there's a freedom from a second. But there's no possible way that the freedom can be free. From what? How can you be free? From what? You are That. How can you be free from That?

– *The Song Of Irrelevance p183*

सम्भूतिवर्जितमिदं सततं विभाति
संसारवर्जितमिदं सततं विभाति ।
संहारवर्जितमिअदं सततं विभाति
ज्ञानामृतं समरसं गगनोपमोऽहम् ॥ ३२॥

Devoid of origin, the Self illuminates forever;
Devoid of mundane existence, the Self illuminates forever;
Devoid of annihilation, the Self illuminates forever;
I am nectarean Jñana, the essence in all
and all pervading like space. [3:32]

K: Whatever you can point to, whatever you can pronounce is unreal and the unreal will never become the real because the real is never coming never going. In Reality there is no coming there is no going. There is no birth and there is no death and that what can be born is already dead. Only dead is born and only dead can die.

Let the idea of dead die! By being what you are. But any moment you believe you are born, that is the only possible suicide you can commit. Then you have a death experience, every experience is a death experience because life can never be experienced. Whatever can be experienced is death. That death experience can never bring you the life experience which is that what you are. But you try hard to make this death – life. You want to bring life into death.

– *Am I – I Am p96*

K: Simply see that whatever is, is already there. Nothing comes and nothing goes. When nothing comes and nothing goes, when there is no birth and death, whatever comes and goes is not coming and not going. So then who is there who has to control something that's not even there?

Maybe here, now, the only thing that can die is the idea of "birth"—which includes ideas of coming and going, of dying, of mortality and immortality, of infinite and finite—these all die at that split second that you see that nothing is ever born, so nothing will ever die.

But no one can take that. Because in that split second, you are gone. That person is living out of that idea that it was born and may die. But in that split second, you see that nothing has ever happened to what you are, or will happen, and you see that you are not born so there is no death for you. Because existence never comes and never goes. What then? That's Zen. No, Zazen.

– *Eight Days in Tiruvannamalai p54*

उल्लेखमात्रमपि ते न च नामरूपं
निर्भिन्नभिन्नमपि ते न हि वस्तु किञ्चित् ।
निर्लज्जमानस करोषि कथं विषादं
ज्ञानामृतं समरसं गगनोपमोऽहम् ॥ ३३॥

You may be spoken of, but you have neither name nor form;
Neither are you separate nor unseparated,
nor are you an object;
Yet nothing exists apart from you;
Why do you grieve, Oh shameless mind?!
I am nectarean Jñana, the essence in all
and all-pervasive like space. [3:33]

K: You have no name, no form, not even no-form. Because no-form is still a form. No-name is still a name. Whatever you say is not it. You're neither name nor no-name. You're neither form nor no-form. You're neither that nor that. That's why this Neti-Neti is perfect. It's not whatever you can imagine. The Absolute Dreamer, the Parabrahman can never dream himself and whatever Parabrahman is dreaming himself as Brahman is already false, it's not what he is. Dreaming himself as Brahman. The origin, the source of everything, even being the source is a dream, is false. False, false, false. But to whom do I talk and say that? It's always a paradox. Who has to know that? Why do I point to that? I have no idea. Just happens. Not out of need.

– Am I – I Am p34

Q: Is there a lot of bliss? In that sense, is there something special or different from before? Or not particularly? Can there can be sadness, unhappiness?

K: Bliss is the absence of one who needs or doesn't need bliss! It is simply the total absence of any need. But this does not taste like one would expect bliss to taste, like the sensation of bliss, because this is not a sensation at all. This is simply being absolutely peace itself. I would call it more of a total immense peace, and I wouldn't swap it for any bliss in the world. I can do perfectly without that which one would call bliss, but I would never swap it for the peace of the Self. This is absolute peace, to be totally in peace with one Self and being that which 'is'.

– Interview

किं नाम रोदिषि सखे न जरा न मृत्युः
किं नाम रोदिषि सखे न च जन्म दुःखम् ।
किं नाम रोदिषि सखे न च ते विकारो
ज्ञानामृतं समरसं गगनोपमोऽहम् ॥ ३४॥

Why do you weep, my friend?
There is no old age or death for you;
Why do you weep, my friend?
There is no misery of birth for you;
Why do you weep, my friend?
There is no imperfection for you;
I am nectarean Jñana, the essence in all
and all-pervasive like space. [3:34]

K: You are Shiva playing with all the puppets and by playing the puppets you yourself became a puppet. You create all the puppets, then you want to play with these puppets and while playing with the puppets you yourself become a puppet. In one moment you realize, Shit! I'm a puppet and now I have to get out of being a puppet. I want to be the puppeteer, but even the Puppeteer is a puppet.

Then you are in this tendency of seeking your way out but you were never in. You imagined yourself in and you want to get out then it becomes a Reality. Then you sit somewhere and cry in self-pity and whine that you cannot get out.

– Am I – I Am p174

K: That's why I am never talking to Betty. I am always talking to That which is the Absolute already and never left what it was. Only that Absolute can take it, to be That infinite, never-born and undying, immortal existence. Whatever is in the idea of "mortality," being mortal, cannot take that immortality, never ever. Because in the infinite embracement of being That which is infinite, you will be annihilated as an idea of separate life, of being born and dying—in that instant.

— *Eight Days in Tiruvannamalai p187*

किं नाम रोदिषि सखे न च ते स्वरूपं
किं नाम रोदिषि सखे न च ते विरूपम् ।
किं नाम रोदिषि सखे न च ते वयांसि
ज्ञानामृतं समरसं गगनोपमोऽहम् ॥ ३५॥

Why do you weep, my friend? You have no independent form;
Why do you weep, my friend? You cannot be deformed;
Why do you weep, my friend? You are ageless;
I am nectarean Jñana, the essence in all
and all-pervasive like space. [3:35]

K: You can say energy takes the form of a so-called human, and then creating another form which is not different, and then having a dialogue, about itself. It's like a self-talk. It's like every morning you wake up there is three waking up - me, myself and I. And then asking 'how are we?' You already wake up in a hospital, in a madhouse. This is your hospital. And there are always doctors who are as sick as you. And the sick doctor wants to help a sick patient. And both are talking about their sickness, infinitely. And everyone is competing who is the sickest. Or someone is even competing who is the healthiest. But the one who competes in health, he must be in hell. Any competition is in hell, in separation. There is one competing with someone else.

— *May It Be As It Is p68*

K: There is a misery of imagination, imagining that you can be imagined. And then you are in that pitiful I. Then you cry about yourself. That's the joke! The Almighty, that what is absolute Energy, feeling powerless. And you cannot avoid it. You are even in the experience of being powerless that what you are. Because that will happen. This is one way of experiencing yourself. Experiencing yourself as someone who is born and now has a body and all of that, and all of that moment by moment is there. But I deny totally that by that experience of birth someone is born. No one is ever born and nothing is ever born. And Life is never born, and you are That. So by no experience you have lost something and now you cannot gain it back. So what can I do?

– *May It Be As It is p27*

किं नाम रोदिषि सखे न च ते वयांसि
किं नाम रोदिषि सखे न च ते मनांसि ।
किं नाम रोदिषि सखे न तवेन्द्रियाणि
ज्ञानामृतं समरसं गगनोपमोऽहम् ॥ ३६॥

Why do you weep, my friend? You have no age;
Why do you weep, my friend? You have no mind;
Why do you weep, my friend? You have no senses;
I am nectarean Jñana, the essence in all
and all-pervasive like space. [3:36]

K: If it starts imagining itself, it has to imagine itself in all possible ways. It cannot just have the comfortable parts. That is what you want and she wants and everyone wants. Just having one part and not the other one. I resist the bad one and only want to have the good one. I only want to feel good. I don't want to feel any pain, no disease, I don't want to age, I don't want to die, I want to be enlightened forever but not have a body. I want to be space-like, I want to be ecstatic moment-by-moment. [Laughter] I want to have an orgasm which never ends. [Laughter] Even if I never had one, I want to have that I could have had. [Laughter] My imaginary one!

– *Worry And Be Happy p102*

Q: How old are you?

K: You don't want to know. Even I don't want to know. [Laughter] I can even speak about the fifties. But now I can say that – I am not even born. [Laughter]

– *Am I – I Am p163*

किं नाम रोदिषि सखे न च तेऽस्ति कामः
किं नाम रोदिषि सखे न च ते प्रलोभः ।
किं नाम रोदिषि सखे न च ते विमोहो
ज्ञानामृतं समरसं गगनोपमोऽहम् ॥ ३७॥

Why do you weep, my friend? You have no lust;
Why do you weep, my friend? You have no greed;
Why do you weep, my friend? You have no delusion;
I am nectarean Jñana, the essence in all
and all-pervasive like space. [3:37]

K: When you are the desirer, the desiring and the desired, then you are that what-you-are. There's no desire any more, there's no ownership of desire. There's still desire but – you are that –

the desirer, desiring what can be desired. Then there's no harm in it, you cannot suffer about it when there's no separation in separation. Then there's an experience of separation but in nature there's no separation. Yes there is, but there's not. This is the end of suffering.

— *Worry And Be Happy p190*

K: I am absolute greedy. I don't go for less than the Absolute. And the absolute is absolute that — what is that and that [pointing to visitors], and that, and that, and that.

— *Am I – I Am p153*

ऐश्वर्यमिच्छसि कथं न च ते धनानि
ऐश्वर्यमिच्छसि कथं न च ते हि पत्नी ।
ऐश्वर्यमिच्छसि कथं न च ते ममेति
ज्ञानामृतं समरसं गगनोपमोऽहम् ॥ ३८॥

Why do you hanker for affluence? You have no wealth;
Why do you hanker for affluence? You have no wife;
Why do you hanker for affluence?
You have nothing that is your own;
I am nectarean Jñana, the essence in all
and all-pervasive like space. [3:38]

Q: How we in India interpret Shivratri as the union of Shiva and Parvati. How do you see it?

K: You can do it on the mundane level. Then there is Shiva, a man, who gets married to his beloved, and then they have a happy marriage. But normally the Shiva moon - Shiva marrying Parvati - is like Parvati and Shiva dissolve into that what is beyond. To the darkness. To the no-moon. So on Maha-Shivratri you celebrate the absence of a relationship between Shiva and Parvati.

Q: The absence?

K: Yes, there is no difference in nature between Shiva and Parvati. So in that absolute no-moon there is no husband and no wife. There is just Existence.

– *May It Be As It Is p50*

लिङ्गप्रपञ्चजनुषी न च ते न मे च
निर्लज्जमानसमिदं च विभाति भिन्नम् ।
निर्भेदभेदरहितं न च ते न मे च
ज्ञानामृतं समरसं गगनोपमोऽहम् ॥ ३९ ॥

The world of false appearances is neither yours nor mine;
This shameless mind appears differentiated;
That which is neither differentiated nor undifferentiated,
is neither yours nor mine;
I am nectarean Jñana, the essence in all
and all-pervasive like space. [3:39]

Q: So all the suffering that we perceive is not suffering at all...?

K: Try to find the sufferer and try to present the sufferer to me. Try. No way! No one can ever present the sufferer. You can present the body or the hurt or the pain and how you measure it but show me the sufferer. No one ever found him. It's just an idea. Where is the sufferer? Who is born? That's the question. Who is that who is born and is now suffering? Who is that guy? Show it to me, show me that idea.

– *Am I – I Am p32*

K: There is no experiencer as a separate one, but there is an absolute experiencer as That which it is. That is not a personal experience or impersonal experience. It is simply experiencing itself, being That which is prior to whatever can be experienced, being That which is prior even to experiencing, being that Absolute— It's a pointer. I don't want to frame it by that. I simply point to That which you are, as you cannot catch it in any way. Uncatchable. "Catch me if you can." There are differences between Tomas and Karl—all the differences of form and non-form, whatever, knowing and not knowing, but in That, there's a total stop of differences. So, for what you are, all the differences make no difference. So there are differences, but there are not.

– *Eight Days in Tiruvannamalai p98*

नो वाणुमात्रमपि ते हि विरागरूपं
नो वाणुमात्रमपि ते हि सरागरूपम् ।
नो वाणुमात्रमपि ते हि सकामरूपं
ज्ञानामृतं समरसं गगनोपमोऽहम् ॥ ४० ॥

Your nature does not have the slightest of dispassion;
Your nature does not have the slightest of passion;
Your nature does not have the slightest of desire;
I am nectarean Jñana, the essence in all
and all pervading like space. [3:40]

K: There is an experience of misery, but who is miserable in misery? You have to say 'me'. But the me, what is the me? Part of the misery. The misery starts with the me in a miserable circumstance. The whole scenery is miserable. Because there is a me, because there is separation, there is mind, time, and all of that is misery. And that's the way you realize yourself. Or that's the way Reality is realizing itself. As an experiencer who is different from what he is experiencing. From a lover who is different from his beloved. And that's misery, and there is passion. Because out of misery there comes passion, to get out of the misery. So you are always moment by moment passionate enough to try to get out of it. But you cannot find any compassion in it. Where is the compassion? How can there be compassion in two? In that imaginary separation, in this love affair, how can there be compassion? When the lover is different from the beloved, how can there be compassion? And when there is no lover and no beloved there is compassion, but no one has it.

– *May It Be As It Is p29*

K: You fear to be soft, too fragile, because you have learned that you have to defend yourself, because there is a second, there is a world; there is "me" and the world. "I have to defend myself." So you make all that armour around you, build a fortress. "Don't touch me!" Then even you want to be detached from everything. You make all the techniques and meditation to be "de-touched." "Don't touch me!"

– *Eight Days in Tiruvannamalai p64*

K: You are that what is ignorance, you are that what is knowledge - there is no second. That's Advaita. Non-duality, or no second, means you are That. And when there is ignorance there is ignorance. So you are absolute. Absolute means there is no second. And the absolute can never be attached to something else because there is nothing it can be attached to. So the absolute detachment, there is no one who can be detached from anything.

– May It Be As It Is p110

ध्याता न ते हि हृदये न च ते समाधि-
र्ध्यानं न ते हि हृदये न बहिः प्रदेशः ।
ध्येयं न चेति हृदये न हि वस्तु कालो
ज्ञानामृतं समरसं गगनोपमोऽहम् ॥ ४१॥

There is no object of meditation in your heart nor in the state of samadhi; There is no inner meditation within your heart nor in the world outside; There is no object of meditation in the heart and nothing that transpires in space-time; I am nectarean Jñana, the essence in all and all pervading like space. [3:41]

K: You want to understand meditation and by that you become a meditator. This is the nature of meditation. You are the question and the answer – Am I? - I Am! That's all. You're the nature of the question and you're the nature of the answer. You yourself are the answer to all your questions. In the main question Am I? – I Am! Just stay in that – that's all. That's the nature of meditation – Am I – I Am.

You're the question and you're the answer permanently. There is nothing to get out of it because you are That what you gain by that question – The answer you already are! Am I – I Am. So it's fantastic!

It's an instant fulfilment. You want to be satisfied and you are instantly satisfied by being what is satisfaction.

– Heaven And Hell p35

K: For forty years Buddha tried to make comfort out of discomfort, he didn't succeed. He just pointed out the failure. You will always fail; you will never make out the unreal or discomfort the comfort you are looking for as much as you try. That's Buddha pointing out – No way of reaching what you are. No religion, no cultivating of what you are by none of that you can become or attain what you are.

– *Am I – I Am p86*

यत्सारभूतमखिलं कथितं मया ते
न त्वं न मे न महतो न गुरुर्न न शिष्यः ।
स्वच्छन्दरूपसहजं परमार्थतत्त्वं
ज्ञानामृतं समरसं गगनोपमोऽहम् ॥ ४२॥

I have disclosed the core essence to you –
There is no you, no me, no cosmic intelligence,
no guru, no disciple; The nature of Self is self-gratifying and
spontaneous; I am nectarean Jñana, the essence in all
and all-pervasive like space. [3:42]

Q: In the master-disciple relationship, I can see why that's duality. But isn't it possible that there's a shared awareness?

K: That's the question if the awareness can be shared. I'm more from the tradition of Ramana, he never took any disciple. He destroyed relationships from the beginning including the master-disciple relationship. He said that's impossible. How can there be two? How can there be one who knows and other one who doesn't?

Just call it good company. In good company, there's no master and no disciple. In good company, there's only Self, there's 'I' to 'I'. So, there's no master and no slave and no one knows more than the other.

– *Worry And Be Happy p22*

Q: There are so many teachers, so many gurus. But we never hear it clearly as we hear it from you...

K: Because I have nothing to gain here. Normally teachers have something to gain. They want to keep you as a disciple – as a slave. It's like a SM (Slave-Master) connection. Guru-disciple connection is like master and slave connection and you cannot even say who's the master and who's the slave, because normally the slave creates the master.

The disciple calls someone a master and makes him a master. So, you don't even know who's creating this slavery. It's a co-dependency, that's a master-disciple relationship. One can only be there because of the other. Then they celebrate the relationship because as long as there is a disciple and master, you can survive in that ignorance.

– *Worry And Be Happy p52*

कथमिह परमार्थं तत्त्वमानन्दरूपं
कथमिह परमार्थं नैवमानन्दरूपम् ।
कथमिह परमार्थं ज्ञानविज्ञानरूपं
यदि परमहमेकं वर्तते व्योमरूपम् ॥ ४३॥

If I am the supreme Reality as all that exists,
How can there be one reality that is blissful;
And how can there be another reality that is not blissful?!
How can there be one reality that is knowledge;
And another reality which is not-knowledge?! [3:43]

K: There is a tendency of what you call seven billion others to go out and look for happiness in the world. It's a mass tendency. And then in very rare cases like this, it turns around. Because that one is totally fed up. It tried everything - relationships, Mercedes, gold, houses, all material things that don't work, still feeling miserable. And then there comes the spiritual experiences. Then you go for have little bliss moments by whatever little understanding. And then you are miserable again. These little orgasms happening by understanding. Then it's like Kundalini rising or something, 'Oh yes, I feel it already in my back! My master told me, if I feel it there I am already on the right path'. And then 'Oh yes, now it's in the shoulders!' And then there are teachers: 'You have to open your crown chakra'.

And then near death experiences, you have to leave your body. And then you leave your body, but back again: 'Shit! I have to leave it again!' And then you have this burning and you think 'Must be an opening of my third Eye. I can see clearly now!' And then suddenly you can say what you have never dreamed about, because this chakra opens here. You are so amazed that you can speak out of the blue, without any speaker. And then you say 'Now I am the oneness of existence, now I made it! Because my heart opened, because now there is heart without heart'.

But even that is fake. Even that experience is false. Wonderful! You expected so much of the Kundalini, being in that flow of the Kundalini. But it was killing you, because if it really works on you, you will be not there any more. So you cannot even harvest. You cannot harvest what you are. There is no harvesting. There is just what you are, and that is harvesting moment by moment. It was already there. You are permanently harvesting what you are by experiencing the next and the next. That was never different.

– May It Be As It Is p112

दहनपवनहीनं विद्धि विज्ञानमेक-
मवनिजलविहीनं विद्धि विज्ञानरूपम् ।
समगमनविहीनं विद्धि विज्ञानमेकं
गगनमिव विशालं विद्धि विज्ञानमेकम् ॥ ४४॥

Know it as That which is neither fire nor air;
Know it as That which is neither earth nor water;
Know it as That which is neither coming nor going;
Know That as infinite space,
pervading everything, everywhere. [3:44]

Q: But as far as I read in the books, Ramana is advising everybody to do self-inquiry.

K: I would advise too.

Q: But if it doesn't bring you closer to yourself, why do anything?

K: If you want to stop suffering, because that is in the dream, then self-inquiry maybe kills the sufferer. But you won't become that what you are by that. So yes, if you want to end suffering, then self-inquiry can maybe end the suffering by ending the sufferer. Because in self-inquiry you just give your attention to that what is attention. There is no time any more, there is no coming, no going, there is no past, no future, there is no place for a me, for a sufferer. So you may end suffering. Or the sufferer. But you cannot attain what you are. Yes, you can maybe end the suffering by self-inquiry. But by self-inquiry you can never attain what you are. So it's still psychotherapy.

— *May It Be As It Is p171*

K: Without Marvin, there would be no universe; there would not even be sun. There would be no belief system without the believer. The very first and imaginary experience of the believer gets burnt out – by itself. That is Ramana's awareness of awareness. The awareness gives awareness to awareness – by being awareness. And there is no one who is or is-not aware in That. That doesn't even know awareness.

– The Song Of Irrelevance p213

न शून्यरूपं न विशून्यरूपं
न शुद्धरूपं न विशुद्धरूपम् ।
रूपं विरूपं न भवामि किञ्चित्
स्वरूपरूपं परमार्थतत्त्वम् ॥ ४५॥

I am neither the void nor the non-void;
I am neither pure nor impure;
I have neither form nor am I formless;
I am That – I am : The Absolute Self [3:45]

K: You are not any part of any purification game. You never know any pure and impure. It needs one who knows purity and impurity, and already that is fake. Thank God no one ever was and will ever be pure enough for that what he is. Never ever. So never ever anyone, by whatever he is doing or knowing, can know that what he is. In any relative way. But in another way, you cannot not know yourself. You are That.

– May It Be As It Is p48

Q: Emptiness?

K: Not even emptiness. Even emptiness is too much. This is That which is emptiness, and this is That which is fullness, and this is That which is whatever you name, but it has no name.

— Eight Days in Tiruvannamalai p37

मुञ्च मुञ्च हि संसारं त्यागं मुञ्च हि सर्वथा ।
त्यागात्यागविषं शुद्धममृतं सहजं ध्रुवम् ॥ ४६॥

Renounce the world in every way;
Renounce renunciation in every way;
Renounce the poison of renunciation and non-renunciation;
The Self is pure, immortal, natural and immutable. [3:46]

K: It's like Ramana's renunciation of renunciation. It's the same, coming out of a necessity of the moment. He had to do it because he was in a court and they wanted to take away his ashram because in India a sadhu cannot own anything. So, he could not own the ashram, someone wanted to take the land and he had to go to the court. Ramana said I even renounce renunciation, so I can own again. By renouncing renunciation, owning is not an obstacle. And then it was invented. That became his biggest saying and I like it the most.

— The Song Of Irrelevance p156

K: But by these experiences I cannot gain or lose anything. So there is no gainer, no loser, that's all. But that is your misery: you are a gainer or a loser. In that instant you commit suicide for what is the absolute owner. You become a relative owner, and now you never get enough. And you don't even have to give it up. I still have my bank account. All of that is there. To be what you are nothing has to go. You don't have to renounce anything. That I like about Ramana – the renunciation of renunciation is what you are. You cannot renounce what you are. So you renounce renunciation and just be that what you are. You devote devotion, because there is nothing you have to devote to anyone. Who can devote something to himself? And who needs that?

– May It Be As It Is p110

Chapter Four

नावाहनं नैव विसर्जनं वा
पुष्पाणि पत्राणि कथं भवन्ति ।
ध्यानानि मन्त्राणि कथं भवन्ति
समासमं चैव शिवार्चनं च ॥ १॥

What is the need of invocations or immersions?
Where is the need to worship with flowers or leaves?
What is the need for meditation or chanting of mantras?
The worshiper and the worshiped (Shiva) are one and the same.
[4:1]

K: Simply see, there is no result coming out of whatever is done or not done. By no understanding can you become what you are. In spite of knowing or not knowing, you are. So if you are totally in spite of whatever you can know or not know, then there is meditation because you cannot not realize yourself.

And realizing yourself is meditating about That which you are. Out of that meditation, the whole dream starts. This dream is meditating about what you are as consciousness. This is a manifestation of what you are. That is meditation without intention.

At the moment intention is part of the meditation; it becomes a personal "me," because there is an advantage idea. "By meditating, I can become what I am looking for, what I am longing for." You make yourself an object of desire, of a goal. Then you are in that control business. You become "the meditator." You are doing meditation.

But you have to be meditation. There is no doership in meditation. That is the "I am" meditating about That which is "I am." That's all.

— *Eight Days in Tiruvannamalai p174*

न केवलं बन्धविबन्धमुक्तो
न केवलं शुद्धविशुद्धमुक्तः ।
न केवलं योगवियोगमुक्तः
स वै विमुक्तो गगनोपमोऽहम् ॥ २॥

Not only am I free of bondage and release;
Not only am I free of impurity and purity;
Not only am I free of separation and union;
I am Freedom itself, all-pervasive like space. [4:2]

Q: So, in this suffering there is a freedom from...

K: There's no freedom from anything. You cannot free yourself from the ocean of realization. And you always realize yourself in separation, in the ocean of discomfort. The presence is always discomfort and then in this discomfort, there is more or less discomfort. Then more intense discomfort is being a person and opening up is less discomfortable. But it's still discomfort – more or less discomfort. You can make levels of discomfort.

Q: So, you were sensing it after it was gone, still was it discomfort?

K: Compared to the comfort you are, not even knowing what is comfort; this less discomfort is just a degree of discomfort. But not the comfort, because the comfort can never be experienced. You can only experience yourself in discomfort – levels of discomfort because That what is comfort, the ease itself, can never be experienced. The bliss itself can never be experienced, the peace cannot be experienced. And the rest is just levels and degrees of war – of tension.

– Worry And Be Happy p145

Q: These practices are somehow working on the mind. Would you say it is a prerequisite that the mind should become quiet, sattvic?

K: No. There will be no mind sattvic enough to become that which is Self. The very idea that the Self has to purify itself is dirty. This word 'purification' in itself is dirty because it implies that the Self is dirty and has to be purified, and the Self would need some purification to be the Self.

It is simply an idea that is coming out of the survival system of 'me', who wants to survive. By having the idea that I have to be purified and by knowing that I cannot be pure enough to be that which is the Self means I can stay as I am, as a little 'me'. It is a trick of this 'me' to stay as a 'me'. Whatever comes out of this 'I' thought is a survival system of this 'I' thought, and you cannot annihilate that which is the 'I' thought.

– Interview

सञ्जायते सर्वमिदं हि तथ्यं
सञ्जायते सर्वमिदं वितथ्यम् ।
एवं विकल्पो मम नैव जातः
स्वरूपनिर्वाणमनामयोऽहम् ॥ ३॥

The notion that phenomena is real;
The notion that the phenomena is unreal;
Such imagination is not mine;
Unblemished and devoid of maya,
I am the nature of Freedom itself. [4:3]

Q: Before you said, by looking, you create, you make this world real.

K: No, by taking that creator as real, there becomes a creator and some creation. But actually, it's all Self, and Self is infinite and never coming and going. In becoming that creator, as "me," by taking that creator as real, you are separate from what you are already. You take an image, a form, as real, but even that "Creator God" is an image, simply an idea. You're still stepping out of that Godlessness you are, out of that paradise of that not knowing, into some idea.

Out of that "creator" idea, you create images and forms. So you become that formless consciousness as a creator, creating all kinds of "in-form-ation." But already that is a dream. It's fake. It's false. So you never created anything, as there was never any creator nor any creation. All that is, is Heart or Self. And in That, there is nothing ever coming or going. So there is no creating, there is not even appearance and disappearance. What to do with that?

– *Eight Days in Tiruvannamalai*

K: There's no life in this life. In this imaginary life, are imaginary differences, by an imaginary phantom who makes differences. There are tendencies of tongue, that which can taste some differences, is already a sickness. Then by taking that as real, the sickness continues. Having a body is already a disease. Who said it? Your master Ramana. Who cares when this disease ends?

– The Song Of Irrelevance p40

न साञ्जनं चैव निरञ्जनं वा
न चान्तरं वापि निरन्तरं वा ।
अन्तर्विभिन्नं न हि मे विभाति
स्वरूपनिर्वाणमनामयोऽहम् ॥ ४ ॥

I have no faults, nor am I without faults;
I have no beginning, nor am I beginning-less;
I am not undivided, nor am I divided;
Unblemished and devoid of maya,
I am the nature of Freedom itself. [4:4]

K: No one wants to make you happy. You have a taste and that's your problem. By having a taste, you already taste shit because you make differences. Making difference is shit and not making difference is shit. You cannot get out of it. So, if you're born and have a taste, it's shit, but what to do? You cannot go against it. Just see that it will be shit.

Every tendency, everything that makes a difference is shit and not making a difference is shit. I just point out to the indifference of shit. None of that will make you happy – nothing, not one of that. So, the moment you are, 'you-are' – it's shit. Whatever comes out of that being, out of existence – it produces shit. All relative concepts coming out of that first concept of existence.

– The Song Of Irrelevance p83

K: The world is there the moment the 'I' appears. Out of this 'I' the spider creates the world surrounded by creation, then the 'I am' as formless consciousness. Then the creative force of the 'I am' creates all this information, which we call world. So this information of universe or world is consciousness in form, coming out of the non-form of formless consciousness.

Consciousness creates by simply getting into form. That which is world is actually consciousness in action, like Shiva dancing with himself and creating this universe out of his dance. The essence of everything that is form and non-form is consciousness. All there is, is consciousness, as cosmic consciousness.

– *Interview*

अबोधबोधो मम नैव जातो
बोधस्वरूपं मम नैव जातम् ।
निर्बोधबोधं च कथं वदामि
स्वरूपनिर्वाणमनामयोऽहम् ॥ ५॥

I know neither knowledge nor ignorance;
How, then, can I claim to be the nature of knowledge?!
How, then, can I claim to have knowledge and ignorance?!
Unblemished and devoid of maya,
I am the nature of Freedom itself. [4:5]

Q: When you say this way is not different...

K: It's in quality not different from the other. The only quality in all the ways is – you-are-That! What can get not more or less in whatever way? You're the quality experiencing yourself in differences. But by none of the differences, you can gain or lose anything and none of them can deliver what you're looking for.

They all promise. At first the world promises satisfaction, then the spirit promises satisfaction, then the awareness promises, then the beyond promises, then the impersonal promises. They're all promising, but they promise something that they cannot deliver – to know yourself!

And your seed of longing is always to know yourself. But none of them can deliver. You fail in all of them – to know yourself. That's what Buddha talks about too – being the absolute failure. He went through all the possibilities and none of them delivered what-he-was. So, the Buddha nature cannot be found in any of that way – so there's no way, the way is the goal.

– *Worry And Be Happy p68*

Q: So, the nature of perception is what?

K: No one will ever know. You will never know – but That is what-you-are. The nature of perception is that perception cannot perceive perception. And whatever the perception is perceiving – especially the perceiver – cannot be That what is perception. That's why they say That perception is closest to That what-you-are – the eye of God. But the eye of God is not God.

So, perception is the closest you can come to That, what is your nature. So, your nature is – whatever is perception, cannot perceive itself – because there's no second. And from there on it becomes like, you perceive an image of a perceiver, perceiving what can be perceived.

– *Worry And Be Happy p96*

न धर्मयुक्तो न च पापयुक्तो
न बन्धयुक्तो न च मोक्षयुक्तः ।
युक्तं त्वयुक्तं न च मे विभाति
स्वरूपनिर्वाणमनामयोऽहम् ॥ ६॥

I am neither virtuous nor sinful;
I am neither bound nor liberated;
I am neither united nor separated;
Unblemished and devoid of maya,
I am the nature of Freedom itself. [4:6]

K: The question is: Is there one who has a relationship and the necessity of liberation? The desire for every union (oneness) is based on the idea of separation. Can something which originates from a lie lead to truth? Can that which is dependent, by its nature dead, subject to time, make you what you are? Where the idea of oneness arises, there is twoness; by uniting is separated, and all comes and goes with something false, the "I". So, back to the root, to the question: To whom or in what does this "I" appear?

– *Interview*

Q: What about the original sin?

K: That's you – that's your spiritual name. [Laughter] The original sin is that God woke up and fell in love with himself and now you are the result of God falling in love with its image. You are the result of God being in love with himself. You are the result of the original sin. You have no business in it; it's all God's business. It's his-story not your story. The narcissistic God! And you are a result of the narcissistic love.

– *The Song Of Irrelevance p191*

परापरं वा न च मे कदाचित्
मध्यस्थभावो हि न चारिमित्रम् ।
हिताहितं चापि कथं वदामि
स्वरूपनिर्वाणमनामयोऽहम् ॥ ७॥

I have no higher, no lower, nor any middle state;
I have no friend, nor do I have any foe;
How, then, can I speak of good and evil?!
Unblemished and devoid of maya,
I am the nature of Freedom itself. [4:7]

Q: Is shit and life same?

K: Yeah. The opposite of live is evil – it's all evil. The moment you experience life, you experience hell – evil.

Q: And you experience heaven?

K: Even heaven belongs to hell because only in hell, there's two. In heaven there would be no hell – if there would be a heaven, but heaven is an idea, as hell is an idea. Only in the idea of hell, there's heaven: both come together. So, both is hell – Hellalujah! Hello – it's very low.

So, if everything is hell, who cares?

– The Song Of Irrelevance p143

Q: That what is called enlightenment, is that another state of mind?

K: It has to be mind because it's different. Whatever is different is mind, enlightenment is different from non-enlightenment. Unenlightened-enlightened: that's mind.

Q: Love and peace are another state of mind?

K: Every state is a state of mind. Whatever you come to, the state of awareness, the state of whatever, is all state of mind. It's a United States of Mind. [Laughter]

– *Am I – I Am p19*

नोपासको नैवमुपास्यरूपं
न चोपदेशो न च मे क्रिया च ।
संवित्स्वरूपं च कथं वदामि
स्वरूपनिर्वाणमनामयोऽहम् ॥ ८ ॥

I am neither the worshiper nor the worshiped;
I neither have any instruction nor any practice;
How, then, can I describe myself,
who am the nature of Knowledge itself?!
Unblemished and devoid of maya,
I am the nature of Freedom itself. [4:8]

Q: Is that the reason that the one without the energy and with the interest, prays to the other one?

K: Yeah. But he cannot do anything because he's not in the dream. So you pray to the Almighty, because you have no energy, you pray to that what is energy. But that what is energy cannot do anything because it is not in the dream.

Q: Understanding the role of probability that you have to be right once in a while, there is some sense that the prayers are answered sometimes. What is that?

K: That is like you have a television set and a remote control without a battery. And you wait for the right moment when the program is changing; you press in the right moment and the program changes.

– *Heaven And Hell p56*

K: So whatever you do against it, is for it. Fantastic! This trap is so fantastic and perfect in its nature – as you are. Absolute trap! And no way out!

And I sit here and tell you that you have to be what you are, inspite of the presence or absence of anything, as you are already. And that you cannot not be. And this relative experience of separation will always be there – if you like it or not. Call it hell, call it whatever. The heaven of oneness and the hell of separation will be there as the way you realize yourself.

And maybe the oneness realization is more pleasant. But this is there as the other one is there. And you cannot have only one side of the metal. Both is there, the pleasant and the unpleasant. The comfort and the discomfort. And if you cannot be in the discomfort of the separation what-you-are, you will not become it in the comfort of oneness. So, what to do?

Q: [Another visitor]: Nothing. You can't do anything...

K: You can do everything but it doesn't work. Just-in-case! Just have fun.

– Heaven And Hell p27

नो व्यापकं व्याप्यमिहास्ति किञ्चित्
न चालयं वापि निरालयं वा ।
अशून्यशून्यं च कथं वदामि
स्वरूपनिर्वाणमनामयोऽहम् ॥ ९ ॥

There is nothing that pervades and nothing that is pervaded;
There is no place to rest nor the absence of a resting place;
How, then, shall I speak of the void and the non-void?!
Unblemished and devoid of maya,
I am the nature of Freedom itself. [4:9]

K: As an idea, a pointer. But the Self doesn't know any Self. There is only "Selflessness," you may call it, "lovelessness," "existencelessness." I am pointing to that "idea-lessness," where all the icons of divinity, of God—are gone. This Godlessness I'm talking about. You are That which is God, but God doesn't know any God, no second or whatever. That which cannot be talked about or defined—that's what I'm talking about.

This paradox cannot be solved. We talk about something that cannot be talked about. So we can talk about it, but it makes no difference. It's just pointing out that it makes no difference whether you talk or not.

For That which you are, it never makes any difference, whatever you say, whatever you define or don't define. There is nothing more or less. There is no quantity in it, of whatever idea of "divine" or anything. All this is gone. This is freedom which has no idea about freedom.

– *Eight Days in Tiruvannamalai p37*

न ग्राहको ग्राह्यकमेव किञ्चित्
न कारणं वा मम नैव कार्यम् ।
अचिन्त्यचिन्त्यं च कथं वदामि
स्वरूपनिर्वाणमनामयोऽहम् ॥ १०॥

I am not the perceiver, nor the object of perception;
I am neither the cause nor the effect;
How, then, can I say, I am the knower or the known?!
Unblemished and devoid of maya,
I am the nature of Freedom itself. [4:10]

K: There is no cause and interrelation between That which is the essence of what you are and That which is the realization of it. You cannot make an influence. It has no cause and effect. It may change something, but not because of that. Whoever said, "Because of this, something changed"—it was not that.

Q: But it's also not an automatic—

K: Side-effect?

Q: Side-effect, yeah.

K: Of a disease? The enlightenment disease? And you have side-effects? That is what enlightenment is, really, that awakening from identified consciousness to non-identified consciousness. Out of this you can make side-effects, out of that identified consciousness as a person then becoming cosmic consciousness. Then you can say there are energetic changes and other things to talk about.

That you can talk about, but not about That, because That is in spite of whatever, never because. But whatever is because of something you have done, sadhana, Self-inquiry, or whatever, and you go from identification to non-identification, maybe, from separation to oneness, all that you can go to—about that you can talk and make side-effects.

– *Eight Days in Tiruvannamalai p52*

Q: As long as form is present, this understanding will just be mental?

K: It will always be mental. Every understanding is mental. That what-you-are, never needs to understand anything to be what-it-is. Every fucking understanding, every realization is mental.

Q: That's what I meant when I said the other day; realization is in the mind...

K: No. You realize yourself in the mind, but you are not the mind and mind is simply two. You can only realize yourself as two – that's mind. Mind means two, that's time, that's two, but there's no other way. You can only realize yourself as a creator which is different from the creation or the seer which is different from what is seen. There is no other way.

– The Song Of Irrelevance p182

न भेदकं वापि न चैव भेद्यं
न वेदकं वा मम नैव वेद्यम् ।
गतागतं तात कथं वदामि
स्वरूपनिर्वाणमनामयोऽहम् ॥ ११॥

I am neither the cause of differences
nor can differences exist in me;
I am neither the knower nor the known;
How, then, can I, my dear, speak of either coming or going?!
Unblemished and devoid of maya,
I am the nature of Freedom itself. [4:11]

K: That is what is meant by If You Meet the Buddha On the Road, Kill Him, because Buddha cannot walk the earth. It's never some form or name or anything. It's a nice book title. It helps you see what is your nature, That which is Buddha himself, that Buddha nature, can never incarnate into anything. It's never in any circumstance or walking the world or whatever. It's never a part of anything, because it cannot be divided from something to another thing. So it is never in any place, but there is no place without it.

– *Eight Days in Tiruvannamalai p300*

K: When you-are – you're shit. When you-are-not – you're not and maybe that's a pointer to That what is not a concept. That what is the Self, knowing the Self – is shit. Not knowing the Self is no-shit, but it cannot avoid knowing itself. So, it cannot avoid realizing itself. The moment it's realizing itself, it's realizing itself as shit. But every night not realizing itself – is chit because there is knowledge without a knower.

But any moment you exist, you realize yourself as knower, knowing, what can be known. That is always realization of what-you-are but not That what-you-are in nature. But you can only realize yourself as shit.

– *The Song Of Irrelevance p91*

न चास्ति देहो न च मे विदेहो
बुद्धिर्मनो मे न हि चेन्द्रियाणि ।
रागो विरागश्च कथं वदामि
स्वरूपनिर्वाणमनामयोऽहम् ॥ १२॥

I have no body, nor am I bodiless;
I have neither intellect, nor mind, nor senses;
How, then, can I speak desire or desirelessness?!
Unblemished and devoid of maya,
I am the nature of Freedom itself. [4:12]

Q: Is there no reason?

K: I didn't say there is no reason. I just said it comes anyway – with or without reason. And the next picture doesn't have to make sense as the picture before never needed to make sense. It's an expression of senselessness. The innocence sensing itself in a chain of events – personal or impersonal or anything. All sensations are sensed by That in-no-sense(innocence). Your very nature is the in-no-sense, realizing itself in senses. There's a sensor, sensing what can be sensed – all that is sensed by what-you-are – without any censorship and not censoring what is sensed. The sensor is sensing what can be sensed.

It's the nature of the sensor to censor. Then there's a story of censorship. It wants to make it a special sense.

– Worry And Be Happy p127

K: Absolute means there is no second. And the absolute can never be attached to something else because there is nothing it can be attached to. So the absolute detachment, there is no one who can be detached from anything. There is not one who sees the world as an illusion and then is detached from the world. Just by being what you are, which is That, there is a total detachment. But not any relative detachment of one who is detached from something else.

– May It Be As It Is p110

उल्लेखमात्रं न हि भिन्नमुच्चै-
रुल्लेखमात्रं न तिरोहितं वै ।
समासमं मित्र कथं वदामि
स्वरूपनिर्वाणमनामयोऽहम् ॥ १३॥

Not even notionally can it be said as different to anything else;
Not even notionally is it hidden;
Then, my friend, what can I call it
to be as similar or different to?
Unblemished and devoid of maya,
I am the nature of Freedom itself. [4:13]

K: The peace that you find in any one of them, will be a relative peace – the peace that's different from something else. The peace that you can find, you land in, you have to leave again. So, in the absolute way – peace off – and be what-you-are inspite of what-is or what-is-not – may it be as it is!

However it is, it cannot make you more or less as you are and it cannot deliver what you're looking for. But you still have to look. The looking cannot stop. This paradox, you cannot understand. Many had this absolute insight – that they cannot find themselves, but they ponder why is this inquiry still going on? Why am I still looking? Why don't I stop?

How can you stop? You have to realize yourself – whether you like it or not – inspite of being what-you-are. And because you are, what you are – reality – you have to realize yourself. The nature of the Parabrahman is the Absolute dreamer and he cannot stop dreaming, because the moment he tries to stop dreaming, he's part of the dream. And That what is part of the dream, is impotent. If the almighty had the wish, he could stop the dream.

– Worry And Be Happy p69

Q: I was wondering about this. So many sages in India for centuries and centuries, and nothing happened.

K: Even in Europe, there were so many! Go to the churches and see the statues of saints and holy people. But that's the beauty of it. It cannot be controlled by any knowing or not knowing. This will go on forever [holds up fingers and then folds them back into fist, over and over, to symbolize infinite movement between states of consciousness]; there is no way out of it. As infinite as you are as the Absolute, that is how infinite is realization. There is no stopping it, because it never started. So what?!

Q: [holding up his fingers and then making a fist] Is this again and again?

K: There is not again and again. There is at once! There is a solid block of realization. And nothing comes and goes.

Q: Who sees that?

K: There is no seeing. You are That. There is no seeing in it. The seeing is part of an aspect of that realization, but there is no seeing in it. There is simply, absolutely being That. It's what is meant by I Am That. Finished.

— *Eight Days in Tiruvannamalai p56*

जितेन्द्रियोऽहं त्वजितेन्द्रियो वा
न संयमो मे नियमो न जातः ।
जयाजयौ मित्र कथं वदामि
स्वरूपनिर्वाणमनामयोऽहम् ॥ १४ ॥

Neither am I free of the senses nor am I bound by them;
Neither is there self-restraint, nor are there any rules for me;
How, then, can I speak of victory and defeat, my friend?!
Unblemished and devoid of maya,
I am the nature of Freedom itself. [4:14]

Q: So what about this saying 'the highest tapas is good company'?

K: There are no tapas. That's the highest tapas. The tapas-lessness. The exerciselessness is exercise. The exercise to be what you are, which never needs to exercise to be what it is. That is the highest tapas you cannot do, you can only be. But any tapa you can do is Vedanta.

Q: So whatever you are trying is Vedanta?

K: Even not trying is Vedanta.

– *May It Be As It Is p17*

K: Only the idea that you hope that someday there will be some help for you, there will be someone or something that helps you, there will be some event of whatever understanding and then you will be happy ever after—this makes war. But if you see there will be no moment like this that helps you, that can get you out of what you are—this is peace. You are in war only because you hope to win something, to gain something. But if you really see there is nothing for you to gain by anything, you are already in that peace of mind, because there is no "so what?" There is always that "so what?" "And then?"

– *Eight Days in Tiruvannamalai p198*

अमूर्तमूर्तिर्न च मे कदाचि-
दाद्यन्तमध्यं न च मे कदाचित् ।
बलाबलं मित्र कथं वदामि
स्वरूपनिर्वाणमनामयोऽहम् ॥ १५॥

I have neither any form nor am I formless;
I have no beginning, no middle, no end;
How, then, my friend, can I be called strong or weak?!
Unblemished and devoid of maya,
I am the nature of Freedom itself. [4:15]

Q: The realization is that there is a lie, that everything is formless...

K: But even that goes away too. Everything is formless, is that a truth?

Q: That there is no form...

K: Is that truth? Whatever you can pronounce and find out, would be covered again. Whatever you say now is separation because the non-form is different from form and formlessness. Then you make another level – emptiness. Then you say I realized that emptiness can never get more or less. Sounds good! Then the opposite of emptiness would not be true.

– *Worry And Be Happy p24*

K: Mind means two and there is no other way of realizing yourself. There will never be any end of the experience of two – it never started. Because you realize yourself even there – no way out. You have to be inspite of that – what-you-are, because it will never end. You cannot end the realization of what-you-are and you will always realize yourself in separation. There is no other way. The dream of realization will always be the dream of separation. No beginning, no end.

– *The Song of Irrelevance p96*

> मृतामृतं वापि विषाविषं च
> सञ्जायते तात न मे कदाचित् ।
> अशुद्धशुद्धं च कथं वदामि
> स्वरूपनिर्वाणमनामयोऽहम् ॥ १६॥

I have neither death nor immortality, neither poison nor nectar;
These opposites do not exist for me, my child;
How, then, can I speak of purity or impurity?!
Unblemished and devoid of maya,
I am the nature of Freedom itself. [4:16]

K: Now I take another approach and show you why you experience this whole dream, the dream of your realization. But maybe it's not even a dream. The pointer is always you cannot leave what-you-are. And that never came and it will never go. There is only silence, the silence of nothing ever happened. Nothing ever came and nothing will ever go.

By all the movements, by all the imaginary coming and going, nothing ever came and nothing will ever go. Nothing was ever born and nothing will ever die. There is no birth in birth and no death in death. The only thing that can die is the idea of death. What is there that is born? What is there to be afraid of? So what to do?

– *Heaven And Hell p116*

K: Whoever wants to be healthy must be sick. But you never became sick, how can you be cured? You are not any part of any purification game. You never know any pure and impure. It needs one who knows purity and impurity, and already that is fake. Thank God no one ever was and will ever be pure enough for that what he is. Never ever.

– *May It Be As It Is p48*

स्वप्नः प्रबोधो न च योगमुद्रा
नक्तं दिवा वापि न मे कदाचित् ।
अतुर्यतुर्यं च कथं वदामि
स्वरूपनिर्वाणमनामयोऽहम् ॥ १७॥

For me there is neither sleeping nor waking-up;
Nor the practice of yogic hand-postures;
For me there is neither day nor night;
How, then, can I speak of transcendental or the relative states?!
Unblemished and devoid of maya,
I am the nature of Freedom itself. [4:17]

Q: You refer to two things; deep sleep and deep-deep sleep...

K: The deep-deep sleep is the absolute absence of any presence. The deep sleep is the presence of awareness. That's deep sleep – awareness, 'I Amness', then comes the world. But deep-deep sleep is the nature of deep sleep. The absence of one who is sleeping or not sleeping. The absolute absence of the presence of the one who is and who is not – that is deep-deep sleep.

And to know yourself as That, which never needs to know itself to be itself – that's the pointer. So what-you-cannot-not-be, never demands any understanding or any knowledge of any kind – whatever can be known to be what-it-is.

– Heaven And Hell p106

Q: So how come this is exhausted?

K: Because you want to grab yourself. You are after yourself. You are already exhausted just by attempting to know yourself. How can knowledge exhaust itself? How can energy exhaust itself? How can meditation exhaust itself? A meditator can be exhausted by doing meditation. What an idea! 'I am going to meditate'. Just to say that!

Ha ha! What a joke! One who claims that he can meditate.

– *May It Be As It Is p49*

संविद्धि मां सर्वविसर्वमुक्तं
माया विमाया न च मे कदाचित् ।
सन्ध्यादिकं कर्म कथं वदामि
स्वरूपनिर्वाणमनामयोऽहम् ॥ १८ ॥

Know me as free of everything and also free of nothing;
Know me as free from illusion
as also free of the freedom from illusion;
How, then, can I speak of the evening, morning
or other rituals?!
Unblemished and devoid of maya,
I am the nature of Freedom itself. [4:18]

Q: But discomfort is also a comfort zone...

K: Comfort knows itself only in discomfort. Knowledge only knows itself in ignorance. How else to know yourself? You can say the nature of ignorance is knowledge, but knowledge only knows itself in ignorance as peace knows itself in war. It's all war! Everywhere!

Q: And both are illusion?

K: No. Where is the illusion? It's all 'what you are'.

Q: There is something that knows itself in something and not in something as part of the illusion.

K: No. It's realization of 'what you are'. The one who says all is an illusion, you can call it illusion. But for 'what you are' there is no illusion. You are the Reality and that is the realization, there is no difference. Reality would never call this illusion.

– Am I – I Am p20

Q: What happens when the body is gone?

K: As I said. First you have to find a body that the body can be gone. If you ask a physicist they say where is the body? It's just a cluster of energy showing itself as a body. But you cannot find a body. You just find an information system of energy that you call body. But how can that go? Did it ever come? Energy taking an information, and then the information becomes something else. But energy is not coming and not going. So what is coming, what is going? Energy always taking a different form. But that what is form is always fleeting. But that what is taking the form, showing itself, will never be known and will never show itself as what it is. It always shows itself in something else. But it will never show itself as what it is. So it will always be different, but does it make a difference? No. Body or no body.

– May It Be As It Is p248

संविद्धि मां सर्वसमाधियुक्तं
संविद्धि मां लक्ष्यविलक्ष्यमुक्तम् ।
योगं वियोगं च कथं वदामि
स्वरूपनिर्वाणमनामयोऽहम् ॥ १९॥

Know me to be endowed with all samadhis;
Know me to be free of both relative and absolute aims;
How, then, can I speak of union and separation?!
Unblemished and devoid of maya,
I am the nature of Freedom itself. [4:19]

Q: I thought that these visions will come out of mind.

K: Even that you cannot think. You cannot decide what you think next. You cannot pre-think.

Q: I thought this was the construction, because I have this aim by my mind.

K: Oh, you cannot aim, but you aim. Just simply see it. You cannot want what you want. You cannot pre-think. You have to think. Then you think, because of the thinking, you think.

– Eight Days in Tiruvannamalai p184

K: If you want to be one with the puzzle, you have to discriminate that being separated is wrong and being one is right. So there has to be one who knows what is right and wrong. Then you are already out of your nature. The moment you know right and wrong you are in what? Never ending game of right and wrong, good and bad, whatever you call it. Knowing or not knowing, being realized not realized, being enlightened not enlightened. All comes from that trying to fix yourself. And I tell you it will never stop - that experience of separation. As much as you try to stop it, as much as you try to be one with yourself, as much you are separated.

But in Reality you were never separate from what you are. In the imaginary realization you will always be separated. All the realizations, all the experiences will be in separation. Whatever you reach will be part of separation. Whatever special reference point, special stand point, special understanding will be a relative understanding in a relative reference point. No way out.

– Am I – I Am p550

मूर्खोऽपि नाहं न च पण्डितोऽहं
मौनं विमौनं न च मे कदाचित् ।
तर्कं वितर्कं च कथं वदामि
स्वरूपनिर्वाणमनामयोऽहम् ॥ २०॥

I am neither stupid nor brilliant;
For me, there is neither silence nor speech;
How, then, can I have arguments and counter arguments?!
Unblemished and devoid of maya,
I am the nature of Freedom itself. [4:20]

Q: I want the answer without any question being asked!

K: It's an old technique: Try to find something which is not hearsay what you picked up from someone, and try to find a question which is your question. Try to find a question which you haven't heard from someone, you have not read somewhere; no one has given to you, which you have not learned. See if that what you are has any question which is not second-hand. Try to find that question of yours. Any original question. Try it. And if you come up with it, show it to me.

Q: I don't know if it is original or not.

K: That would be the question. What is not what you have learned, what you have read, or your mother or your guru told you? What is that? What would you be without that hearsay, without that learning? Not even nothing you can claim. So that would be my advice: try to find that question which is yours, which is not second-hand. That would be the direct path. And I tell you, that what you are never had any question, never needs any answer for anything.

– May It Be As It Is p101

Q: I'm reading about Meher Baba...

K: The one who never spoke until the last ten minutes of his life. [Laughter] He promised that he will never speak again because he said the moment I speak again, there will be an energetic explosion and every one will be enlightened. That would be too much for humanity. But in the last ten minutes he started to talk because he had to go to the hospital and the taxi was late. He sat there and yelled – 'Where is my taxi?' And that was the explosion of the world...

— *Worry And Be Happy p86*

पिता च माता च कुलं न जाति-
र्जन्मादि मृत्युर्न च मे कदाचित् ।
स्नेहं विमोहं च कथं वदामि
स्वरूपनिर्वाणमनामयोऽहम् ॥ २१॥

I have neither father nor mother, neither lineage nor caste;
I have not the slightest knowledge of birth, nor of death.
How, then, can I speak of affection or attraction?!
Unblemished and devoid of maya,
I am the nature of Freedom itself. [4:21]

K: You try every possible way to end that bullshit, but trying to end the bullshit is part of the play. So, even that is cheating yourself – but who cares of being cheated by oneself? No one else can cheat you as you can cheat yourself. You are the trapper, the trapping and the trapped – in persona. The Absolute persona trapping itself in a relative persona. Who else can make you believe that you have a bloody body as you can make yourself believe in that bullshit?

There's no mother who can do that, there's no father, there's no conditioning. If you would not do what you do to yourself, no one else can do that to you. In the form of your mother, in the form of your father, in the form of your whole world – you betray yourself. But being betrayed by yourself, who fucking cares?

– *The Song Of Irrelevance p154*

K: Neti-neti is always fine – neither-neither. There will be never anyone who will be worth listening to what I say. I think in Radha Ma's (Tiruvannamalai) case there was still an expectation that she can help somebody with energy. And there is something going on with energy, but it's always disappointing. There's always like a child God who wants to find his mother where he can go back and find home with someone and rest forever in the presence.

And you cannot stop it. It will be like this forever. It's like this in every relationship, every romance, every friendship in the school. You thought you found your perfect mate. This is made for me, only for me, your soul mate. All those satsangs in America, people are going for soul mates. Not for truth.

– *The Song Of Irrelevance p105*

अस्तं गतो नैव सदोदितोऽहं
तेजोवितेजो न च मे कदाचित् ।
सन्ध्यादिकं कर्म कथं वदामि
स्वरूपनिर्वाणमनामयोऽहम् ॥ २२॥

Never do I disappear, I am never-never;
Never do I illuminate nor do I not illuminate;
How, then, can I speak of evening, morning and other rituals?!
Unblemished and devoid of maya,
I am the nature of Freedom itself. [4:22]

K: I always try to make it the last talk. I really mean it. I really try to make it the last talk so that no one comes back again. But look how successful I am. [Laughter] Failure! I'm failing even in failing.

How can I go? A master would say, 'I never came, I never can go, I will always be there for you'. That's the doctor again. [Laughter] Whenever you turn your attention, I will be there for you. Ramana was like a doctor. They asked him where will you go when your body will be burnt? What shall we do without you? Ramana said, wherever you lift a stone, wherever you are, I shall be there for you. How can I go? I never came. Sounds good!

– Heaven And Hell p219

Q: When I look at you, I see luminosity. Am I hallucinated?

K: I don't know from where you look. You're right, whatever is – is light. Light is all there is. And sometimes light can present itself in all the different ways. But light is never the way it is presenting itself. So that light you can experience is not the nature of light. But I know what you talk about.

In that sense Arunachala was the biggest master for me. Arunachala, make me bala-bala. It was the last home that I found in the eighties which was light. [Gesturing dramatically] This luminous light, the presence of awareness light, it was – superior. And I was walking around being a messiah of light. Light, Light, Light. You are all light, just shining; you are like a sun walking around.

Then I went to Arunachala to the light of Shiva. I was able to go into the cave and sit there with the perception penetrating the whole mountain. And yes! The whole mountain is pure light. The origin of all universes, of all existence, all the little structures and sculptures and constructions. The whole thing coming out of that light of Arunachala. Being the origin of the whole existence of all possible milky way's and cosmos...

But the moment I saw the light of Arunachala was the origin of everything, there was like – shit. I can experience it, so it can only be a dream. Shit! Even the light of Shiva, the origin of all existence, of all manifestation is all just a dream. What Am I? Shit! No-home, nowhere to land. What to do?

– *Heaven And Hell p215*

असंशयं विद्धि निराकुलं मां
असंशयं विद्धि निरन्तरं माम् ।
असंशयं विद्धि निरञ्जनं मां
स्वरूपनिर्वाणमनामयोऽहम् ॥ २३॥

Know, without doubt, that I am limitless;
Know, without doubt, that I am changeless;
Know, without doubt, that I am stainless;
Unblemished and devoid of maya,
I am the nature of Freedom itself. [4:23]

Q: I cannot follow that...

K: You cannot follow that, as you never followed anything. [Klara laughs] You try to follow something that you cannot follow anyway. You try to understand some mystery of existence, but you will never understand.

There will be total understanding when you are that mystery. Only by being that mystery, there is absolute understanding, only by the total absence of a "me" who is in the idea of "understanding." In that absence, there is absolute understanding without any doubt. But in that doubter, "me," you'll always doubt. Whatever is understanding or non-understanding, you will always doubt. This is a functioning of "me." It has to doubt. Undoubtedly. So let the doubter doubt what the doubter can doubt about.

– *Eight Days in Tiruvannamalai p133*

Q: Why such a waste of power?

K: It's not a waste of power because nothing happens – energy cannot be wasted. When the Parabrahman wakes up, nothing wakes up because it was already there. So, there's nothing to create, so there's nothing to waste. That's why it's inexhaustible – the whole universe, the whole thing is so inexhaustible, because nothing happened. And nothing changes because it's a solid block of what-is. So, there's nothing to waste.

This is eternal life. [Whistling with a bird singing in the background]

– *Worry And Be Happy p70*

ध्यानानि सर्वाणि परित्यजन्ति
शुभाशुभं कर्म परित्यजन्ति ।
त्यागामृतं तात पिबन्ति धीराः
स्वरूपनिर्वाणमनामयोऽहम् ॥ २४ ॥

The wise renounce all meditation;
Renouncing all actions, good and bad,
Drink the nectar of renunciation;
Unblemished and devoid of maya,
I am the nature of Freedom itself. [4:24]

Q: There is no advantage of having fewer desires?

K: No, because for an advantage, it would need one who could have an advantage.

Q: Right, because this really something that we heard all the time, that there is advantage in being more desireless.

K: How can the desirelessness become more desireless than desirelessness? Because you are desirelessness right now. And desire and no-desire are just a shadow, or a reflection of that what is desirelessness. So you cannot get less or more than you are. With or without desires you are still what you are. Good deeds, bad deeds.

– Interview

K: Grace is devoting the devoter, renouncing the renouncer – being what-you-are. Just by being what-you-are, which absolutely doesn't know itself. The absolute absence of any idea of what-you-are and what-you-are-not – your very nature.

Simply by being That, what-you-cannot-not-be, this is renunciation of the renouncer. The dropping of the dropper and nothing else can drop the dropper as you being what-you-are – in nature. The rest is the rest. It cannot give you the rest of what-you-are. The whole restaurant of the world, of light and spirit cannot give you the rest you are looking for. But it seems like, first, second, third and – [makes a popping sound]. From there, no one comes back, as no one came out of That in the beginning. There was never anyone who came out of it.

– The Song Of Irrelevance p68

विन्दति विन्दति न हि न हि यत्र
छन्दोलक्षणं न हि न हि तत्र ।
समरसमग्नो भावितपूतः
प्रलपति तत्त्वं परमवधूतः ॥ २५॥

Where there is neither knowledge nor anyone who knows;
Where prose and poetry are rendered meaningless;
As the all-pervasive essence, absorbed in not-knowingness;
The Avadhut simply prattles about the Truth. [4:25]

Q: It sounds like...

K: It sounds like many things. It sounds like Jesus when he says – 'Me and my father is one, but I am not the father'. It's like 'me' and 'awareness' is one – but I am not the awareness. Just pointing to That – you are That what-is. Like Nisargadatta says – 'I Am That', but not knowing what-it-is. But I Am That – That what is the knowing and That what is the not-knowing. The knower and the not-knower. You are That what is realizing itself.

And you will always 'be'. Wherever 'you' are, you will 'be' – That – which never comes, never goes. You are not that ghost phantom who believes that something has to happen. You cannot help experiencing yourself as that, because your nature is helplessness. You cannot want what you want, you cannot decide what you decide. You cannot realize the way you want to realize yourself because there is no 'one' who could want that.

– Worry And Be Happy p28

K: I was doing karate for twenty years – with the empty hand and now I do the tongue karate – with the empty tongue. First I started with the material, the empty hand and now it's the empty tongue, empty words, empty questions, empty answers.

– Worry And Be Happy p62

Chapter Five

ॐ इति गदितं गगनसमं तत्
न परापरसारविचार इति ।
अविलासविलासनिराकरणं
कथमक्षरबिन्दुसमुच्चरणम् ॥ १॥

 (OM) pervades everything, equally like space;
Without distinctions of high or low;
Being neither manifest nor unmanifest;
How, then, can it be subject to expression
either as a syllable or even a dot?! [5:1]

K: The first notion, the first experience of light, the first Om or sound, is "I." Out of that "I"-thought comes "I am"-ness and "I am so"-ness. But this [fist] is always what is realizing itself as "I" [thumb] "am" [thumb and index finger] "the world" [thumb, index, and middle fingers]. This [fist] you never lose; this you never left. So whether you go from this state [thumb, index, and middle fingers] to this state [thumb and index finger] to that state [thumb], it cannot make you this [fist], as you are this [fist] in any state. Simply this, Heart itself, not knowing what is Heart and what is not Heart.

– *Eight Days in Tiruvannamalai p95*

इति तत्त्वमसिप्रभृतिश्रुतिभिः
प्रतिपादितमात्मनि तत्त्वमसि ।
त्वमुपाधिविवर्जितसर्वसमं
किमु रोदिषि मानसि सर्वसमम् ॥ २॥

The Shrutis proclaim – 'That thou art';
They go on to prove that you are indeed That;
You are free from limitations, the Self itself, pervades all;
Why then, do you,
the identity in all and as all – grieve, O heart? [5:2]

K: You just stay in the 'am I, I am, am I', it just becomes like a sound of Om, like a light and sound, permanent stream of existence. That is like when Ramana said that sound remained, the Shruti in Indian music, this basic sound of a vibration of existence. And the rest of all the other sounds are just like notes on a screen of that. But the basic sound is uninterrupted. So all the other informations are varying, but this is uninterrupted that. And if you can just stay in that, I promise you after whatever time there will be no me any more. Simply staying in that, being that, there is a total annihilation of any idea of any relative I. If you can do that. But you cannot do it. If it will happen it will happen by itself.

– *May It Be As It Is p221*

Q: Is the Shruti still one when the mind is jumping?

K: Ramana talks about the flat line of the Shruti, like the awareness line.

Q: And that's the base of everything?

K: When you wake up in the morning, that's the first and just to stay there in that awareness is the technique they all used. Shruti is the basic tone, the basic sound of Om, staying there and from there all the orchestral, universal information system of sounds are always there. But you just are That – by staying there. That's what they mean by canvas where all the projections, information, differences are projected and it doesn't make you more or less as That.

So that's the first and the last you can experience. Then you just don't move from there. You abide in the first and the last notion. Even that is maybe an effort in the beginning, but after a while, it becomes your nature.

– The Song Of Irrelevance p46

अधऊर्ध्वविवर्जितसर्वसमं
बहिरन्तरवर्जितसर्वसमम् ।
यदि चैकविवर्जितसर्वसमं
किमु रोदिषि मानसि सर्वसमम् ॥ ३॥

Devoid of higher or lower,
I am the same, the identity in all;
Devoid of inner and outer,
I am the same, the identity in all;
Devoid of the sense of oneness,
I am the same, the identity in all;
Why then, do you,
the identity in all, grieve – O heart?! [5:3]

Q: When you speak of deep-deep sleep, you speak of the absence?

K: It's just a pointer that everyone knows. Every night you are that absence. So, know yourself as you know yourself in absence and in the presence – what-it-is. Your nature does not change in anything. It's not that you should only stay in deep-deep sleep.

Know yourself as That knowledge which is with and without the knower. The presence would be the knower. But with and without the knower – you are. That's the knowledge of your nature. The nature That doesn't need to know itself. In the presence, there's a starting point of a knower and all relative knowledge comes with That. All the ideas of what can be known – that's called ignorance.

– *Worry And Be Happy p22*

Q: So what happens is, the mystical states, the mystical experiences, the siddhis, all these are like the candy in the window.

K: They are all just different realizations of what you are. All of this is self-experiencing, but they are not better or worse than a sip of coffee for what you are. So for what you are it doesn't make any difference, there are no levels in it. There is no higher or lower experience. You are experiencing yourself moment by moment in whatever state, and all the seven states are there. You cannot deny them. So not talking about them would not help. I can just point to them, and you have to transcend them all by being what is that what is dreaming them all.

– *May It Be As It Is p142*

न हि कल्पितकल्पविचार इति
न हि कारणकार्यविचार इति ।
पदसन्धिविवर्जितसर्वसमं
किमु रोदिषि मानसि सर्वसमम् ॥ ४॥

There are no concepts, nor conceivability;
Neither is there discrimination between cause and effect;
The Self is beyond rhymes and words;
Why then, do you,
the identity in all, grieve – O heart?![5:4]

K: Whatever can be known or not known, whatever you can imagine, whatever you can give a name to, is all dream. And whatever in that dream can be dreamed and you can experience, can never lead you to that what is the absolute Dreamer. There is no bridge. Thank God that what you are can never be reached, not even by yourself. As it cannot be reached, it cannot be affected. By anything. So there is no cause and no effect in what you are. And that's Advaita, because Advaita means there is no second. And when there is no second, there is no effect from anyone. Who can be affected by what? It needs two for being affected. And effects are only in the dream. So only dream objects are affected by other dream objects. And that continues, like a chain of reactions. Effects, effects, effects.

But you cannot find the cause. The action you cannot find. Energy cannot be found. You can only experience the effects of energy. And not by one of these effects can energy be controlled. Only effects controlling effects. Very effective sometimes. But who cares?

– May It Be As It Is p60

K: All the masters before, they all pointed to that. All the Buddha's pointed to that: there was never any Buddha walking this earth. A Buddha never shows up and can never be realized. And Ramana answered the same when he was asked 'Are you realised?' Ramana said, that what you call Ramana will never realize that what is the Self. And that what is Self is ever realized. Never needs to realize anything. And there is no bridge between that.

He pointed out there was never any master, there was never any Guru who was ever realized. Thank God and praise the Lord and Hallelujah just in case! And you will not be the first one, that I tell you as there was no one before you who ever realized himself. There was never anyone before anyone of you in the whole story of mankind and the whole universe and whole consciousness who ever realized its true nature. Whoever claims that he realized his true nature for sure, is a liar.

– All liars! The absolute lineages of all liars.

Q: What about you?

K: Thank God I don't need to know myself to be myself.

Q: Are you lying too?

K: I'm one of the biggest liars. [Laughter] Whatever can be said is a lie, I said that. And I say a lot! And it doesn't matter.

No, I can just sit and say the same that Buddha and Ramana have been pointing out: that there is no master, no disciple in Reality. I can just point to that. And no master can ever give you what-you-are. No words or any master or whatever can be said can deliver what you are looking for. They cannot even help themselves, all those masters.

– Heaven And Hell p87

न हि बोधविबोधसमाधिरिति
न हि देशविदेशसमाधिरिति ।
न हि कालविकालसमाधिरिति
किमु रोदिषि मानसि सर्वसमम् ॥ ५॥

There is neither knowledge nor ignorance,
nor any meditation;
Nor any differences of place such as here or there;
There is no time or absence of time;
Why then, do you,
the identity in all, grieve – O heart? [5:5]

Q: Absolute ignorance?

K: Doesn't know any ignorance, as absolute knowledge doesn't know any knowledge, but the moment you know one of it, there's relative ignorance and relative knowledge. Relative knowledge and relative ignorance – is misery. You know that.

So, know yourself as you know yourself in deep-deep sleep. The knowledge of what-you-are, you cannot lose and you cannot gain. So, inspite of all the shadow experiences, all what you can call whatever experience, not because. So, being absolute ignorance is not knowing any ignorance. For sure there's no one who's ignorant in ignorance. If there's one who's ignorant in ignorance – that's relative ignorance.

When you are ignorance, you don't even know what is ignorance and what's not-ignorance. So, not knowing ignorance or not-ignorance is the nature of knowledge – and ignorance. That's the nature of nature. That what never knows anything about nature of what-is and what-is-not nature. So, the absolute presence of one who knows or doesn't – That is what-you-are. That, you are, every night and now you try to.

– The Song Of Irrelevance p205

न हि कुम्भनभो न हि कुम्भ इति
न हि जीववपुर्न हि जीव इति ।
न हि कारणकार्यविभाग इति
किमु रोदिषि मानसि सर्वसमम् ॥ ६॥

There is neither pot nor the space within the pot;
There is no body embodying the soul,
nor is there any soul to be embodied;
There is no cause and there is no effect;
Why then, do you,
the identity in all, grieve – O heart? [5:6]

Q: When you say that it is never affected...

K: There is no cause and effect in nature. Only in imaginary phenomenal experiences there is cause and effect, the idea of cause and effect. But for that what is the nature – there is no cause and no effect.

Q: But you experience this...

K: Who?

Q: Me.

K: That is already an imaginary phenomenal experience for sure which is always affected by other imaginary phenomenal experiences. It's always affected; there is a dream of cause and effect. Then there is fear because you fear to be effected.

– Am I – I Am p200

Q: There's something I don't understand. You said there can be a sense of individuality with no one there.

K: Why not?

Q: How can you have a sense of individuality while no one is there?

K: It was before, and why should something change? Like Nisargadatta said in his last ten days there's a little booklet of that—even the last day, one hour before he died, he said that the last traces of individuality were leaving him. What would you say about that?

Q: Is this no one?

K: More or less sense of individuality—why not?

Q: But in this case, there is someone.

K: Yes, of course, there is an absolute one!

Q: No, you said there is no one.

K: What "no one"? There is no person. But there is still the Absolute. As you are, there is no difference. You are still the Absolute who thinks there is a little absolute, little self. But it's still the Absolute. Makes no difference. What?

– *Eight Days in Tiruvannamalai p220*

इह सर्वनिरन्तरमोक्षपदं
लघुदीर्घविचारविहीन इति ।
न हि वर्तुलकोणविभाग इति
किमु रोदिषि मानसि सर्वसमम् ॥ ७॥

Here is only freedom, which is All and undifferentiated;
Devoid of distinguishing concepts of long and short;
Devoid of divisions of circularity and angularity;
Why then, do you,
the identity in all – grieve, O heart? [5:7]

K: You can be here in the relative experience, as you can be in the Absolute tra...la...la... or not, for what-you-are in nature it makes no difference and I can only point to That. The quality of your existence does not depend on the way you experience anything. You have nothing to gain by going to the seventh state or lose by staying in the first. You don't lose anything here and you don't gain anything there. Because you are not a loser and you are not a gainer. You are That what is life – which has nothing to lose in any way of experiencing itself.

— *The Song Of Irrelevance p27*

Q: What do you mean by Reality?

K: Reality is that what is this. Reality knows no difference. In the absolute absence of the word reality and any imaginary reality there is Reality. And there is no difference between Reality and realization for what is Reality. And now talking about what is Reality, you make it an image. You make it an object. And then it becomes a religion. The Reality religion. Or the Truth religion. And then you create all these religions about imaginary so-called images.

— *May It Be As It Is p54*

इह शून्यविशून्यविहीन इति
इह शुद्धविशुद्धविहीन इति ।
इह सर्वविसर्वविहीन इति
किमु रोदिषि मानसि सर्वसमम् ॥ ८ ॥

Here is neither the void nor the voidlessness;
Here is neither purity nor impurity;
Here is neither the whole nor an absence of the whole;
Why then, do you,
the identity in all, grieve – O heart? [5:8]

K: I'm not pointing at the knowingness, I'm pointing at the knowledge. Knowingness is ignorance. It's a realization, but realization is not the Reality. The aspects of realizations are aspects of realizations, not of Reality. It's not different from Reality, but That what is Reality you cannot find in realization because it was never lost. There is no between. The illusion is that you call something illusion. You make yourself apart from something else. Then you become Bonaparte.

— *Am I – I Am p20*

K: I try to take away all the ... even the invisible rugs I pull or I try to pull. Because what-you-are, never needs any landing place or any home or anything. There is an uninterrupted fulfilment of what-you-are. It's never neither empty nor full or anything. There is no-anything that can be full or empty and that what can be anything – is always ignorant. It's always false, whatever can be known.

— *Heaven And Hell p95*

न हि भिन्नविभिन्नविचार इति
बहिरन्तरसन्धिविचार इति ।
अरिमित्रविवर्जितसर्वसमं
किमु रोदिषि मानसि सर्वसमम् ॥ ९ ॥

There is no distinction of different or the non-different;
There is no distinction such as
within, without or the in-between;
Devoid of friend and foe, it is and remains the same in all;
Why then, do you,
the identity in all, grieve – O heart? [5:9]

Q: I am meeting too many happy puppets and they are telling me that I am not happy enough.

K: You are not depressed enough if you ask me [laughter]. You are not deep-rest enough, undisturbable because your nature is rest, what is rest. It never needs to be happy, happiness is just another concept, joy another concept, all of that makes you unhappy. Then you have teachers who tell you that you have to be happier. No. Kill them all! Actually we should kill all the awakened ones. Happy people are the worst, they give hope and hope is hell.

But that's bit too much work. Just be lazy as you are and be what you cannot not be and forget them all and let there be awakened ones or not who fucking cares if there is one who is awakened? It's amazing, people just wake up and they are sharing. Having friends is the worse, they always ask you – How are you?

Enemies are fine because you don't expect anything from them, but friends. You have to be friendly, you have to lie to them all the time, I like you. You don't even like yourself, how can you like someone else? [Laughter] How can you tell somebody I love you? Bloody liars. It looks like inflation of bloody 'I love you'.

'I hate you' makes everyone smile, 'I love you' is always like a bargaining, a business. What do you want? [Laughter]. Naturally, if someone says 'I love you' you think – what does he want? It's like a business proposal. Even God cannot control his willy, who do you think you are?

– Am I – I Am p135

K: You look infinitely and then, at one point, the seeking simply drops because there is a resignation by seeing you cannot find yourself in any place or object or experience. Then it's collapsing. And then you look inward for That which is, but even there, you don't find it within. So there is a "not finding" on the outside and a "not finding" on the inside. So then, the total resignation comes, and you stop – full stop. Then you see you are already That which you are looking for.

— *Eight Days in Tiruvannamalai p137*

न हि शिष्यविशिष्यस्वरूपैति
न चराचरभेदविचार इति ।
इह सर्वनिरन्तरमोक्षपदं
किमु रोदिषि मानसि सर्वसमम् ॥ १० ॥

There is neither disciple nor a non-disciple;
There is no (one) living or not-living;
There is only the state of freedom – The Absolute:
undifferentiated;
Why then, do you,
the identity in all, grieve – O heart? [5:10]

Q: Why did he [Maharaj] say that I am here to make Gurus?

K: Because you believe that you are a disciple and that is a false belief system. Even by trying to become a master, you will be a disciple but by destroying all the ideas that you can ever become what you are, you are the master not knowing the master because it takes even the idea of master away.

Neti-Neti-Neti. Whatever comes gets destroyed, all the rugs get pulled and you have to stay alone as you are. Not even knowing or not knowing who you are. No one else as what you are as nature can be that. Being absolutely independent of any presence of absence of any friends or enemies or any experiences of any kind. That what tries to become that will never become that. That's what they call good company of fearlessness.

– *Am I – I Am 66*

K: It's like, you're a puzzler and there is a big puzzle in front of you. You think you're the puzzler, who is different from the puzzle. But actually the puzzler is part of the puzzle. But the puzzler is always missing one little piece of the puzzle – himself. It's crazy! And sometimes during the day, you forget that you're the puzzler and naturally you become one with the picture. There is no difference between you and the picture, because then there is no puzzler and no puzzle.

– *Worry And Be Happy p81*

ननु रूपविरूपविहीन इति
ननु भिन्नविभिन्नविहीन इति ।
ननु सर्गविसर्गविहीन इति
किमु रोदिषि मानसि सर्वसमम् ॥ ११॥

Without form and formlessness, is it not?
Without difference and non-difference, is it not?
Without evolution and involution, is it not?
Why then, do you,
the identity in all, grieve – O heart? [5:11]

Q: So, the development of consciousness is another nice illusion?

K: Sounds good – evolution. For me it's evil-lution because it's an evil idea. That there has to be a transformation of consciousness. That consciousness gets to a higher level. That only puts consciousness down and makes it a bullshit consciousness because there's a consciousness that needs to transform, that needs to evolve in itself to become what-it-is? What kind of consciousness is that which needs to change?

Q: In an absolute way it doesn't need an evolution...

K: And in the relative way?

Q: There are all kinds of levels...

K: What kinds of levels are that? Shit, shit, shit – levels of shit.

– *Worry And Be Happy p196*

K: You have no name, no form, not even no-form. Because no-form is still a form. No-name is still a name. Whatever you say is not it. You're neither name or no-name. You're neither form nor no-form. You're neither that or that. That's why this Neti-Neti is perfect. It's not whatever you can imagine. The Absolute Dreamer, the Parabrahman can never dream himself and whatever Parabrahman is dreaming himself as Brahman is already false, it's not what he is. Dreaming himself as Brahman. The origin, the source of everything, even being the source is a dream, is false. False, false, false.

– *Am I – I Am p34*

न गुणागुणपाशनिबन्ध इति
मृतजीवनकर्म करोमि कथम् ।
इति शुद्धनिरञ्जनसर्वसमं
किमु रोदिषि मानसि सर्वसमम् ॥ १२॥

Neither by the gunas (tendencies) nor by anything else
am I bound;
How can actions pertaining to this life or any after-life
affect me?
I am the pure, stainless Self, the essence in all;
Why then, do you,
the identity in all, grieve – O heart? [5:12]

K: Thank God life never needs any peace. And that life which needs peace is a piece of shit. Peace never needs peace. The quality never needs any quality and that what needs quality is already too much.

So be what-you-cannot-not-be is pointing to that quality you are which never needs any quality. Which is never-never that what it is. And that needs a quality of life or anything, tries again to make something more pleasant than before.

– *Heaven And Hell p45*

K: Whatever you can point to, whatever you can pronounce is unreal and the unreal will never become the real because the real is never coming never going. In Reality there is no coming there is no going. There is no birth and there is no death and that what can be born is already dead. Only dead is born and only dead can die.

Let the idea of dead die! By being what you are. But any moment you believe you are born, that is the only possible suicide you can commit. Then you have a death experience, every experience is a death experience because life can never be experienced. Whatever can be experienced is death. That death experience can never bring you the life experience which is that what you are. But you try hard to make this death – life. You want to bring life into death.

– Am I – I Am p96

इह भावविभावविहीन इति
इह कामविकामविहीन इति ।
इह बोधतमं खलु मोक्षसमं
किमु रोदिषि मानसि सर्वसमम् ॥ १३ ॥

Here is neither existence nor non-existence;
Here is neither desire nor desirelessness;
Here, the wisdom learned is of the nature of freedom;
Why then, do you,
the identity in all, grieve – O heart? [5:13]

Q: It's like desiring desirelessness...

K: Yes. It's impossible. There is only a wish because wishlessness is there. So it comes out of what it is, the wish is rising from wishlessness, and will go back to wishlessness. Automatically. Naturally. There is a natural rising and going again. And the wishlessness is uninterrupted what it is. So the realizer starts and whatever is realizing, and then it will be gone one day. But by that dropping of the unrealized one, no one becomes realized. So there is enlightenment, but in enlightenment there is no one who becomes enlightened. There is just a drop of the unenlightened one. Naturally, as it was rising, it will drop again. It is already gone now. It cannot even drop any more. It never rose, that's the problem. So we can talk about realization. Realization may happen. But it never creates any realized one.

– May It Be As It Is p92

K: That which is in deep sleep as That which is here, now—Absolute. Absolute from any idea of "to be" or "not to be," in spite of knowing or not knowing, in spite of defining yourself or not defining yourself, you are. Never because. So be That, here, now, what you are in deep sleep, absolutely independent of any idea of existence or non-existence.

– Eight Days in Tiruvannamalai p45

इह तत्त्वनिरन्तरतत्त्वमिति
न हि सन्धिविसन्धिविहीन इति ।
यदि सर्वविवर्जितसर्वसमं
किमु रोदिषि मानसि सर्वसमम् ॥ १४ ॥

Here is the truth, undifferentiated by truths;
Here is neither union nor separation;
Though devoid of all, it is the same in all;
Why then, do you,
the identity in all, grieve – O heart? [5:14]

Q: So what is the one thing that is right?

K: It's never right, not even nothing is right, even truth is a lie. The biggest lie is truth. There is a Zen master who wrote a book, Zen – the biggest lie ever.

Q: So the fact that the truth is a lie, is a truth?

K: It's not a consequence [laughter]. But nice try, that is called logic. The famous logo, in Germany log means lie. Logo has already created another lie.

Q: How is truth a lie?

K: Because it's an idea now, you can pronounce it. Whatever you can pronounce is a lie. If truth is the truth, then what about lies? We always make differences, the polarities. Truth is opposite to untrue. So how can that what is truth which is different from untruth be the truth? It's a relative truth and the relative truth will stay as relative truth. The relative freedom, relative peace is all relative.

Be that what has no idea what it is and what it is not. That what has an idea, already is an idea. An idea has an idea, then it becomes idealistic, it's a list of ideas.

– Am I – I Am p139

अनिकेतकुटी परिवारसमं
इहसङ्गविसङ्गविहीनपरम् ।
इह बोधविबोधविहीनपरं
किमु रोदिषि मानसि सर्वसमम् ॥ १५॥

Here is the Self, having no place, no home and no sheath;
Devoid of association and disassociation;
Here is the Self, devoid of knowledge and ignorance;
Why then, do you,
the identity in all, grieve – O heart? [5:15]

Q: In this association, whatever, of no expectation, no getting –

K: No, it's not "no expectation, no getting." I'm not talking about "no expectation."

Q: Okay, expectation, but not getting.

K: There may be expectations, but who cares?

Q: Some merit, or something is there.

K: Maybe not.

Q: It makes no difference. But I don't even understand.

K: She thinks, "If that German can do it, I can do it too." But there is no one who has done it. I tell you over and over again, I never reached anything, as I never left anything. I cannot reach again what I am. So I didn't reach anything. So from me, for sure, there is nothing to get.

– *Eight In Tiruvannamalai p323*

K: Your nature you can call it restlessness. You cannot rest anywhere. There is no rest for you. There is no peace for you. There will be no happiness for you. No knowledge. None of that what can be named will be there for you. There will always be relative ignorance for you.

And I tell you be happy that you cannot find yourself, not know yourself, never find yourself in anything. What to do? Can you call off the search? No. Because even trying to call off the search is part of the search because you expect by calling off the search, an advantage. Strange isn't it?

– *Am I – I Am p50*

अविकारविकारमसत्यमिति
अविलक्षविलक्षमसत्यमिति ।
यदि केवलमात्मनि सत्यमिति
किमु रोदिषि मानसि सर्वसमम् ॥ १६॥

Change and changelessness, both are untrue;
Purposeful and purposelessness both are untrue;
If truth is the Self alone;
Why then, do you,
the identity in all, grieve – O heart? [5:16]

Q: You haven't undergone any change?

K: No.

Q: No experience of change?

K: There are experiences of change, but no one is changed.

Q: The one is never changed.

K: There is no one. That unchangeable, you make it different again to that which is changing. You want to make a difference. That what can be changed and that what cannot be changed. Even that what cannot be changed is stupid. The same stupid as that what is not Self.

Q: But the Self is unchangeable.

K: But the unchangeable is another concept only. You make it different from that what is a change. That what is unchanged is still part of the dream. Already the spirit is unchanged. So you think the spirit is different from what is this? Who makes a difference?

Q: So there is not something that you call Absolute?

K: I call it Absolute but I don't call it unchanged.

Q: Ok. So the Absolute is not unchanged.

K: It is neither unchanged nor changed.

– *May It Be As It Is p136*

> इह सर्वसमं खलु जीव इति
> इह सर्वनिरन्तरजीव इति ।
> इह केवलनिश्चलजीव इति
> किमु रोदिषि मानसि सर्वसमम् ॥ १७॥

Here is the all-inclusive Conscious Being, the one Absolute;
Here is the ever-present, Undivided Being.
Here is the one and only Immutable Being;
Why then, do you,
the identity in all, grieve – O heart? [5:17]

K: The good thing is no one can comprehend what that is. There is no possible way of understanding it. Because the moment you would understand it, you would not be there. And whatever you do, you try against that. From that what you now believe in. The believer instantly wants to make even that a belief system.

Q: So it's all futile?

K: It's not futile. For who? It's wonderful! This is what you are, this is your realization of what you are and the next is the next. And as the last one didn't deliver, the next one will not deliver what you are. Wonderful! So it's all empty. It's all pffff – the next sip of coffee. The next, the next, the next. The next word flows out and nothing is said and the next listening happens and the next movie happens – and nothing happens.

Q: Ground zero...

K: Yes, you are the zero of the zero. You are what they call the groundless ground, the groundlessness.

– *May It Be As It Is* p22

K: You can shift infinitely between all of that and by all the shifts of differences of experiences, you can never be changed, or gain or lose anything. Because what-you-are, is not more there or less here. That's the quality of life which has nothing to gain or to lose by any experience. So what's more natural as being That, which by being all of that, is unchangeable. Never gaining or losing anything.

– *The Song Of Irrelevance p37*

अविवेकविवेकमबोध इति
अविकल्पविकल्पमबोध इति ।
यदि चैकनिरन्तरबोध इति
किमु रोदिषि मानसि सर्वसमम् ॥ १८॥

Where neither mindfulness nor mindlessness can be validated;
Where neither intention nor intentionlessness can be validated;
If there is just the perpetual Knowledge itself;
Why then, do you,
the identity in all, grieve – O heart? [5:18]

K: Ramakrishna Parahamsa's basic teaching was that I can doubt myself. But prior to the doubter – that I experience myself as a doubter doubting myself – the doubtlessness of the existence has to be there. Without the doubtlessness of the existence, there is no possibility of the presence of a doubter, doubting to exist or not to exist. That's all.

The doubtlessness is the absolute omnipresence, which is never-never – has to-be before even the imaginary doubter can doubt or not doubt. Even the possibility of one who could or could-not can only be there because the doubtlessness of what-is – has to-be. Prior beyond of all presences and absences – That doubtless is. That there can be a presence or absence at all – That has to-be – and That is what-you-are, That you cannot-not-be, and That is realizing itself as all that whatever doubting or not doubting.

– *The Song Of Irrelevance p181*

K: There is a dream of the seer, the scene and what can be seen. And there is always a guest experience – coming, going. That's the presence. And then every night in deep-deep sleep, there is the absence of it. But you still are what-you-are.

In experiencing you are the presence of the seer, the presence of scene and the presence of what can be seen, then there is maybe a disturbance of separation. But by that disturbance of separation, no one is disturbed. You cannot find anyone who is disturbed. Even calling it disturbance is too much. But your nature does not depend on presence or absence of that.

– *Heaven And Hell p135*

न हि मोक्षपदं न हि बन्धपदं
न हि पुण्यपदं न हि पापपदम् ।
न हि पूर्णपदं न हि रिक्तपदं
किमु रोदिषि मानसि सर्वसमम् ॥ १९॥

There is no state of liberation and no state of bondage;
There is no state of virtue, and no state of sin;
There is no state of perfection and no state of imperfection;
Why then, do you,
the identity in all, grieve – O heart? [5:19]

K: When he asked me what is final liberation? That is when there's no one to be liberated – never was, never will be. As there was never any one who needed to be liberated. Who cares if the phantom is liberated? Only the other phantoms.

Moksha is the absolute absence of a necessity of liberation.

Q [Another visitor]: Does That happen to someone?

K: No, never happened to anyone. No one needs to be jealous because it never happened to anyone. No one ever reached liberation. No one ever became himself. Imagine! Does your Self become you? No, because when Self is, you are not.

— *Worry And Be Happy p166*

K: Perfection that needs to be perfect is relative perfection. The absolute Perfection is – there is no need for any perfection to be what it is. But all ideas are that it has to be perfect. Everyone wants to be perfect.

— *May It Be As It Is p225*

यदि वर्णविवर्णविहीनसमं
यदि कारणकार्यविहीनसमम् ।
यदिभेदविभेदविहीनसमं
किमु रोदिषि मानसि सर्वसमम् ॥ २० ॥

If I am always the same, beyond colours and colourlessness;
If I am always the same, beyond cause and effect;
If I am always the same, with and without differences;
Why then, do you,
the identity in all, grieve – O heart? [5:20]

K: In cause and effect, ignorance is the cause and ignorance is effect. The origin of whatever you say is ignorance. From knowledge nothing comes. Just know that, that whatever comes is ignorance and where it comes from is ignorance. Even the origin of whatever is ignorance.

Whatever you can name, whatever you can frame, whatever you can understand – is ignorance. If you can understand the origin and the cause, even the cause is ignorance.

— *Heaven And Hell p137*

K: You cannot want what you want, because That which is wanting it already wanted it. The movie is already shot. So that there can be wanting, out of that wanting, something will happen, because this is part of the movie. It's a cause and effect. There is an action-reaction chain, and everything is interrelated, but no one is there who can want it. Even the wanting, you cannot want. You cannot think before you think. You cannot want before you want.

— *Eight Days in Tiruvannamalai p183*

इह सर्वनिरन्तरसर्वचिते
इह केवलनिश्चलसर्वचिते ।
द्विपदादिविवर्जितसर्वचिते
किमु रोदिषि मानसि सर्वसमम् ॥ २१॥

Here is eternity, where everything is universal Self;
Here is sheer tranquillity, where everything is universal Self.
Devoid of men or other beings, everything is universal Self;
Why then, do you,
the identity in all, grieve – O heart? [5:21]

K: You are the unmovable spectator – the Absolute 'I' – the Absolute seer, who's experiencing itself frame by frame coming from illusionary future and going into an illusionary past. But you're not moving. The frames are coming and going in front of your eyes. Then you make a movie out of it, with an imaginary movement.

You're not moving in it. Never! It's an imaginary movement of frames – moments coming and going. But even to know all of that, you better know yourself what-you-are in nature – That never needs to know the mechanics. It's magic in a way! Just enjoy your show – by being That what is trying or not trying anything – just to realize yourself.

– Worry And Be Happy p67

K: When you are what-you-are – your natural state – is neither born nor unborn. There was no one who was ever born. So who can stop that wheel of incarnation? Was there anything ever incarnated? That's the question. Was there any life that was born, ever? Show me any life which is born!

Q: What we call 'myself'; isn't it that life which we believe in?

K: It's a 'maybe' life. Can that be life? Can you call something life which is born and dies? Can that what is life, die? Would you call something that can die as life?

– Heaven And Hell p125

अतिसर्वनिरन्तरसर्वगतं
अतिनिर्मलनिश्चलसर्वगतम् ।
दिनरात्रिविवर्जितसर्वगतं
किमु रोदिषि मानसि सर्वसमम् ॥ २२॥

The Self, transcending all, is perpetual and all-pervading;
Free from the stain of attachment,
it is immovable and all-pervading;
It is without day or night and is all-pervading;
Why then, do you, the identity in all, grieve – O heart? [5:22]

K: That detachment is so totally attached to that detachment. When I am asked what you do, I say – Be totally attached to what you are, be that absolute being, as you cannot not be attached to what you are, being that attachment itself. You cannot leave what you are.

In absolute identification, there is no separate identification any more, and the separate one is simply dropping – but that cannot be done. That absolute identification that you are That cannot be done – you have to be It! But not by any understanding, not by choice, not by anything, as you are That anyway, as you cannot not be It, that's all! So be It!

– Eight Days in Tiruvannamalai p80

K: Ramana is a rare one who said when there is oneness there is twoness, instantly. It comes together as day and night. Then you shift through all of them or so it seems like but what you are never shifts through anything and what shifts through something is a fisherman who wants to fish something. Always tries to catch a bigger fish, an impersonal fish because he thinks that the impersonal fish tastes better than the personal fish. Both stink. All the fishes stink after a while.

– Am I – I Am p65

न हि बन्धविबन्धसमागमनं
न हि योगवियोगसमागमनम् ।
न हि तर्कवितर्कसमागमनं
किमु रोदिषि मानसि सर्वसमम् ॥ २३॥

Nothing can be freed as nothing is bound;
Nothing can be united as nothing is separated;
Nothing can be reasoned as there is no disputation;
Why then, do you,
the identity in all, grieve – O heart? [5:23]

Q: So the bondage is really the freedom. Because the bondage is the evidence of freedom.

K: Yes, but freedom is just an idea. Freedom is bondage. You will never be free.

Q: As long...

K: There is no as long!

Q: The moment you believe there is a way out, you are already in.

K: In what? Even that doesn't matter. Believing or not believing, does it make you different? It is a joke. It seems like I just remind you that you made a joke and now you have to start to laugh about it. This is your joke! The joke that you believe that you have to know yourself to be yourself. And now to suffer about the joke is quite a drama.

Q: Seven billion must not be wrong if they suffer.

K: If there is two it's already wrong, so whatever one says is wrong. Seven billion wrong or one wrong - whatever can be said is wrong. That's the beauty, that's the entertainment, everything is empty. Whatever you do or don't do is empty.

– *May It Be As It Is p186*

Q: Can you dissolve in oneness? Is that a different way to lose the mind?

K: No. From the oneness, everyone comes back. What is love is oneness, and it always goes back to the separation of a lover and something beloved. Many people go from the relative love to the oneness love, but then a beautiful girl or man comes their way and they step into the same thing again. It's worth nothing anyway. That heaven of oneness is fleeting. It's promising a lot but it's not delivering.

– Eight Days in Tiruvannamalai p17

इह कालविकालनिराकरणं
अणुमात्रकृशानुनिराकरणम् ।
न हि केवलसत्यनिराकरणं
किमु रोदिषि मानसि सर्वसमम् ॥ २४॥

It is inspite and not because of time and timelessness;
It is inspite and not because of atoms and particles;
Absolute Reality is inspite and not because of reason;
Why then, do you,
the identity in all, grieve – O heart? [5:24]

K: It's all too late. You're like a little child in the dark.

Q: It's too late, but still the time is there...

K: Where? No one could ever prove time. You repeat something what you heard about but no one could ever prove time. Time just means two – separation. But no one could ever prove it. The whole quantum physics, the whole scientists could not even find matter.

It may not matter. Maybe there is not even two.

Where is the movement? They can only say sometimes it's a particle, sometimes it's a wave. But they cannot find the movement. Where is the movement? What is moving? And where? And who is observing it? And who is witnessing? If you really look for it, you cannot find anything.

Where is something? The moment you look for it, it's gone. Only when you not look at it, it can be there. But when you look at it, it's gone. Crazy!

– Heaven And Hell p22

Q: So all of this is the Absolute looking for itself…

K: I don't know what happened, that's just a concept too. That's why I say Am I-I Am is the only thing you cannot deny. Even to deny it, you have to be to deny it, that's Ramakrishna's basic teaching. There is this I am which you cannot deny, even to deny it you have to be. There is no way out!

– Am I – I Am p198

इह देहविदेहविहीन इति
ननु स्वप्नसुषुप्तिविहीनपरम् ।
अभिधानविधानविहीनपरं
किमु रोदिषि मानसि सर्वसमम् ॥ २५॥

Here is the Self, devoid of body and bodylessness;
The Supreme state is neither the dream
nor the dreamless deep sleep;
Here is the Supreme, with and without nomenclature;
Why then, do you, the identity in all, grieve – O heart? [5:25]

Q: So I understand you correctly when you say you cannot be what is realizing itself, you mean one is already realized?

K: You already realize yourself. This is your realization.

Q: So everybody is realized?

K: No, there is no 'everybody' in that. Everybody is a realization of that what is everybody. But there is no everybody. That what is everybody doesn't know everybody. So that what you are is nobody. And neither is a body or a no body. It is neither something nor nothing. Even nothing is too much. Or too less. You are that what is nothing, and you are that what is everything. But you are not nothing and you are not everything. And you are not even beyond. You are that what is the beyond. And you are that what it this. You cannot find what you are not. But you can never find yourself in what you find. This paradox is not for any simple me trying to understand it. Because that is not an understanding. This is being what you are. And that is in spite of understanding, in spite of all this tra...la...la....

– *May It Be As It Is p64*

Q: Are we in dream right now? Are you in the dream?

K: Do I have to know that? Who wants to know that? If I say yes, I'm lying and if I say no, I'm lying. The closest to that is that I have absolutely no idea about what I Am or what I Am not, in whatever dream or no-dream.

I can only give these pointers to that what never needs to know anything, or doesn't need to know. But by all the knowing it doesn't know and by all the not knowing, it doesn't not know. All of that are just pointers to what? [silence]

– *Heaven And Hell p185*

गगनोपमशुद्धविशालसमं
अतिसर्वविवर्जितसर्वसमम् ।
गतसारविसारविकारसमं
किमु रोदिषि मानसि सर्वसमम् ॥ २६॥

Pure, infinite and like space;
The Self is the same in all yet independent of all;
It is divested of the essential, the inessential and ills;
Why then, do you,
the identity in all, grieve – O heart? [5:26]

Q: You said that in absolute nothing, there is Absolute...

K: I never said that. Nothing is not Absolute. The nature of nothing is Absolute and the nature of everything is Absolute, but 'nothing' is not Absolute. If 'nothing' would be Absolute, there would be no-everything. If 'nothing' would really be the nature of things, then this would be not what is. Then 'nothing' would be different to this.

How can anything that is different to this be the Absolute without a second? Only that. How can that be? How can nothing be the Absolute? How can emptiness be the Absolute?

Whatever you say or don't say – it is not. It has no 'attribute' or 'no-attribute', neither it has nor it has not. Neither it is nor it is not, it neither exists nor doesn't exist. Whatever you say is false. Whatever you say, whatever you don't say, whatever you hear, think or not think is all false. False, false, false, false, false!

Because whatever you come up with or not come up with needs opposites, needs to exist. Even emptiness needs to exist to be emptiness.

– Am I – I Am p147

Q: What is the essence of consciousness?

K: Consciousness.

Q: Substratum?

K: Consciousness. Why do you have to repeat it? Consciousness. It's like what's the essence of Self? Self!

Q: That's true for everything. The nature of fun is fun...

K: Yeah. That's called noumenon. The nature of beauty is beauty, the nature of knowledge is knowledge, the nature of world is world, the nature of a man is man, the nature of a woman is a woman. It's easy. The nature of real is real. The nature of unreal is unreal. You can go on and on. Everything is as it is.

– Worry And Be Happy p147

इह धर्मविधर्मविरागतर-
मिह वस्तुविवस्तुविरागतरम् ।
इह कामविकामविरागतरं
किमु रोदिषि मानसि सर्वसमम् ॥ २७॥

Here, I am unattached, to virtue or vice;
I am unattached, to the material and the non-material;
Here, I am unattached, to desire and detachment;
Why then, do you,
the identity in all, grieve – O heart? [5:27]

Q: What do you say about Karma?

K: [Teasing] I like it – actually Karma-sutra. I like cow-ma too. No. It's all a Karma of consciousness. But there is no personal

Karma in it. All this is – is an incarnation of that consciousness or energy. Call it energy, all that you see is a vibration of energy. The next moment is the next incarnation of that energy which was incarnated in this moment. This moment is an incarnation of energy that would incarnate in the next moment in a different way - and then and then. But that what is incarnating, getting into this Karma, in-car-nation or in-formation is always That what it is. Life always shows itself in differences, in moment by moment, but That what is life is not different because of it.

– *Am I – I Am p88*

Q: What is the first and last hindrance to find out?

K: There is no hindrance, that's the problem. What can hinder you to be what you are? There are no others. There is no second who can hinder you to be what you are. There was never any hindrance. Hindrances are only in the dream, when you are one of these three. And only God as a creator wants to change his creation. In this (fist) – there is silence. Peace creates peace. So harmony can never be in disharmony. There is no disharmony for harmony. Disharmony can only be in those differences when you landed in one of those landing places. And then you are already in a disharmony of separation. But it is a dream separation. It's a dream disharmony. Any moment you want to change this dream disharmony – you cannot kill it, you cannot get rid of it. Because how can you get rid of a dream? How can you get rid of an illusion? It is not even there. It has no substance. How can you kill it? How can you get rid of something what is not even there? So the main problem is, there is no problem!

– *May It Be As It Is p151*

सुखदुःखविवर्जितसर्वसम-
मिह शोकविशोकविहीनपरम् ।
गुरुशिष्यविवर्जिततत्त्वपरं
किमु रोदिषि मानसि सर्वसमम् ॥ २८ ॥

Untouched by happiness and suffering is the Self;
Untouched by grief and grieflessness is the supreme Self;
Untouched by the guru-disciple relationship is the Self;
Why then, do you, the identity in all, grieve – O heart? [5:28]

Q: I have a dual reaction to it because of the strong sense of sympathy that I feel for my brother-in-law...

K: You didn't feel for him. You had a sense of sympathy for your sister. You only experience for the leftovers, who suffer – they are left over when someone went. Who's more pitiful? The one who is dead or the one who has lost someone? I don't know.

No one grieves for the one who's dead – never. You're always grieving for yourself or your leftover family. Everyone is actually unhappy that he's not the one who died. Then you imagine how it would be when you would die. Maybe you're jealous of the dead person. Why him, not me?

Q [Another visitor]: Ramana just laid down his life when he was fifteen...

K: He imagined what it would be to die. But he didn't die. He went through all the experiences of dying but in none of those experiences what-he-was could die. The body could die, the ideas of spirit could die. All what you can imagine could die but still you are what-you-are. You are Absolute, without all of that you can experience – even without the experiencer you-are. And that cannot die because That was never born. That's what he experienced.

– Worry And Be Happy p202

K: Every tendency, everything that makes a difference is shit and not making a difference is shit. I just point out to the indifference of shit. None of that will make you happy – nothing, not one of that. So, the moment you are, 'you-are' – it's shit. Whatever comes out of that being, out of existence – it produces shit. All relative concepts coming out of that first concept of existence.

What else do I point to? Don't say you will be happy. That's why I get angry because I say you'll never be happy and you expect that you'll get happy, by what I say. You go totally against what I say – since years! I say no one is here to make you happy, because you'll never be happy. There's no happiness which you can experience. But you say [in a whining tone] 'I cannot be happy' and then I say 'Fuck you! Go and kill yourself somewhere else. Who gives a shit?'

I say every moment 'you' can only experience misery but not 'what-you-are' – that's all. And still after fifteen years you say 'But I don't feel happy by that' and then I get a bit pushy.

– *The Song Of Irrelevance p84*

न किलाङ्कुरसारविसार इति
न चलाचलसाम्यविसाम्यमिति ।
अविचारविचारविहीनमिति
किमु रोदिषि मानसि सर्वसमम् ॥ २९॥

There, indeed, is no conception of essence or non-essence;
Of movable or immovable, of identical or non-identical;
The Self is devoid of enquiry and the absence of enquiry;
Why then, do you,
the identity in all, grieve – O heart? [5:29]

K: You can say it's the statelessness that is your natural state, That which has not, and never will have, any state. All the states are from that absolute Source, but That which is the absolute Source has no source. So it's a statelessness wherein all the other states and ideas and images appear.

There is no state without That, but itself, it has no state. You may say there is no place for it, but no place is without it. It is always this absolute essence of existence, never the form or non-form, or whatever you give it as a name or frame or belief system.

I Am That means "I am that—question mark." Absolute question mark. That absolute mystery of what you cannot frame, and as much as you try, you cannot put it into any system. By not finding what you are, whatever you found, in whatever experience, drops. By not finding that absolute experiencer, as that relative experiencer which comes up in the morning is already part of the experience, you cannot be that experience of that experiencer. That absolute experience has to be prior to that. That's all.

Always prior, prior, prior. It's a pointer, but simply go to That which is prior, what they call "the total abstract," "the total substratum." It's a concept, but just the concept that you cannot be a concept.

– *Eight Days in Tiruvannamalai p311*

Q: You were speaking of absolute block of what-is. Does it come with all possibilities?

K: It comes with everything.

Q: And all the possibilities of each person?

K: Each person is just a part of it, a fragment of the total block. It comes with whatever you can imagine. Whatever can be and cannot be. Instantly by that absolute waking up – Bang! – It's there. You can even say this moment is absolute in absolute action and it's a potential of all possible futures and pasts. So, everything is here and now – infinite now.

Q: For no reason at all?

K: It's just a realization of reality. That's a reason enough for me, at least. It doesn't need any reason to-be. It's just a pointer of peace that nothing ever happened. That everything is already there and nothing comes and nothing goes. Nothing is born, nothing will die. Just pointing to the eternal life which is this, what you just experience.

— *Worry And Be Happy p80*

इह सारसमुच्चयसारमिति ।
कथितं निजभावविभेद इति ।
विषये करणत्वमसत्यमिति
किमु रोदिषि मानसि सर्वसमम् ॥ ३०॥

Here is the essence of all essences –
Apparently appearing separate from its own perception;
It has no object of perception other than or outside Itself;
Why then, do you,
the identity in all, grieve – O heart? [5:30]

Q: So, no direct perception?

K: How can that happen? What is direct and what is indirect? You must know. What is in psychology direct and indirect perception?

Q: Direct perception perceives like a baby without a language...

K: Then there is no perceiver and nothing to perceive. How can that be direct? There is no direction in it. Only when there is indirect, there is direct and in baby there is neither – neither direct nor indirect. Otherwise from a position of an indirect perception, you have an imaginary idea of direct perception. From now on, it's all imaginary. It was always imaginary. Even the baby has an imaginary non-perception.

Q: Non-perception?

K: Experiencing no images is still – non-perception. It's still different from perception. Perceiving the absence and perceiving the presence is different – it needs a presence of one. That's too late. It needs a presence of awareness and it's already too late. God is aware to be and then he has a child consciousness and then a grown-up consciousness. The one who has a language to describe what-he-is and an absence of describing of what-he-is. But there is no advantage for a baby.

Q: So, the nature of perception is what?

K: No one will ever know. You will never know – but That is what-you-are. The nature of perception is That perception cannot perceive perception. And whatever the perception perceives – especially the perceiver – cannot be That what is perception. That's why they say That perception is closest to That what-you-are – the eye of God. But the eye of God is not God.

– *Worry And Be Happy p95*

बहुधा श्रुतयः प्रवदन्ति यतो
वियदादिरिदं मृगतोयसमम् ।
यदि चैकनिरन्तरसर्वसमं
किमु रोदिषि मानसि सर्वसमम् ॥ ३१ ॥

In various ways the Vedas proclaim –
The observed universe is like a mirage in the desert;
If there is only One indivisible Self, same in all and as all;
Why then, do you, the identity in all, grieve – O heart? [5:31]

Q: The nature is the Self?

K: It's called Sat and Sat is satisfaction – absolute satisfaction, uninterrupted satisfaction. The absolute absence of any idea of existence, and how existence has to be, and could be, and shall be. All those ideas depend on a dream character. The dream character is a phantom and it has all the ideas of masters and servants and slavery – ideas of how it has to be.

But That what-you-are in nature, has absolutely no idea about itself or anything else. So, your nature would say, it's absolute absence of any presence of any idea of what-you-are and what-you-are-not – the absolute absence of any presence of whatever you can imagine. So, you are not an image. But the moment you try to imagine yourself, you become an image of yourself – like a shadow and when you are the shadow of yourself, you miss yourself – that's called suffering, and longing.

So, you suffer out of bullshit – that you found yourself – that's the misery. It's unavoidable. The moment you found yourself, you know yourself, you suffer – anything. That what-you-are cannot be known by itself but when what-you-are knows itself as a person that is born, any idea, any experience – already there's misery.

— *Worry And Be Happy p14*

विन्दति विन्दति न हि न हि यत्र
छन्दोलक्षणं न हि न हि तत्र ।
समरसमग्नो भावितपूतः
प्रलपति तत्त्वं परमवधूतः ॥ ३२॥

Where there is neither knowledge nor anyone who knows;
Where prose and poetry are rendered meaningless;
As the all-pervasive essence, absorbed in not-knowingness;
The Avadhut simply prattles about the truth. [5:32]

K: All these words, crazy! You start as King-Kong then you want to be the king. Words, words, words. And if no one told you want they mean, you would be [talking gibberish] brmm, brmm, brmm, bam, bam, brmm, zrrppp, brmm. I can talk like that for the whole day [Laughter].

For me it would be the same as the high, profound or brmm... brmm.... There's no difference. Makes no difference. All the day brmm...... is no different than talking all the day about the substratum and the absolute and the highest of the highest. And all the levels of the underlying truth. All the blah, blah, blah, brmm.. brmm.. brmm... The resonance would be no different. Different resonance but that what is resonating to itself would not be different in nature. It would be just resonating to itself in the absolute resonance to that what is – That. It never needs this high – tra...laa...laa... Of this abstraction of abstraction.

But it's fun too. You can talk very high and very profound and then [making sounds of trumpet] The entire spectrum of all the bullshit you can do and none of them makes you more or less as you are. You can be professors and professors of Upanishads with Yoga-vashishta up and down. And you can go to the zoo and play with the monkey. As you play with yourself, or you press an ant between your fingers.

– *Heaven And Hell p159*

Chapter Six

बहुधा श्रुतयः प्रवदन्ति वयं
विषयादिरिदं मृगतोयसमम् ।
यदि चैकनिरन्तरसर्वशिव-
मुपमेयमथोह्युपमा च कथम् ॥ १॥

In various ways the Shrutis declare;
The observer and the observable are like a mirage;
If there is only the One, perpetual Shiva (Absolute);
How, then, and to what, can the Self be compared? [6:1]

K: Only from the reference point of a human, there are comparisons. Then you compare the point of views, from your point of view or my point of view. But already in the vertical spirit, there is no comparison. Comparison only happens in the relative – horizontal or human or personal point of views. Then you can compare. Already in vertical there is no comparison, there is knowing. In no time, you cannot compare.

Q: Knowing or not-knowing...

K: But still it's different from comparison. The non-comparison is different from comparison, so it's relative. A relative vertical, a relative horizontal, then relative awareness. It's all relative. Relative means it's different from something else. The awareness is different from being unconscious – all of that is relative.

– The Song Of Irrelevance p131

K: I destroy the concept that you have to destroy any concept to be what-you-are. I destroy the idea that something has to be destroyed for you to be what-you-are. Nothing has to be changed, nothing has to come, and nothing has to be different for you to be what-you-are.

So I destroy the idea that something has to be destroyed. That is destroying your idea that something is too much – 'You'. You are not too much for anybody. The ego can stay forever, no one cares. No one needs the phantom to go. Only a phantom needs the phantom to go. That what is your nature never needs anything to come or to go for you to be what it is.

And that what needs something to go or to come to be what it is – is a lie. It's a phantom. And it will always try to survive.

Q: So we would come back again and again to have the same fun?

K: I have fun with phantom, that's why it's called a fun-tom; it's not a sad-tom. [Laughter] It's a fun-tasty, that's why it's all fun. Fun-tactic! All fun-tasty. Mirage, all the ME's are me-rage. And they are in a total rage – me-rage.

– Heaven And Hell p96

अविभक्तिविभक्तिविहीनपरं
ननु कार्यविकार्यविहीनपरम् ।
यदि चैकनिरन्तरसर्ववशिवं
यजनं च कथं तपनं च कथम् ॥ २॥

The Self is devoid of both divisibility and in-divisibility;
The Self is devoid of both activity and non-activity;
If it is, the one-and-only,
perpetual all-encompassing Shiva (Absolute);
How, then, can there be worship or how can there be austerity?!
[6:2]

Q: Is it that the formless can only be known in forms?

K: The ultimate can only know itself in something relative as the ultimate cannot know the ultimate. The Absolute never knows the Absolute because for knowing, it needs two. So, it imagines a dream of separation to know different aspects of what-it-is but it will never know its nature. It always has to divide itself as subject-object to know itself. But it will never know its nature. For sure not in any relative way. Absolutely you know that 'you are'. No one can take it away and no one can give it to you. You know that 'you are'.

– *Worry And Be Happy p207*

K: You have to practice until a point where no practice would help you. That by no practice, the suffering would stop. And if in that instant of split-second you see the suffering, that there's no way out of that – the idea drops. The idea that there's a way out of it, that's the 'me'. This little hope idea that one day you would get out of That.

But by all the practices, by all the years of practices, Buddha was a total failure and by being a total failure, failing to reach by all means, the idea of a way out drops. And with no idea of a way out, there's no 'me'. There's a peace which was always there. But this little hope of a way out is the 'me'. This little tendency – the tendency of avoidance – that makes the 'me' and the idea that you really can make it.

Mahabharat is the same – Yudhishthir in hell with the question – If this would be for eternity, are there any tendencies left to avoid that? Then by whatever accident, there was no tendency left. He said – May it be forever, who cares? And then – Okay. But not by his choice – never ever. So, nothing can be done for it. But nothing can be done against it too. If it's meant to happen, it will happen. That you cannot avoid this total moment of despair and you cannot close your eyes any more for That what-is unavoidable. That you are that what is realizing itself and any moment you realize yourself, you realize yourself in separation. You cannot get out of it. That this is discomfort – moment-by-moment. You may call it hell.

– Worry And Be Happy p143

मन एव निरन्तरसर्वगतं
ह्याविशालविशालविहीनपरम् ।
मन एव निरन्तरसर्वशिवं
मनसापि कथं वचसा च कथम् ॥ ३॥

The mind, which is never-never and is all-pervasive;
Is devoid of enormity and lack of enormity;
The mind is, indeed, the eternal,
perpetual all encompassing Shiva (Absolute);
How, then, can it be reached by mind or speech?! [6:3]

K: You are the absolute dreamer who dreamed the whole dream.

But now it's too late. Now you cannot change it any more.

Q: But now I think I am this phantom.

K: Yes, and that's part of this dream. That's the way you realize yourself now in a personal way. But it doesn't make you less, or more. The Energy you are, the Life you are, doesn't get less if it's realizing itself in this relative little me. The experience of being small doesn't make you small. The experience of a little 'me' doesn't make you little. That's the beauty of that what is the absolute Experiencer; it doesn't become what is experienced. It still remains as the Nature it is.

– May It Be As It Is p209

Q: Maharaj says, behind the mind is consciousness...

K: But consciousness is mind.

Q: Do you call the vibrations in consciousness as mind?

K: I call everything as mind. Whatever can be called is mind, everything. You always want to make something what is not mind. That for sure is mind.

Q: Even the body you call it tendencies, you don't use the word body...

K: I call it a cluster of energetic tendencies.

Q: That is again part of mind?

K: It is all mind. Part of mind? All is mind! Even no-mind is mind. So never mind. But he wants to find something that is not mind. And he really minds the mind. Mining the mind, to maybe find something in mind that is not mind. [Laughter] The miner of the mind, which is the mind mining the mind. Creating problems which would not be there without the mind.

And especially the problem that the mind doesn't want to be the mind, that's the biggest problem.

– Heaven And Hell p112

दिनरात्रिविभेदनिराकरण-
मुदितानुदितस्य निराकरणम् ।
यदि चैकनिरन्तरसर्वशिवं
रविचन्द्रमसौ ज्वलनश्च कथम् ॥ ४ ॥

In Self are neither distinctions of night and day;
Nor are there distinctions of rising and setting;
If it is, the one-and-only,
perpetual all-encompassing Shiva (Absolute);
How, then, can there be a sun, moon or fire?! [6:4]

Q: It's nice what you say that samadhi and when you have a cup of coffee is not different.

K: No difference. Yes, a few guys said that, like Nisargadatta or Ramana: all the seven states are different states of realizing yourself, samadhi or not samadhi, relative or not relative, they are all in nature not different. They are all just different ways of realizing yourself. So the quality is always Reality, which is what you are in all circumstances. There is no difference in quality. So the next sip of coffee, the next breathing in and breathing out, is as good as samadhi or not samadhi. Or whatever highest experience you can have. And in nature the highest doesn't know any highest. And the lowest doesn't know any lowest. So in the highest there is no highest and in the lowest there is no lowest.

— *May It Be As It Is p195*

K: This is simply pointing to that absolute unborn you are, which was never in any suffering system. But the first moment you step out of that, by taking any idea or belief system as real, the sufferer starts, the suffering starts. For you, it's unacceptable that there is a second, because you step out of that absolute peace, out of the freedom from a second, into that idea of "a second," and then there is war. Even if you call it "love," that love is war. The defence system starts, the conserving of whatever is there then, as you make an individual existence, a separate being.

Even this idea becomes so real, because whatever you give your attention to is reality. Whatever you take as real is real. So at the moment that you take that separation as real, it is as real as it can get. Only when That which is awareness turns around to That which is awareness, it's like a mirror that is totally mirroring That which is prior They call it "the inner sun rising," but this has no cause, it comes and goes, not by any effort, not by any doing or not doing in front of it. So in spite of all your effort, you are, but you cannot avoid any effort. This paradox you cannot solve.

That helplessness—to see that as paradise—that's what I'm sitting here for. I'm pointing to That which you are, that helplessness, as there is no second.

– *Eight Days in Tiruvannamalai p294*

गतकामविकामविभेद इति
गतचेष्टविचेष्टविभेद इति ।
यदि चैकनिरन्तरसर्वशिवं
बहिरन्तरभिन्नमतिश्च कथम् ॥ ५॥

Here is neither desire nor desirelessness;
Here is neither activity nor inactivity;
If it is, the one-and-only,
perpetual all-encompassing Shiva (Absolute);
How, then, can differentiations
such as exterior or interior apply to it?! [6:5]

K: It's very easy and natural to tame the bull – by being the bull. But the moment you have the bull, the bull controls you. The bull leaves you with a bloody nose.

Q: Does the same apply to desire?

K: Everything. When you are the desirer, the desiring and the desired, then you are That what-you-are. There's no desire any more, there's no ownership of desire. There's still desire but – you are That – the desirer, desiring what can be desired. Then there's no harm in it, you cannot suffer about it when there's no separation in separation. Then there's an experience of separation but in nature there's no separation. Yes there is, but there's not. This is the end of suffering.

The same is with the mind. When you are mind, you cannot suffer about the mind. Only when you have mind, you suffer. It's all ownership. If you're a relative owner, you suffer. When you're the absolute owner, there's no possibility of suffering. And there's no bridge. There cannot be 'half' ownership or something. You are what-you-are – fine. If you are not – poor 'me'.

– *Worry And Be Happy p190*

Q: Which manifests itself in living as total ease of existence?

K: Total ease? No. The Ease cannot be experienced.

Q: Which cannot be experienced, but which is the Ease itself.

K: But that is not an experience, that is your Nature. It's not an experience. Whatever is 'ex', it's an ex-ternal dream. But that what has no inside and no outside cannot be experienced.

– *May It Be As It Is p115*

यदि सारविसारविहीन इति
यदि शून्यविशून्यविहीन इति ।
यदि चैकनिरन्तरसर्वशिवं
प्रथमं च कथं चरमं च कथम् ॥ ६॥

If the Self is devoid of essence and lack of essence;
If it is without void and non-void;
If it is, the one-and-only,
perpetual all-encompassing Shiva (Absolute);
How, then, can there exist
any first or how can there be any last?! [6:6]

Q: Sometimes there's a void, a feeling of complete emptiness. It's like there's nothing to cling on to. Once I had a panic attack with this sense of emptiness. It seems contradictory. Why does that happen?

K: That's what you are longing for – that's grace but when that happens, you piss in your trousers.

Q: Why?

K: Because 'you' cannot exist in there. It's the most dangerous absence. The 'me' cannot exist in the absence of the second. It's impossible. Even Jesus went into the desert for forty days. He went not to the desert but to the void and then the mind came back, the devil tempting him.

– *The Song Of Irrelevance p171*

Q: When you say 'realize yourself'...

K: No, I don't say that! I say 'what you are has to realize itself'.

Q: This is what I mean, I am paraphrasing.

K: And there will be no end to it. There was no beginning and there will be no end of it. The next sip of coffee is the realization of what you are. I don't say you have to realize yourself. It is the realization.

– *May It Be As It Is p142*

यदिभेदविभेदनिराकरणं
यदि वेदकवेद्यनिराकरणम् ।
यदि चैकनिरन्तरसर्वशिवं
तृतीयं च कथं तुरीयं च कथम् ॥ ७ ॥

If Self is the negation of difference and non-difference;
If it is the negation of the knower and the knowable;
If it is the-one-and-only,
perpetual all-encompassing Shiva (Absolute);
How, then, can there be
a third (state of consciousness) or any fourth?! [6:7]

Q: I love the fact that everyone's nature is the same...

K: Call it stupid, but everyone is stupid.

Q [Another visitor, laughing]: She really likes that everyone is as stupid as I am...

K: That's fun! We are one in stupidity. As no one can know himself, he must be very stupid and I sit here and tell you, enjoy the stupidity – that's all. Because it will never change. You are knowledge, which will never know itself and from the relative position, it must be stupid. It cannot know itself – How stupid can it be? But from that position of knowledge, it is absolute. Because even knowledge doesn't know there is knowledge, or who has to know itself or not.

So the absence of anyone who is or is-not, is not so bad. Not good either, but not so bad.

– The Song Of Irrelevance p35

K: That's why I say, the shit reacts and shit always has differences of shit. The difference of shit between the personal shit and the impersonal shit and even that beyond shit. Shit, shit, shit. And only that shit reacts, because reactions are only reactions of action, but action never reacts to anything. Only in the realization there are differences of reactions from different reference points. But in the Absolute – that what is That – it's absolutely indifferent on how it reacts. It makes no difference.

– The Song Of Irrelevance p96

गदिताविदितं न हि सत्यमिति
विदिताविदितं नहि सत्यमिति ।
यदि चैकनिरन्तरसर्वशिवं
विषयेन्द्रियबुद्धिमनांसि कथम् ॥ ८ ॥

> *Whatever can be spoken or unspoken is not the truth;*
> *Whatever is knowable or unknowable is not the truth;*
> *If it is the-one-and-only,*
> *perpetual all-encompassing Shiva (Absolute);*
> *How, then, can there be*
> *objects or senses, intellect or mind?! [6:8]*

K: As deep as you can go with your realization, it's a lie. As profound as it can get, it's a lie – lie, lie, lie. Every master is a lie and every disciple is a lie. Whatever can be said is a lie, whatever can be experienced is a lie. Lie, lie, lie. The question is – was there any master who ever helped anybody? Do you really think the Self needs any help from a master?

— *Worry And Be Happy p23*

Q: This what is called split-second, is it same as recognition?

K: No, it's not recognition. It's the Absolute knowledge that what you can-be, cannot be known — which was always there and is not something new. Splitting the second is destroying the hope, that by whatever, you can know yourself. That's the split second.

Q: So the split-second is the recognition that the phantom never existed?

K: No. It's simply being what-you-are — that's the split second and by being what-you-are — everything-is. There is nothing but what-you-are and that is splitting the second and not by any other thing you can split the second. Just by being what-you-cannot-not-be and that is what-is. That is splitting the second — the idea of duality. Just by being what-you-are and not by anyone who is splitting the second.

— *The Song Of Irrelevance p28*

गगनं पवनो न हि सत्यमिति
धरणी दहनो न हि सत्यमिति ।
यदि चैकनिरन्तरसर्वशिवं
जलदश्च कथं सलिलं च कथम् ॥ ९॥

In neither space nor air lies the truth;
In neither earth nor fire lies the truth;
If it is the-one-and-only,
perpetual all-encompassing Shiva (Absolute);
How, then, can there be
a cloud, and how, then, can there be rain?! [6:9]

K: The scientists they say they cannot find matter. So they created an idea of matter. But if you look for it, it's not there. But you have to exist even not to exist. Even that there can be no matter; you have to be that what you are. So it's like a total confirmation, moment by moment, even that you cannot know yourself, you have to know yourself as That. This is not like what you can doubt. Even that you can doubt to doubt, you have to exist. Prior to the doubter. And beyond the doubtful I, you are. Because otherwise there could not even be a doubter doubting himself.

– *May It Be As It Is p53*

यदि कल्पितलोकनिराकरणं
यदि कल्पितदेवनिराकरणम् ।
यदि चैकनिरन्तरसर्वशिवं
गुणदोषविचारमतिश्च कथम् ॥ १०॥

If it is the negation of imagined worlds;
If it is the negation of imagined gods;
If it is the-one-and-only,
perpetual all-encompassing Shiva (Absolute);
How, then, can one talk of good or evil?! [6:10]

Q: Are all the mythological stories fragmentation of the mind?

K: It's all a psychological explanation of how you are, how Shiva works in you. I'm just pointing out that it's all the nature of the Self – different tendencies, patterns of Shiva. So, even when Shiva gets married, he gets jealous like you. In the Bible, there are similar stories of God getting jealous and having revenge. It's everywhere. It's just a pointer to the Self in its different facets of experiencing itself. So, even God himself is not safe. If he exists, he gets the same bullshit as everybody. No way out.

– The Song Of Irrelevance p73

Q: You said that the one we imagine is already imagined...

K: Yeah. The absolute seer is imagining a relative seer. So, out of the absolute seer, the Parabrahman, he imagines Brahman. And already Brahman is an imagination of Parabrahman and only the Parabrahman is real. The Parabrahman not knowing reality and that's the nature of reality. For reality, there is no reality. There is not even an idea of reality and only in unreal; there are ideas of reality – of real and unreal. In reality, there is no such thing as real or unreal. It doesn't even know itself.

So, Parabrahman is Brahman not knowing itself in its absolute nature. But the moment he knows himself, he becomes relative – relative creator, creating relative ideas of imaginary events and worlds and universes.

– Worry And Be Happy p94

मरणामरणं हि निराकरणं
करणाकरणं हि निराकरणम् ।
यदि चैकनिरन्तरसर्वशिवं
गमनागमनं हि कथं वदति ॥ २१॥

If it is the negation of death and deathlessness;
And the negation of doing and non-doing;
If it is the-one-and-only,
perpetual all-encompassing Shiva (Absolute);
How, then, can one speak of coming or going?! [6:11]

Q: So, you don't have a story?

K: The phantom always has a story, but who cares if the phantom has a nice story or a bad story? It was always a phantom that was unrealized and whatever the phantom realizes is a phantom realization. It's called fun-tom – have fun with it because it's a never ending story of a phantom who believes in himself and then believes in being realized or not realized. Who cares about an enlightened phantom? Only the other phantoms. It always needs a community of ignorant ideas and one of them maybe is a master-ignorant. The master of ignorance! There are no masters of knowledge. How can there be a master of knowledge? How can there be a master of Heart? You can only be a master of shit. [Laughter]

And I call it shit, because it is shit – compared to what is your chit – the knowledge, whatever you realize, whatever you know, whatever has a knower or can know – is shit. Even knowing himself, is shit – shit knowing shit. Sat-shit-ananda. Sometimes it's unavoidable, the phantom will always carry a story and sometimes it's a story of 'no-story' – the story of being unborn. Even that is a story. Even Osho's grave – never born, never died – is a story. What to do with it? I leave you my dream! Okay. [Laughter] Why not?

— *Worry And Be Happy p26*

Q: I feel guilty about not doing things…

K: Then you are not lazy, then you just resist. But who gives a shit about what you said a minute ago? All the promises you gave to yourself. Now you define yourself as lazy – that's too much work. You better be really lazy because you are too lazy to be lazy. Right now you are working too much on your laziness. I am too lazy to be lazy because it's hard work to be lazy.

— *Worry And Be Happy p162*

प्रकृतिः पुरुषो न हि भेद इति
न हि कारणकार्यविभेद इति ।
यदि चैकनिरन्तरसर्वशिवं
पुरुषापुरुषं च कथं वदति ॥ १२॥

Distinction of prakriti (phenomenon) and purusha (noumenon)
does not exist here;
Nor the difference between cause and effect;
If it is the-one-and-only,
perpetual all-encompassing Shiva (Absolute);
How, then, can there be talk of Self or non-self?! [6:12]

Q: What is the true understanding of the world?

K: The world is there the moment the 'I' appears. Out of this 'I' the spider creates the world surrounded by creation, then the 'I am' as formless consciousness. Then the creative force of the 'I am' creates all this information, which we call world. So this information of universe or world is consciousness in form, coming out of the non-form of formless consciousness. Consciousness creates by simply getting into form. That which is world is actually consciousness in action, like Shiva dancing with himself and creating this universe out of his dance. The essence of everything that is form and non-form is consciousness. All there is, is consciousness, as cosmic consciousness.

– *Interview*

तृतीयं न हि दुःखसमागमनं
न गुणाद्द्वितीयस्य समागमनम् ।
यदि चैकनिरन्तरसर्वशिवं
स्थविरश्च युवा च शिशुश्च कथम् ॥ १३ ॥

Where no suffering arises due to infancy (third stage);
Nor the suffering of youth (second stage)
which arise due to gunas (tendencies);
If it is the-one-and-only,
perpetual all-encompassing Shiva (Absolute);
How, then, can there be any infancy, youth or old-age?! [6:13]

K: People always ask 'what do you think about unknotting the karmic knots? That's Vedanta. Your tendencies - unknotting them by techniques, by meditation or something. You come to me, we are doing the opposite! I put so many knots in your bloody brain that you cannot even imagine that they ever will be gone. It's all knotty-knotty. Because succeeding by unknotting knots makes the first knot, that there is one who has knots, stronger and stronger. No, I go the opposite way. I make so many knots for you; maybe there is a point of giving up even trying to unknot them. Because then laziness is there, your nature. The laziest of the laziest.

– *May It Be As It Is p39*

Q: I assume being alive is a speck from coming out of a woman till buried into the ground...

K: Being alive is already a punishment because you get a life sentence and on top of a death penalty [laughter].

Q: Some people would call it annihilism.

K: No, it's just absolute irrelevant. When there is an 'ism' it's already a chism. It's all if, if, if and it's all fiction. It is like it is anyway so saying if, if, if is just a game.

Q: So it's all a story...

K: It is his story.

Q: Who is he?

K: The phantom, the guest who comes without being invited. Then this guest has a story and then he has other guests around. Then he has guests talking about their story and guess what would happen. It's all guessing and by guessing they become guests.

– Am I – I Am p178

ननु आश्रमवर्णविहीनपरं
ननु कारणकर्तृविहीनपरम् ।
यदि चैकनिरन्तरसर्वशिव-
मविनष्टविनष्टमतिश्च कथम् ॥ १४॥

It is without caste and stage of life;
It is without cause and effect;
If it is the-one-and-only,
perpetual all-encompassing Shiva (Absolute);
How, then, can there be
anything perishable or imperishable?! [6:14]

Q: Is there no reason?

K: I didn't say there is no reason. I just said it comes anyway – with or without reason. And the next picture doesn't have to make sense as the picture before never needed to make sense. It's an expression of senselessness. The innocence sensing itself in a chain of events – personal or impersonal or anything. All sensations are sensed by That in-no-sense(innocence). Your very nature is the in-no-sense, realizing itself in senses. There's a sensor, sensing what can be sensed – all that is sensed by what-you-are – without any censorship and not censoring what is sensed. The sensor is sensing what can be sensed.

It's the nature of the sensor to censor. Then there's a story of censorship. It wants to make it a special sense. Like Constans wants to make a special sense of real life, because he has a censorship up here. This cannot be it, so it has to be something better, something more. You make a censorship – comparison. This is not it, there has to be something what is more real – that's called censorship. That's called mind and the nature of mind is always censoring – judging how it is. That's one way of realizing yourself. Does it make you more or less? Or does it matter?

— *Worry And Be Happy p127*

ग्रसिताग्रसितं च वितथ्यमिति
जनिताजनितं च वितथ्यमिति ।
यदि चैकनिरन्तरसर्वशिव-
मविनाशि विनाशि कथं हि भवेत् ॥ १५॥

The destroyed and the un-destroyed, both are false;
The born and the unborn, both are false;
If it is the-one-and-only,
perpetual all-encompassing Shiva (Absolute);
How, then can there be
the perishable or the imperishable?! [6:15]

K: That is Nisargadatta's ultimate medicine: You will not find the knower. You will not find the loser, as you cannot find the finder. There was in the first place no loser, so out of not finding the loser, you cannot make a gainer.

I can just repeat, repeat, repeat.

Q: On what basis do we say that your nature is unborn and uncreated and eternal?

K: Even that unborn is too much. It's a lie. If you would be the unborn, you would still be too much. There is still one who is unborn and then experiencing all this but he is not involved. Then you are in the world but from not the world and all of that. But you are still one too many who is not involved. It's all [blowing in the wind]...

– *Heaven And Hell p109*

पुरुषापुरुषस्य विनष्टमिति
वनितावनितस्य विनष्टमिति ।
यदि चैकनिरन्तरसर्वशिव-
मविनोदविनोदमतिश्च कथम् ॥ १६॥

It has no distinctions of masculine or non-masculine;
Nor does it have distinctions of feminine or non-feminine;
If it is the-one-and-only,
perpetual all-encompassing Shiva (Absolute);
How, then, can there be
pleasure or lack of pleasure?! [6:16]

K: It's amazing, the competition never stops. The moment you wake up, even when there is no one around, you compete with yourself. There is already a competition, who is ruling today? The one who wants to wake up quickly or the one who wants to stay in bed? There are many definers waking up in the morning and everyone wants to be the main definer today, and has a concept of what is better for today – What to do. Competition! Who rules today? My mother or my father or me? My genes or my understanding? Out of what should I live today? Out of that – I am not? Or out of that – I am? What is my basis today? Then you start your baseball.

At first you have to remember what-you-are, a man or a woman. That's already a big decision every morning.

– *Worry And Be Happy p31*

K: In relative sense, awareness is better than the body experience. So, if you can stay there, good luck! I give a shit, if you ask me. So, all this precious choiceless awareness that is mentioned in the books, is fine, but it's only fine because no one needs it. If you really would need to be there, to be what-you-are, you still would be fucked by yourself in a delusion of a dream.

So, be aware that you don't need to be aware. Be happy that you don't need to be happy. Enjoy, that you don't need to enjoy. All these paradoxes are the pointers to the paradox. Know that you don't have to know. Stay in that knowledge that you don't have to know – to know. And that one who needs to know, to know – bye bye. It came and it will be gone. But what-you-are will still be what-it-is.

– *The Song Of Irrelevance p133*

यदि मोहविषादविहीनपरो
यदि संशयशोकविहीनपरः ।
यदि चैकनिरन्तरसर्वशिव-
महमेति ममेति कथं च पुनः ॥ १७॥

If it is free of delusion and depression;
If it is free of doubt and grief;
If it is the-one-and-only,
perpetual all-encompassing Shiva (Absolute);
How, then, can there be
any 'I' or 'mine'?![6:17]

K: Whatever I do is trying to destroy the falsity in front of you. But the instant you are what you are, there was not even an idea of falsity. Or right and wrong. Or something that has to be changed. Even someone going to Ramana and claiming to be a disciple, who cares? For that there is the absolute 'Who cares'. But if you ask me, that relative one, and I see myself being trapped in that idea that he can attain himself by just behaving like Ramana, then I have to hit him, or myself, because I don't see anyone else. So if I hit someone I hit myself. So if I destroy all the teachers, I destroy all my own ideas of teachers. It's not that I see any Ramana or someone who is false. I just see myself in that delusion of suffering about an image. So I rather destroy it. I do my best, but still I don't expect anything to come out of it. It's all futile. So it has to be more like fun. It's an entertainment. I cannot take it seriously. But the moment this energy is there, it's very serious. But it's an empty seriousness, it's an empty energy.

– *May It Be As It Is p109*

ननु धर्मविधर्मविनाश इति
ननु बन्धविबन्धविनाश इति ।
यदि चैकनिरन्तरसर्वशिवं-
मिहदुःखविदुःखमतिश्च कथम् ॥ १८ ॥

If it is the annihilation of virtue and vice;
And the annihilation of bondage and freedom;
If it is the-one-and-only,
perpetual all-encompassing Shiva (Absolute);
How, then, can there be
any suffering or absence of suffering?! [6:18]

K: In deep-deep sleep you are that happiness without the experience of the one who is happy or unhappy. At first you experience the unhappy one and then by effort, you come to the absence of the unhappy one. That you call happiness. Then you define – this is happiness and that is unhappiness. Then in deep-deep sleep, you are That what is your nature, you can call it happiness itself which is inspite of the presence or absence of the one who is happy or unhappy – what-it-is. But you cannot say what happened. There was even no one who was 'not'. That's more the nature of – what-you-are. The happiness that's inspite.

– *Worry And Be Happy p211*

K: God not knowing himself, he is awareness, he is I Amness and he is the world and there is no difference in it. This is the end of separation but in all the first three, there is separation. But the way back is like you come out. You come back from the unknown to someone who knows himself. God knows himself – God oh God! Then he becomes out of that a lover and by loving, he comes from unknown to someone who knows himself. God knows himself –

God oh God! Then he becomes out of that a lover and by loving, he creates a beloved – in his love affair.

And how to get out of that love affair? How to break this hypnotic love affair with yourself? First you drop the beloved, then only loving happens – loving as oneness. Then you see that even loving is not it. Then you remain as the lover himself, being the origin himself, but from there, you can start again.

So by grace alone – not even God can help himself, he just ceases away in to the total black sun – which never knows the sun – it's being the sun. The black sun is the sun, not knowing any sun. From the black sun, only what-is, the sun-is and whatever-is – is That.

– The Song Of Irrelevance p67

न हि याज्ञिकयज्ञविभाग इति
न हुताशनवस्तुविभाग इति ।
यदि चैकनिरन्तरसर्वशिवं
वद् कर्मफलानि भवन्ति कथम् ॥ १९ ॥

No distinction of sacrifice and sacrificer exists here;
Nor the distinction between fire and the offerings offered to it;
If it is the-one-and-only,
perpetual all-encompassing Shiva (Absolute);
How, then, can there be
any rewards of (one's) actions?! [6:19]

K: I cannot change what you are. I have nothing to give and nothing to share here. The Absolute you are doesn't need anything from me, from That which is sitting here talking. It cannot add something to what you are. I'm always pointing out that there is no teaching, no teacher, and no disciple. Whatever I say is a total pointer to that, if I am in a good position. The rest is—I don't know. So by grace, you are sitting here and I am, by grace, sitting here, and grace is all there is. And grace talks to That which is grace, telling grace, "Don't wait for grace, because grace will not come."

Q [A visitor]: My name is Grace! [Group laughs]

Q [Another visitor]: Thank you for coming...

Q [Another visitor]: Grace just arrived!

Q [Another visitor]: Have another coffee!

K: So don't wait for grace, because grace is already here, and grace will never come because grace is what you are. Whatever is, is grace. So you'd better not wait for it, because it will never come. It's already here. It never left you, so you cannot gain it back. You cannot lose what you are, as you are grace itself.

– *Eight Days in Tiruvannamalai p108*

ननु शोकविशोकविमुक्त इति
ननु दर्पविदर्पविमुक्त इति ।
यदि चैकनिरन्तरसर्वशिवं
ननु रागविरागमतिश्च कथम् ॥ २० ॥

It is verily free of grief and absence of grief;
It is free of pride and absence of pride;
If it is the-one-and-only,
perpetual all-encompassing Shiva (Absolute);
How, then, can there be
any attachment or non-attachment?! [6:20]

K: You only want to be enlightened because you want to make a business out of it. That's a phantom business. A holy business. And then you are one enlightened one who talks to other unenlightened ones. Then you are in the holy business. So it's all about money. There is nothing without that, money.

Q: So even this Ramana business was for money?

K: Ramana? Ramana had no business. That he always said, I have no business here.

Q: So there is something which is not for money or business?

K: No, everything is for money. Even bhakti is business. Jnani is business. You only want to understand because by understanding you want to buy yourself. Because then you think you have enough spiritual money inside that you can pride yourself.

– *May It Be As It Is p167*

न हि मोहविमोहविकार इति
न हि लोभविलोभविकार इति ।
यदि चैकनिरन्तरसर्वशिवं
ह्याविवेकविवेकमतिश्च कथम् ॥ २१॥

No distinction of illusion or freedom from illusion exists here;
Nor distinction of greed or freedom from greed exists;
If it is the-one-and-only,
perpetual all-encompassing Shiva (Absolute);
How, then, can there be
discrimination or lack of discrimination?! [6:21]

Q: So whenever one goes through the experiences - some of them call them calamities, changes, transformations -even to say all that is imaginary?

K: Bogus!

Q: You haven't undergone any change?

K: No.

Q: No experience of change?

K: There are experiences of change, but no one is changed.

Q: The one is never changed.

K: There is no one. That unchangeable, you make it different again to that which is changing. You want to make a difference. That what can be changed and that what cannot be changed. Even that what cannot be changed is stupid. The same stupid as that what is not Self.

Q: But the Self is unchangeable.

K: But the unchangeable is another concept only. You make it different from that what is a change. That what is unchanged is still part of the dream. Already the spirit is unchanged. So you think the spirit is different from what is this? Who makes a difference?

– May It Be As it Is p136

Q: So, the development of consciousness is another nice illusion?

K: Sounds good – evolution. For me it's evil-lution because it's an evil idea. That there has to be a transformation of consciousness. That consciousness gets to a higher level. That only puts consciousness down and makes it a bullshit consciousness because there's a consciousness that needs to transform, that needs to evolve in itself to become what-it-is? What kind of consciousness is that which needs to change?

– Worry And Be Happy p195

त्वमहं न हि हन्त कदाचिदपि
कुलजातिविचारमसत्यमिति ।
अहमेव शिवः परमार्थ इति
अभिवादनमत्र करोमि कथम् ॥ २२॥

Never was there any 'you' nor an 'I';
The discrimination of family and race is false;
I am indeed Shiva, the ultimate Truth;
How, then, should I worship?!
To whom do I bow?! [6:22]

K: You are That what is life and life has to live life – in whatever possible way. Sometimes is not attractive the way you live life. But still you have to live life in that way. What is the problem? You will never be free. How can one become free? There was never anyone who was born. What is there to be free from?

— *Worry And Be Happy p131*

K: You are Self-guilty. You woke up and by waking up you became aware of what you are. You became aware to exist and from there on you start realizing yourself. So you cannot blame anybody else. There is no God, no devil, no family, no parents whatever you can blame that you have to realize yourself moment by moment. From this point, or that point, or the other point it doesn't matter. You are just that what you are realizing itself in that way right now and later in another way.

— *Am I – I Am p146*

गुरुशिष्यविचारविशीर्ण इति
उपदेशविचारविशीर्ण इति ।
अहमेव शिवः परमार्थ इति
अभिवादनमलं करोमि कथम् ॥ २३ ॥

There is no distinction of guru or disciple;
Nor is here any teaching;
I am indeed Shiva, the ultimate Truth;
How, then, should I worship?!
To whom do I bow?! [6:23]

K: I cannot change what you are. I have nothing to give and nothing to share here. The Absolute you are doesn't need anything from me, from That which is sitting here talking. It cannot add something to what you are. I'm always pointing out that there is no teaching, no teacher, and no disciple. Whatever I say is a total pointer to that, if I am in a good position. The rest is—I don't know. So by grace, you are sitting here and I am, by grace, sitting here, and grace is all there is. And grace talks to That which is grace, telling grace, "Don't wait for grace, because grace will not come."

– *Eight Days in Tiruvannamalai p122*

न हि कल्पितदेहविभाग इति
न हि कल्पितलोकविभाग इति ।
अहमेव शिवः परमार्थ इति
अभिवादनमत्र करोमि कथम् ॥ २४॥

Division between bodies is mere imagination;
Division between places is mere imagination;
I am indeed Shiva, the ultimate Truth;
How, then, should I worship?!
To whom do I bow?! [6:24]

Q: So, even the phantom is a thought?

K: It's just a popping up thought with all the surrounding thoughts. It's like a sun surrounded with planets of secondary thoughts. It's like the main thought 'I', and then it gathers a universe of other thoughts. That's called the cluster – 'me'. A cluster of concepts which are the functioning of a 'me', of a personality. It's just like a cluster of concepts. And when this body dies, this cluster just disappears and the person was never there. It was just a cluster of ideas.

Q: So, there is no phantom?

K: A cluster of ideas is the phantom – of a personal story – that's all. Just an energetic cluster of memory effects, of stories – past, present and future stories. The whole blah, blah, blah – 'me' – coming from another cluster of blah, blah, blah. Cluster creating clusters.

– *Worry And Be Happy p157*

K: You will always talk to yourself – if you like it or not. You cannot stop talking to yourself. You realize yourself by talking to yourself and explaining what-you-are. You have to explain the door that there can be a door, you have to explain the universe that there can be a universe. You have to give it a name otherwise you cannot experience it. This is the way of realizing yourself in all the different ways. How else can you experience your finger if you don't call it a finger?

You can only realize yourself in differences. By not giving it a name, there's no finger, you don't even see it. Like a baby that doesn't see any world. Then slowly by words, it starts seeing the world more and more. It puts a pattern of a world together – like a puzzle. Without naming something, it's not there. It's amazing.

– Worry And Be Happy p158

सरजो विरजो न कदाचिदपि
ननु निर्मलनिश्चलशुद्ध इति ।
अहमेव शिवः परमार्थ इति
अभिवादनमत्र करोमि कथम् ॥ २५॥

Neither with passion nor devoid of passion;
Spotless, immovable and pure;
I am indeed Shiva, the ultimate Truth;
How, then, should I worship?
To whom do I bow? [6:25]

K: The caring and the not-caring, the knowing and the not-knowing belongs to this body. Even the vertical knowing belongs to the body. It comes with this body and will leave with this body, but the carelessness is the screen where the caring and not-caring, the knowing and the not-knowing, the discussion, the fucking and the not-fucking happens. It's un-spoiled, there's no spot on it. It's as it was before – spotless.

– The Song Of Irrelevance p126

K: That Heart, the "I"-thought as an "in-form-ation" flowers or blooms. But you are not what is coming as an "I"-thought, so stay in That which is permanent, absolutely permanent, as solid as it can be, that Heart itself, unmoved by that idea. That is abidance.

Be that unmoved Heart itself—which was never touched or untouched, never shaken or changed in any sense—simply by seeing that "I"-thought already as a phantom thought and staying at That which is prior to that thought.

– *Eight Days in Tiruvannamalai p118*

न हि देहविदेहविकल्प इति
अनृतं चरितं न हि सत्यमिति ।
अहमेव शिवः परमार्थ इति
अभिवादनमत्र करोमि कथम् ॥ २६॥

No distinction such as with-body or without-body exists;
Nor is there right-action or wrong-action;
I am indeed Shiva, the ultimate Truth;
How, then, should I worship?
To whom should I bow? [6:26]

K: In Germany we have different names and they mean something else too – different tendency. I never tried to get another name because Karl means free man – one who doesn't have to bow down to anyone. That was fine with me and then that vibrates in you and maybe you behave like one. You never bow down or obey to anyone's wish.

– *The Song Of Irrelevance p75*

K: Even if you claim not to know, there is knowledge. But inspite of one who knows or doesn't know, there is knowledge. That's what I always point to and there is always perception inspite of a presence of a perceiver or absence of a perceiver. I don't say anything else.

So you may say that what is your nature is with and without one who is 'experienced'. So saying that there is no one, is still one too many and it doesn't work. You are with and without.

— The Song Of Irrelevance p15

विन्दति विन्दति न हि न हि यत्र
छन्दोलक्षणं न हि न हि तत्र ।
समरसमग्नो भावितपूतः
प्रलपति तत्त्वं परमवधूतः ॥ २७॥

Where there is neither knowledge nor anyone who knows;
Where prose and poetry are rendered meaningless;
As the all-pervasive essence, absorbed in not-knowingness;
The Avadhut simply prattles about the Truth. [6:27]

K: You will fail. You will never know yourself. I'm talking to That what will always fail because what-you-are will never know itself. And I can just put you into That absolute absence of a knower, because there is no knower. The knower already means knowing – to exist. But that knowledge of existence is already ignorance.

— The Song Of Irrelevance p135

K: By not knowing what-you-are or what-you-are not, you are always what-is. And there is only the quality of what-you-are. There is no quantity of more or less or deeper or higher, in anything. But you can still experience higher. But in this experience of higher, you do not become higher. And in lower, not lower. And the brmmm [talking gibberish] is not different from what I just said.

– Heaven And Hell p169

Chapter Seven

रथ्याकर्पटविरचितकन्थः
पुण्यापुण्यविवर्जितपन्थः ।
शून्यागारे तिष्ठति नग्नो
शुद्धनिरञ्जनसमरसमग्नः ॥ १॥

A rag picked off the road serving as his garment;
The Avadhut walks a path devoid of merit or sin;
Naked, in an empty abode he stays;
Merged in and as the pure, stainless Self,
  the essence in all. [7:1]

K: Nine years ago, I was in Vienna, I thought I would never go back here. Two hundred people in front of me, trying to kill me. [Laughter] Attacking me verbally. You still have glasses, you cannot be enlightened. You wear a watch; you cannot be enlightened because you still want to know what's the time. Bullshit questions and I thought what's going on here? They were attacking me from all sides and my master is a master of light and you cannot be like him.

And after two hours, I said it was like it was, but if you don't see me any more, don't miss me. Bye bye. Then two hundred people started clapping – Bravo! That killed me. [Laughter] They were just checking me out with all those possibilities and saw that I survived. [Laughter] And since then, I have to go there. Now they're okay. [Laughter] But they were all attacking with all possibilities, from the lowest to the highest. Like a machine gun.

— *Worry And Be Happy p79*

लक्ष्यालक्ष्यविवर्जितलक्ष्यो
युक्तायुक्तविवर्जितदक्षः ।
केवलतत्त्वनिरञ्जनपूतो
वादविवादः कथमवधूतः ॥ २ ॥

He aims for aimlessness itself;
Skillfully steering clear of what is appropriate or inappropriate;
He remains Absolute, stainless and pure;
How can the liberated engage in discussions and debates? [7:2]

Q: I have this tendency to question 'Is this correct or is this an illusion? Is it something I imagine or is it something real?' This I always question for everything.

K: That is called dream. The dreamer dreaming about the dream, about a real dream or an unreal dream. Only when there is a relative dreamer he has a real or unreal dream. For what you are this question never applies. It only applies to one who is already false. Good and bad and right and wrong only applies to one who is already false.

— *May It Be As It Is p105*

K: I enjoy the helplessness as nothing else. There is no conflict in anything. Where is the conflict? With what? How can you be in conflict with something? It even needs an effort to be in a conflict. I am much too lazy for that. I am even too lazy to be lazy. That's my problem. Otherwise I could not sit here. Because trying to be lazy is much too much effort. I rather let the words flow, like being the flow and the words come out or not. There is a carelessness of talking. I don't know. Not to talk would be much too much effort.

– *May It Be As It Is p98*

आशापाशविबन्धनमुक्ताः
शौचाचारविवर्जितयुक्ताः ।
एवं सर्वविवर्जितशान्त-
स्तत्त्वं शुद्धनिरञ्जनवन्तः ॥ ३ ॥

Freed from bondage of the traps of hope;
Freed of purificatory and ceremonial conduct;
Freed of all, having thus attained peace;
He is stainless, pure and the Absolute [7:3]

K: All the stories of passion of Christ and crucifixion is not an outside story. It's an inside way of reaching that helplessness and helplessness is the symbol of the cross – being crucified. That you cannot absolutely move any more. Being totally fixed on what-you-are. It's not a story of a drama or something. It's like you being crucified. This is like you are being crucified more and more so that the helplessness taking over – that's grace.

The Self becomes more and more – that what is unmovable. Crucifying itself in the helplessness, that it cannot do anything. You will be crucified on what-you-are. In the horizontal time, in the vertical spirit and the Heart in center – you are that and you will be crucified. Part of the preparation for this crucifixion is that the void becomes more and more. The senselessness of your surroundings becomes more and more. Nothing makes you happy any more, everything becomes empty. The relation-shit(ship) – all of that becomes like shit.

Nothing gives you satisfaction. All is empty. No drinking, no friends, no family, no work. All of that becomes [blowing in the wind] – empty! Like a void. No hope any more in anything. No comfort you can find in any little thing. Before you were in the ashram and you were so happy with the energy and the Shakti bullshit. Now it's so empty. Even this light bullshit, the kundalini – who bloody needs it? All of that becomes completely empty and that's called grace.

– The Song Of Irrelevance p172

कथमिह देहविदेहविचारः
कथमिह रागविरागविचारः ।
निर्मलनिश्चलगगनाकारं
स्वयमिह तत्त्वं सहजाकारम् ॥ ४॥

Where is the question of being embodied or bodiless?
Where is the question of passion or dispassion?
Tranquil and unmoving like the infinite sky;
Here is Reality itself, spontaneously, in Its natural form. [7:4]

Q: They say men have forgotten to be men, but for women it's easier to know who they are because they give birth...

K: Good luck babies! [Laughter] Actually I'm not so jealous. Even if women know who they are, that's bullshit. It's more bullshit because then there's a woman, who knows who she is. Shit! Should

I be jealous that they know more shit than me?

It's like they have a near death experience while giving birth. The pain is so immense that sometimes they're out of the body and have near death experience. It happened quite often when there was no anaesthesia. In that sense, the ladies should not have any anaesthesia, they should have pain of the lifetime so that they may disconnect from the body because of that pain.

And then you claim that they know who-they-are because they have had this out of body experience? It's like a satori that you get by sitting in front of a wall for ten or twenty years. And then the pain in your legs is so immense and your Zen master hits you so very hard, that your perception disconnects from the whole circumstance and you're in that oneness space. Sounds good!

But whoever went out, came back. How many concepts do we have? How many advantages of being a woman or man? It all makes you feel bad.

– *Worry And Be Happy p65*

कथमिह तत्त्वं विन्दति यत्र
रूपमरूपं कथमिह तत्र ।
गगनाकारः परमो यत्र
विषयीकरणं कथमिह तत्र ॥ ५॥

How can anything be known about it by anyone?
How can there be any form or formlessness?
For the Supreme, infinite as the sky;
How, then, can there be any objectification?! [7:5]

Q: How can you say that even if consciousness is not there, we are what we are? How can you know it?

K: It's not a knowing. But before consciousness wakes up, you are already what you are. And then waking up happens. Otherwise there cannot be waking up. It is not logic. It's your daily experience. Before waking up, before the first purest notion of awareness can be there, you are already there. And then awareness happens.

Q: That's not my experience...

K: That will never be your experience. But still you are prior to that first experience.

Q: How do we know that?

K: There is no 'how'! You are that! You have to be what you are that even awareness can be. And you will never know that as a person. You cannot put it in your personal pocket, saying 'I know now that I am before'.

— May It Be As It Is p191

Q: What-you-are is also a lie?

K: I don't have to know what I Am. I don't have to pronounce what I Am. Why should I pronounce any bullshit?

Q: But what do you see?

K: I don't see anything.

Q: Why? Is it because everything is a lie?

K: No. Because What I Am is not a seer. How can I see something? What I Am never sees anything. The seer sees what can be seen. But all of that is part of the seer, the story of the seer but is not what 'I Am'. You cannot make That what I Am the story of a seer. Whatever you see is already past, you know that. You need to explain what you see. There needs to be an explainer for what you see, otherwise there is not even seeing.

— Heaven And Hell p145

गगनाकारनिरन्तरहंस-
स्तत्त्वविशुद्धनिरञ्जनहंसः ।
एवं कथमिह भिन्नविभिन्नं
बन्धविबन्धविकारविभिन्नम् ॥ ६॥

The Self is perpetual, like the sky;
It is the pure and stainless Reality;
How, then, can there be difference or non-difference,
Bondage or liberation, division or multiplication?! [7:6]

K: If it really would help some existence to become That which is Self, it would stop right away, because there was Buddha, there was Jesus, there was Ramana, there were so many big sages. If it really would help—those experiences of whatever transformation, coming from identified consciousness into cosmic consciousness, all that energy happening, then back to it—if it really would help, this would simply stop. It could not continue. For one Self, that would be the end. By whatever transformation or transmutation into something else, the whole existence would simply drop. If you could control That which is existence itself, as That which is Self, by whatever experience of heat, or whatever transformation, what kind of freedom would it be? So all this is part of the show, but it makes no difference.

— *Eight Days in Tiruvannamalai p321*

केवलतत्त्वनिरन्तरसर्वं
योगवियोगौ कथमिह गर्वम् ।
एवं परमनिरन्तरसर्व-
मेवं कथमिह सारविसारम् ॥ ७॥

There is just the Absolute: the All and perpetual;
How, then, could there be union, or separation, or pride here?!
If there is only the Supreme, the never-never and the all;
Where, then, arises the question of
essence or absence of essence?! [7:7]

K: Harmony can never be in disharmony. There is no disharmony for harmony. Disharmony can only be in those differences when you landed in one of those landing places. And then you are already in a disharmony of separation. But it is a dream separation. It's a dream disharmony. Any moment you want to change this dream disharmony – you cannot kill it; you cannot get rid of it. Because how can you get rid of a dream? How can you get rid of an illusion? It is not even there. It has no substance. How can you kill it? How can you get rid of something what is not even there? So the main problem is, there is no problem!

– *May It Be As It Is* p151

केवलतत्त्वनिरञ्जनसर्वं
गगनाकारनिरन्तरशुद्धम् ।
एवं कथमिह सङ्गविसङ्गं
सत्यं कथमिह रङ्गविरङ्गम् ॥ ८ ॥

Only the stainless, all-encompassing Reality exists;
Pure, perpetual and infinite as the sky;
How can association or dissociation occur here?
If there is only the One Reality,
How, then, can there be a stage or a drama? [7:8]

Q: Some people say that you have to listen to your satguru...

K: You don't have to listen to it; you just have to be in the company. In That, there's no understanding. Good company means the absence of company. The absence of a teacher or a disciple. The absence of something to do or not to do – just to be That.

Q: What is satguru?

K: It is 'I' talking to the 'I'. It's not one who's happy talking to the one who's unhappy. It's not that there's one who knows and one who doesn't know. Even to make that special, is bullshit. Even making a standard of good company is bullshit. Even Ramana and Nisargadatta repeated it – If there's at all, it's good company. But you have to see good company as never-never because you're always in the company of what-you-are. Then you get pointers for That – that you cannot not have good company. All there is – is the Self and the good company is uninterrupted. It's not something that you can see as if 'there-is' and 'there-is-not'.

Good company is good company without one pointing out that one is better than something else. Even if someone's pointing that this is better, it is the same lie as everything else. That all the paradoxes appear and disappear and with it, sometimes you disappear.

– *Worry And Be Happy p186*

योगवियोगै रहितो योगी
भोगविभोगै रहितो भोगी ।
एवं चरति हि मन्दं मन्दं
मनसा कल्पितसहजानन्दम् ॥ ९ ॥

He is a yogi devoid of yoga and whatever is not-yoga;
He is a bhogi (enjoyer),
devoid of enjoyment and non-enjoyment;
He, thus, wanders lazily, leisurely;
His mind having merged in the spontaneous bliss of Self. [7:9]

K: Be aware that you don't need to be aware. Be happy that you don't need to be happy. Enjoy, that you don't need to enjoy. All these paradoxes are the pointers to the paradox. Know that you don't have to know. Stay in that knowledge that you don't have to know – to know. And that one who needs to know, to know – bye, bye. It came and it will be gone. But what-you-are, will still be what-it-is.

In Zen they say, what was your face before you were born? No one knows. Stay in That what has no face, no persona, no reference point at all. Neither having nor not-having. Because the root thought is always the owner thought – having or not-having. Even not having is having too much. Owning or not-owning is not the question.

– *The Song Of Irrelevance p134*

K: You may cut some branches, but it means nothing, because the tree will grow back even further. So controlling the mind is making it grow even more. You have to go to the root of the mind, that "I"-thought. Without rooting that out totally, it always will grow again even more, even making a religion out of it. Then comes a religion out of experiences of whatever spiritual kind, but the "I"- thought is still there, and it makes a personal history of religious experiences. There are many enlightenments and awakenings and experiences, but they are taken personally. And then comes a religion out of it, or a technique, or even a Yoga technique, of cutting some branches.

Ramana was very radical, in a sense, to go directly to what is the root-thought. Because without that root-thought, there is no tree any more—never was, never will be. That's the meaning of that supreme Yoga, which is the direct path to annihilating the first thought, the first card of your card-house of concepts. The first card of the idea even of "existence," the first notion of existence as "I," which is awareness, the "I"-awareness—already that is a phantom.

– *Eight Days in Tiruvannamalai p134*

बोधविबोधैः सततं युक्तो
द्वैताद्वैतैः कथमिह मुक्तः ।
सहजो विरजः कथमिह योगी
शुद्धनिरञ्जनसमरसभोगी ॥ १० ॥

How does one, ceaselessly bound by knowledge and ignorance,
become free of duality and non-duality?
How can a yogi gain spontaneity and dispsasion?
Being stainless purity itself,
he is the enjoyer of essence in all. [7:10]

K: The one who wants to control you, you control them by letting them control you. The controller is controlled by that what he wants to control. What you try to control, controls you if you like it or not. That's hell. But you want to be free; you want freedom so freedom controls you. You are a slave of freedom. Freedom is your master, and then you are a slave.

If truth is your master, then you are a slave of truth. If Self is your master then you are a slave of the Self. Whatever you make higher or an icon you become a slave. Love makes you a slave of love. But why not?

Not to be a slave, you become a slave of not being a slave. No way out. You will always be in Self-service.

– Am I – I Am p212

Q: Karl, if you imagine being a sufferer, you're a sufferer; if you imagine being an enjoyer, you're an enjoyer—but you cannot control it.

K: You have to be, in spite of being a sufferer and suffering, only That which you are. It's unavoidable. You cannot avoid what you are. That which is whatever aspect of existence, you are. And you cannot not imagine yourself as it, and by imagining it, you become it. And then there is the sufferer, the suffering, and that which is suffered about.

But you are That which is the sufferer, That which is the suffering, and That which you suffer about. You are always that experiencer, that experiencing, and what is experienced—as you are whatever is. You cannot not experience what you are. And by experiencing yourself, you become an experiencer experiencing what is experienced. But there is no difference. There is no separation between the experiencer, the experiencing, and what is experienced. It's all the realization of what you are as consciousness.

Q: But I'd rather experience myself being the enjoyer rather than the sufferer.

K: But that is part of the imagination.

Q [Another visitor]: You're saying there's no control.

K: No.

— *Eight Days in Tiruvannamalai p91*

भग्नाभग्नविवर्जितभग्नो
लग्नालग्नविवर्जितलग्नः ।
एवं कथमिह सारविसारः
समरसतत्त्वं गगनाकारः ॥ ११ ॥

As destroyer, it is devoid of the destroyed and the un-destroyed;
As sustainer, it is devoid of the sustained and the un-sustained;
How, then, can there be any essence or absence of essence?
For the Self, which is the essence in all, infinite as the sky.
[7:11]

K: The Self is always stupid because the Self is already a lover and out of love for himself, it wants to end whatever is there. Shiva knowing Shiva, when there is a Shiva, it wants to destroy everything, whatever can be destroyed – even himself. But he cannot. He always tries, but he'll never succeed. Crazy! So, even Shiva is crazy! Shiva knowing Shiva is totally crazy and stupid. That you really didn't expect.

— *The Song Of Irrelevance p198*

K: What I am really doing is demolishing the demolisher. It is like this is Shiva destroying Shiva. Because even in the destruction there is a hope that one day everything is destroyed and then you will be better off. No! I destroy the destroyer. That's your worst nightmare.

I am sitting here destroying even the destroyer for you. Demolishing the demolisher. Because nothing can be demolished at all. And who needs to demolish something? No, I am not demolishing anything. And telling the phantom: 'No one needs you to go!' That's the worst scenario the phantom can be not in. Because if no one cares if there is one or not, that kills the phantom right away!

— *May It Be As It Is p157*

सततं सर्वविवर्जितयुक्तः
सर्वं तत्त्वविवर्जितमुक्तः ।
एवं कथमिह जीवितमरणं
ध्यानाध्यानैः कथमिह करणम् ॥ १२॥

Forever connected to all, yet independent of all;
Liberation is devoid of all principles (tattvas);
How, indeed, can there be birth or death here?
And what will meditation or no-meditation
accomplish here?! [7:12]

Q: Karl, are you in love with yourself?

K: I have no idea about love or no love or hate or anything. I'm talking about That which is prior to love and hate and all this. There is no idea. There is a total absence of that love or hating or all that polarity of concepts about myself. That all belongs to that dream.

That dream figure, Karl, maybe he is in love or not in love. For That which is Karl, what is in spite of Karl and never because of Karl, there is no concept of love or no love or anything. There's a conceptlessness about everything.

— *Eight Days in Tiruvannamalai p228*

K: Try to find the sufferer and try to present the sufferer to me. Try. No way! No one can ever present the sufferer. You can present the body or the hurt or the pain and how you measure it but show me the sufferer. No one ever found him. It's just an idea. Where is the sufferer? Who is born? That's the question. Who is that who is born and is now suffering? Who is that guy? Show it to me, show me that idea.

– Am I – I Am p32

इन्द्रजालमिदं सर्वं यथा मरुमरीचिका ।
अखण्डितमनाकारो वर्तते केवलः शिवः ॥ १३ ॥

Everything is magical hallucination – like a mirage in the desert;
Beyond all imagined forms and differences,
pervades Shiva alone. [7:13]

K: The final healing is giving you the total knowledge of what you are, by giving you the knowledge of being That, unborn, never dying—and not healing some body. Because that healing, that pointing to the nature of that Heart that you are, that is the absolute healing. The healing of the body is maybe a side-effect, or whatever, but whoever's body was healed is dead now. It's a temporary adjustment.

All these wonders and miracles are temporary too, simply relative, like an amazing show, like David Copperfield, who can make a whole plane disappear, or Sai Baba, who can produce a linga. What to do? Doesn't matter. Both mean nothing. Both are the magic of consciousness that can do everything. It can make a mountain appear and disappear. It can make the whole universe appear and disappear.

What is more magical? You are the total magician. You let the whole universe appear by simply taking it as real. You are creating everything simply by looking at it.

– Eight Days in Tiruvannamalai p267

K: This bloody love that makes you so stupid. Only love makes you so crazy that you are after yourself. What else can make you so crazy and stupid? Only love! Tell me anything else that can make you so stupid to try to become what you are? Tell me? This bloody love is the only magic that can make you so stupid that you really believe that you can know yourself. Fantastic! You are crazy for yourself by love. So only love can make you so stupid that you suffer about yourself. You suffer about being in love with yourself. That's your suffering. That's the whole reason you suffer about yourself, because you are in love with yourself. And because you love yourself and you don't know yourself you suffer about not knowing yourself. This bloody love is like a high icon, that's really the reason of suffering.

This bleeding heart for yourself. Bloody love. Valentine's Days and all of that. And then people tell you that you have to love yourself, so what is all that? It's all the devil's work or what? Selling you what he doesn't have? Bloody love? How can you not love yourself? Try! So whatever you do is out of love. Love is running the whole show.

You sit here for love.

– May It Be As It Is p262

धर्मादौ मोक्षपर्यन्तं निरीहाः सर्वथा वयम् ।
कथं रागविरागैश्च कल्पयन्ति विपश्चितः ॥ १४ ॥

If we are completely oblivious to everything –
From the performance of duties to the attainment of liberation;
How, then, can we have anything to do
with attachment or detachment?
Only the learned imagine such things. [7:14]

K: You try to create the harmony which was never gone. Even by trying to create harmony you are so arrogant that you think you can create harmony by you being still. What is more arrogant? Bloody meditators. Kill them all, put them in Ganga.

Just see it, you try to make the harmony more harmonious, the harmony was never gone. You try to make it your harmony, you want to make it your bloody harmony and you want to control it by meditating. What can be more arrogant? Then you should suffer about it. Even the fly on the wall disturbs you. The little insects making little noise while you are meditating and you get disturbed, totally freaked out. And that's exactly how it has to be.

– Am I – I Am p52

K: You are the seer which is not different from what it seen, in nature. But that is darkness for itself. So whatever is experienced is a dream for what you are. But still is not different from what you are. The only dream is that you try to find yourself in that what you imagine, and that makes you an imagined poor me. There is a misery of imagination, imagining that you can be imagined. And then you are in that pitiful I. Then you cry about yourself. That's the joke!

– May It Be As It Is p27

विन्दति विन्दति न हि न हि यत्र
छन्दोलक्षणं न हि न हि तत्र ।
समरसमग्रो भावितपूतः
प्रलपति तत्त्वं परमवधूतः ॥ १५॥

Where there is neither knowledge nor anyone who knows;
Where prose and poetry are rendered meaningless;
As the all-pervasive essence, absorbed in not-knowingness;
The Avadhut simply prattles about the Truth. [7:15]

K: All of that is absolute not needed to know, all of that is mechanics. If what you are would demand to know all of that, it would still be depending on all of that. What you are never needs to know anything, not even the mechanics of whether it happens or not. That who is now interested in what happens and if it happens is already false. What you are never needs to know that to be That.

— *Am I – I Am p167*

Q: How is truth a lie?

K: Because it's an idea now, you can pronounce it. Whatever you can pronounce is a lie. If truth is the truth, then what about lies? We always make differences, the polarities. Truth is opposite to untrue. So how can that what is truth which is different from untruth be the truth? It's a relative truth and the relative truth will stay as relative truth. The relative freedom, relative peace is all relative.

Be that what has no idea what it is and what it is not. That what has an idea, already is an idea. An idea has an idea, then it becomes idealistic, it's a list of ideas.

— *Am I – I Am p139*

REFERENCES

References for Karl Renz

- The Song Of Irrelevance – Meditation Of What You Are
- Worry And Be Happy – The Audacity Of Hopelessness
- Heaven And Hell
- Am I - I Am
- May It Be As It Is – The Embrace Of Helplessness
- Eight Days In Tiruvannamalai – Dialogues In The Presence Of Arunachala
- Interviews

References for Avadhut Gita

- Avadhut Gita Of Dattatreya By Swami Ashokananda
- Dattatreya: Song Of The Avadhut By Swami Abhayananda
- Dattatreya: The Way And The Goal By Sri Jaya Chamarajendra Wadiyar Bahadur
- Avadhut Gita In Hindi By Shri Banmali Chaturvedi

- The Avadhut Gita Of Dattatreya By Kanoo Mal
- Avadhut Gita By Anandaghana

Other References
- Dattatreya Upanishad

www.ingramcontent.com/pod-product-compliance
Lightning Source LLC
Chambersburg PA
CBHW070717160426
43192CB00009B/1225